IC PACKAGING UPDATE

Editor
Eric Bogatin

1999

1964 35th 1999
Serving The IC Industry Since 1964
ICE
INTEGRATED CIRCUIT ENGINEERING

17350 N. Hartford Dr.
Scottsdale, Arizona 85255
Phone: 480-515-9780
Fax: 480-515-9781
E-mail: ice@ice-corp.com
Internet: http://www.ice-corp.com

ISBN: 978-1-7325670-0-9

Graphic Artists
Chad Chase
Jay Karcher
Hope M. Litten
Heather Miller

Printed on Recycled Paper

Table of Contents

List of Illustrations

Figure	Title	Page

Figure	Title	Page

1 Overview

INFORMATION OVERLOAD

"Silicon, germanium, gallium arsenide, optoelectronic, MEMS, aluminum pads, gold wire bonds, aluminum wire bonds, TAB ILB, lead-frame, eutectic die attach, thermo-compression bond, thin film redistribution with balls, gold bumped, nickel bumped, polymer bumped, eutectic solder bumped, high-temp solder bumped, stud bumped, silicon, thin film on glass, thick or thin film on ceramic, build up organic, microvias, decals, organic or thin film on metal, buried resistors, buried capacitors, bumped, tiered, chip first build-up, organic solderability preservatives, copper/nickel/gold, palladium, tin, solder-coated, solder-plated, COB/gold, COB/aluminum, overmolded, encapsulated, eutectic reflow, high-temp reflow, no-flow underfill, quick-flow underfill, print paste, dispense paste, solder-jet, conductive adhesive, nonconductive adhesive, anisotropic adhesives, isotropic adhesives, adhesive film and through-hole"

-Philip Yates, in HDI Magazine, July 1998, p. 48.

And then there's...... BGA, PBGA, CPBA, CCBGA, CDBGA, SBGA, CSP, LOC, BUM, SLC, C4, FC, DCA, EDA, PCA, QFP, PQFP, C2BGA, CLCC, COL, D2BGA, DBGA, EPBGA, LGA, MBGA, MQFP, NCSP, PLCC, SLICC, SOP, SOT, SQFP, TBGA, TSOP, VSOP...

There is a seemingly bewildering array of choices to be made in the selection of package and interconnect solutions. Decision makers new to the field see a jumbled forest, with each tree having a flag placed by a proponent proclaiming their offering to be the greatest and most optimal solution for all packaging needs. This is a direct result of the rapidly evolving state of the industry, and the increasingly important role that packaging and interconnect plays in system performance.

Every product is a custom design, with its own set of cost-performance-risk-schedule tradeoffs. Because the packaging choices will touch every aspect of the product, the selection process increasingly involves more engineers than just the packaging group. As for any consumer product, to effectively make an optimized decision, requires an informed consumer.

This book, as a supplement to **Roadmaps of Packaging Technology**, available from ICE, provides an update on the latest packaging and interconnect choices which are arising from the revolutionary changes, rocking the industry. In addition to the "what and the how", this book offers the "why", a perspective and analysis that will facilitate the decision making process so that packaging technology consumers can be informed consumers. It is a map of the trails through the packaging and interconnect forest.

The Packaging and Interconnect Industry

Ultimately, it is the integrated circuits (ICs) that perform the function in most products. By any metric, the actual content of silicon in a product is very small. The fractional volume and weight of silicon is typically less than 0.1% and the cost of the silicon is less than 10% of the product price.

The "rest of the system", the interconnects, represent the majority of the weight, volume, and cost to a system. Yet, they can never add performance to the silicon, only subtract from it. The goal in selecting the optimum interconnect strategy is to minimize the detrimental impact to the silicon in terms of cost, weight, size, power consumption and speed.

The interconnects extend from the pads on the chip, to the chip attach, the package, the multichip module, the daughtercard, the motherboard, the backplane, the racks and to the cabinets. This hierarchy of interconnects, illustrated in Figure 1-1, is designed to protect the delicate chips and interconnect them electrically and thermally to each other and the outside world.

Historically, the packaging was always a separate function and structure from the interconnects. "Packaging" used to refer to the specific component that protects the bare die from the harsh environment and allows the flow of heat, power and signals to and from the chip. This is illustrated in Figure 1-2.

The package was a well-defined, easily partitioned piece of a system and could be optimized independent of the rest of the system. A variety of traditional IC packages are shown in Figure 1-3.

The die is typically attached to the inside cavity of the package and wire bonded to the bonding shelf. The inner row of connections fans out to an array of leads that are either surface mounted to the printed circuit board (PCB), or through hole mounted. In either case, conventional pick and place equipment is used to automatically place the part on the board and it is then reflow soldered with all the other components.

The package represents a clean interface to the system it is integrated into. On one side is the bare die. On the other side are leads that are mounted to the circuit board. The package is a robust vehicle for testing, transporting and handling the fragile, bare die.

INTERCONNECTION HIERARCHY, FROM CHIP TO SYSTEM

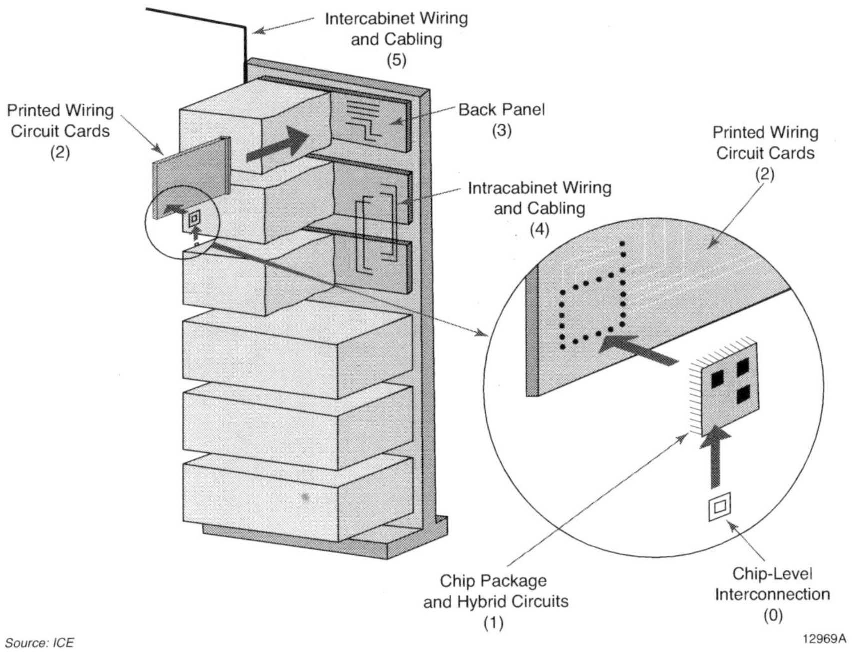

Figure 1-1. Interconnect hierarchy from the chip pads to the enclosure. Packages, passives and the circuit boards are the major packaging and interconnect elements.

THE ROLE OF THE PACKAGING

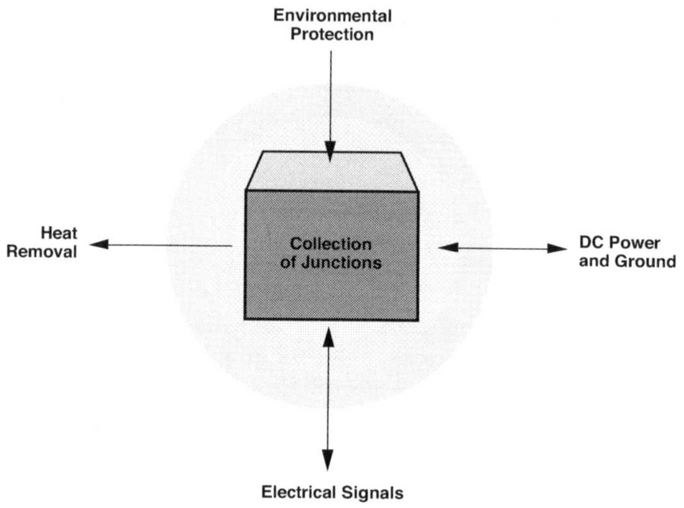

Figure 1-2. Role of packaging in isolating the chip from the environment and interconnecting power, signals and heat.

MYRIAD ARRAY OF SINGLE-CHIP PACKAGES

Figure 1-3. Examples of single chip packages (SCP) which cleanly partition the bare die from the system.

However as the IC features, such as I/O count, bandwidth and power dissipation, advance, the package must also advance to meet these increasing needs. In turn, the circuit board must advance to meet the increasingly complex needs of the package. As package pin count increases, the interconnect density in the substrate must increase. As the surface pad pitch decreases, the via density in the substrate must increase. As the bandwidth increases, new designs must be implemented, and new materials with enhanced electrical properties must be used in the substrate to rescue the last psec of performance.

Today, there is a strong interdependency on the chip features, the package features and the substrate features. The partitioning of the chip from the package and from the substrate is no longer clean and independent. Trying to optimize one element independent of the others will leave performance on the table.

For example, the Sony DCR-PC7 Digital Camcorder, shown in Figure 1-4 was the world's smallest digital camcorder when it was introduced in September, 1996. What made it possible to fit the functionality of a larger handheld device into a palm size device was the new Chip Scale Package (CSP) technology, with microvia build up multilayer (BUM) technology substrates.

SONY DCR–PC7 DIGITAL CAMCORDER

Source: Portable Design, May 97, p. 28 and Prismark Partners 24663

Figure 1-4. Introduced in 1996, was the first high volume consumer product that used CSPs.

In this Sony Camcorder, there are 18 chip scale packages (CSPs) on the main circuit board. Each of these CSPs contains a single chip, flip chip attached to an interposer substrate. This substrate is a geometry transformer. It is typically a two layer circuit board with pads on the top having a pitch of 9mils (0.225mm) to match the pads of the die and pads on the bottom having a pitch of 32mils (0.8mm) to match the pads of the circuit board. To interconnect the 18 CSPs, in a very tight space, a microvia printed circuit board is used. It consists of a six layer core of conventional circuit board with two layers of fine line, microvia interconnect on both sides. A cross section of this board, through one of the CSPs, is shown in Figure 1-5.

DIAGRAM OF THE STACKUP OF THE MAIN CIRCUIT BOARD IN THE SONY DCR-PC7 CAMCORDER

CROSS SECTION OF SONY CAM BOARD SHOWING FLIP CHIP CSP MOUNTED ON THE MICROVIA CIRCUIT BOARD

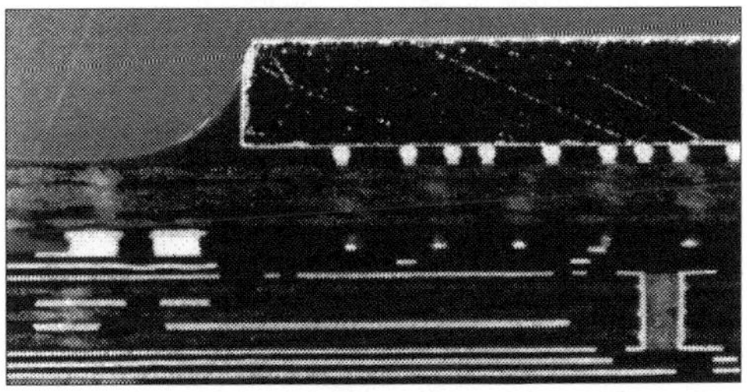

6 LAYER CORE WITH 2 MICROVIA LAYERS ON EACH SIDE

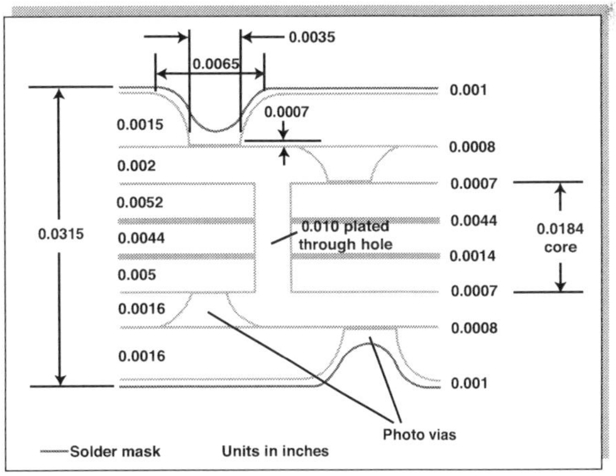

Source: Portable Design, May 97, p.28, and Prismark Partners 24664

Figure 1-5. (Top) Cross section of Sony Camcorder board, showing a 6 layer core with 2 microvia layers on each side, and a flip chip mounted on a CSP printed circuit board interposer. (Bottom) Diagram of the stackup of the main circuit board.

To achieve the higher density of functionality required by this camcorder application, an optimized "system" of flip chips, CSPs and microvia substrates was required.

Driven by reducing cost and board area, and increasing performance, there is beginning a comparable advancement in the integration of passive components. Historically, passives have been discrete resistors or capacitors either surface mounted or through hole mounted to the substrate. These discretes are now being integrated into small modules, or even built into the substrates as integral passives. Using technologies and materials borrowed from IC, package, MCM and PCB designs, the next generation of integrated passives can reduce the part count and board surface area used by the passives by over 90%. Along with the reduced size can come better performance at high clock frequencies. An example of this new transition in passives is shown in Figure 1-6.

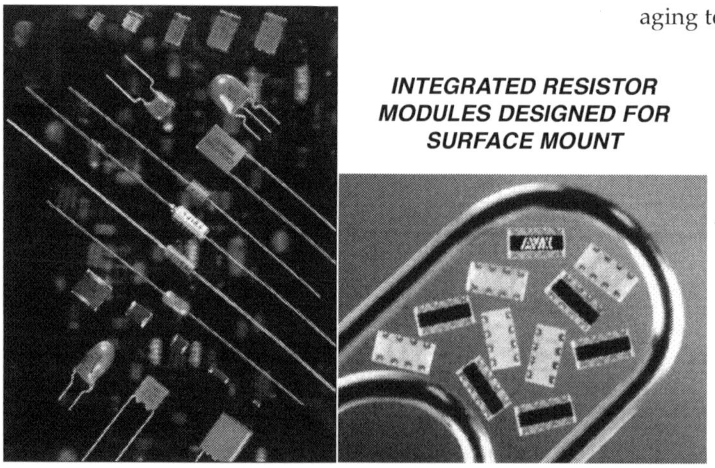

Figure 1-6. (Left) Individual discrete capacitors for through hole and surface mount attach to a PCB. (Right) Integrated resistor modules designed for surface mount, with over 90% reduction in mounted surface area of comparable discretes.

The futures of these four elements in the system: the chip form factor, the packages, the passives and the circuit boards, are tightly intertwined. Together, they represent a major percentage of all the interconnects in a final product, from the pads on the die, to the outer enclosure. The other significant element is composed of the connectors between each of the circuit board cards. Connector technology, just beginning its own revolution, is reviewed in a future publication.

As there is a blurring between the technologies used to design, manufacture and assemble these four elements, they are all grouped together into the packaging and interconnect industry. These technologies and their revolutionary changes underway, are reviewed in this book.

Driving Forces

Faster, smaller, cheaper, lower power consumption, NOW! are the strategic goals of the system Original Equipment Manufacturers (OEMs). These goals stem from their customers, the consumers, who are demanding ever higher functionality, in ever smaller form factors and at ever lower price. This expectation is partly in response to the ability of IC technology to have met these expectations in the past. These forces are driving the adoption of new packaging technologies and methods, such as:

- Flip chip (area array attach with a high I/O density off the chip)
- BGA (ball grid array package, with large I/O density off the package)
- CSP (Chip Scale Package, with fine pitch area array leads in a small package)
- BUM (Build Up Multilayer, micro via substrates with very high via density)
- Concurrent engineering (enabling faster time to market)
- Virtual prototyping (increasing the probability that the first article will meet specs)

This is summarized in Figure 1-7.

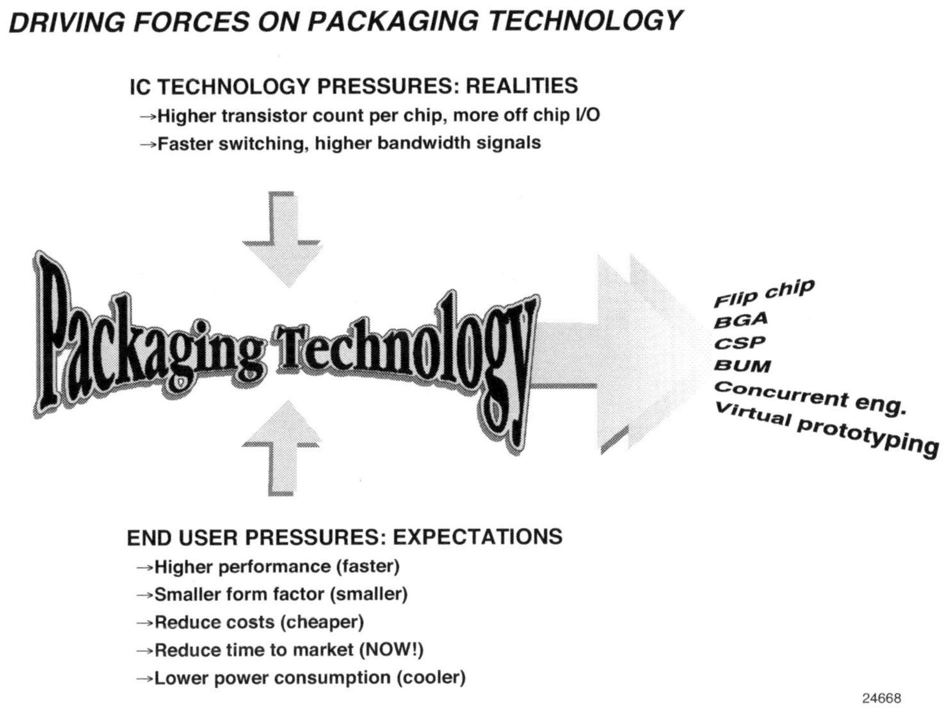

Figure 1-7. Driving forces on packaging technology gives rise to new packaging technologies.

Each decade has had its primary market that drove the development of the electronics industry. In the 70's, it was the military and aerospace industry. In the 80's, it was the mainframe computer industry. In the 90's, it was the microprocessor and telecom industries. And, in the early part of the next millennium, it will be the personal, consumer products, both portable and networked.

Personal electronic products are more than just the cell phone, PDA (personal digital assistant), pager and laptop. They also include the emerging generation of information appliances that will provide instant Internet access to the individual, anywhere and anytime. An example of some of these next generation devices is shown in Figure 1-8. For these products, higher functional density, lower power consumption, lower cost and rapid evolution, will be the primary driving forces from the final customer.

SAMPLING OF THE NEXT WAVE OF PORTABLE OR NETWORKED CONSUMER PRODUCTS THAT INTEGRATE MANY FUNCTIONS

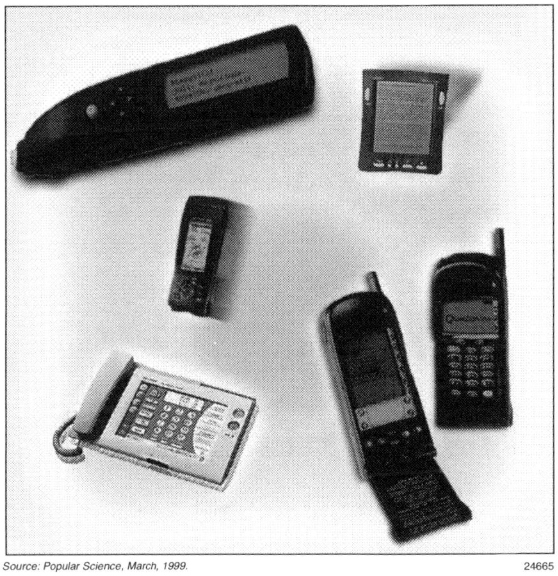

Source: Popular Science, March, 1999. 24665

Figure 1-8. The functionality and time to market pressures required for these new generation products will have significant impact on the implementation of the nine packaging revolutions.

By 2001, the unit volume of information appliances will exceed personal computers. The rapid growth of this new generation of products is described in Figure 1-9.

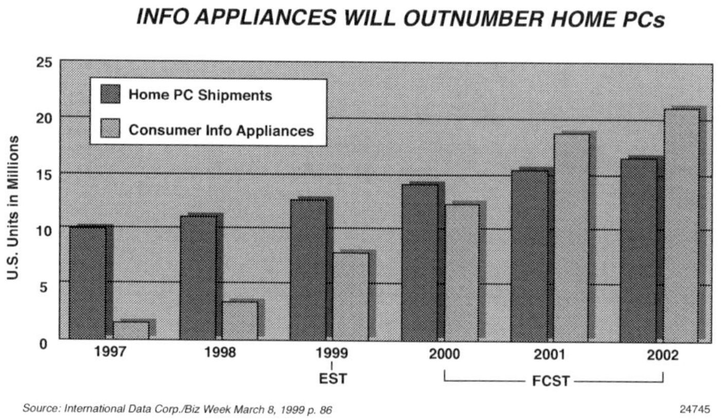

Figure 1-9.

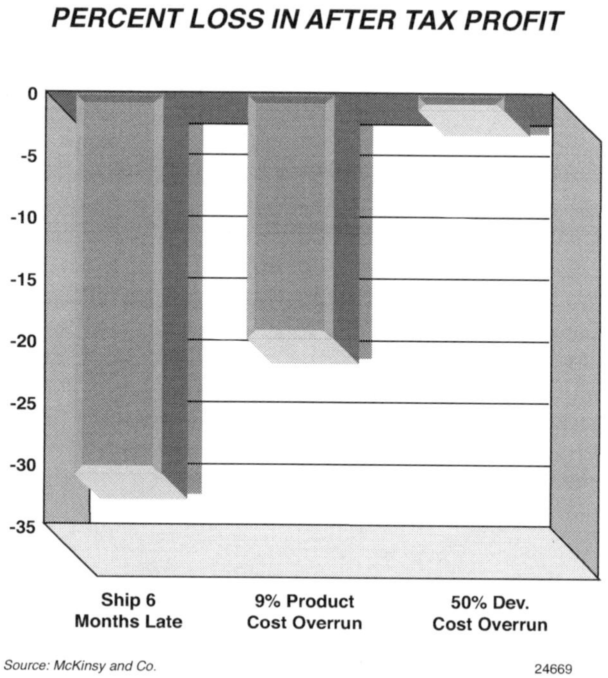

Figure 1-10. Summary of the conclusions from McKinsey and Co, illustrating the profit loss in being late to market compared to spending more for being on time.

In this new globally competitive, fast paced consumer based marketplace, time to market is as important a competitive edge as features. As product life cycles have dropped from 10 years for mainframes, and 3 years for PCs, to 6-9 months for some consumer products, missing a market launch window by a few months can erode the total profits from a product.

McKinsey and Co. completed a cost study in the early 1990s evaluating the importance of time to market on profit. From their model, they concluded:

"A new product with a 5 year life cycle which is 6 months late to a market growing at 20% per year with a 12% annual price erosion can be expected to lose fully 33% of its net profit. Even with a 50% development cost overrun, net profits are only reduced by 4%."

This is summarized in Figure 1-10.

Though the precise numbers depend strongly on the assumptions about the product and life cycle, its conclusion will remain: it is more profitable to spend more to reduce the development cycle time, either in R&D or component cost, if it means getting the product to market earlier rather than later.

In the example of the Sony hand held camcorder, the product was redesigned within a year to reduce the chip count to only 5 chips by the use of silicon integration. However, by performing the integration initially on the substrate, time to market was significantly reduced.

Evolution vs Revolution

The electronics industry has been in a state of perpetual change. Electronics, with active devices, came into use in the early 1920s' with the introduction of the vacuum tube. Since this time, when electronics began to set expectations among consumers, we have witnessed seven significant revolutions in the technologies used for the active devices and in their integration into systems. These are summarized in Figure 1-11.

SEVEN SIGNIFICANT REVOLUTIONS IN THE HISTORY OF ELECTRONICS

FROM	TO
Vacuum tubes	Transistors
Discrete wiring	Printed circuit boards
Transistors	Integrated circuits
Metal can packages	Leaded DIP and PGA packages
Through hole mounting	Surface mounted
Hermetic packages	Non hermetic plastic packages
Manual ruby lithography tape layout of boards	CAD (Computer Aided Design) tools for package and board design

24670

Figure 1-11.

IC DENSITY TRENDS

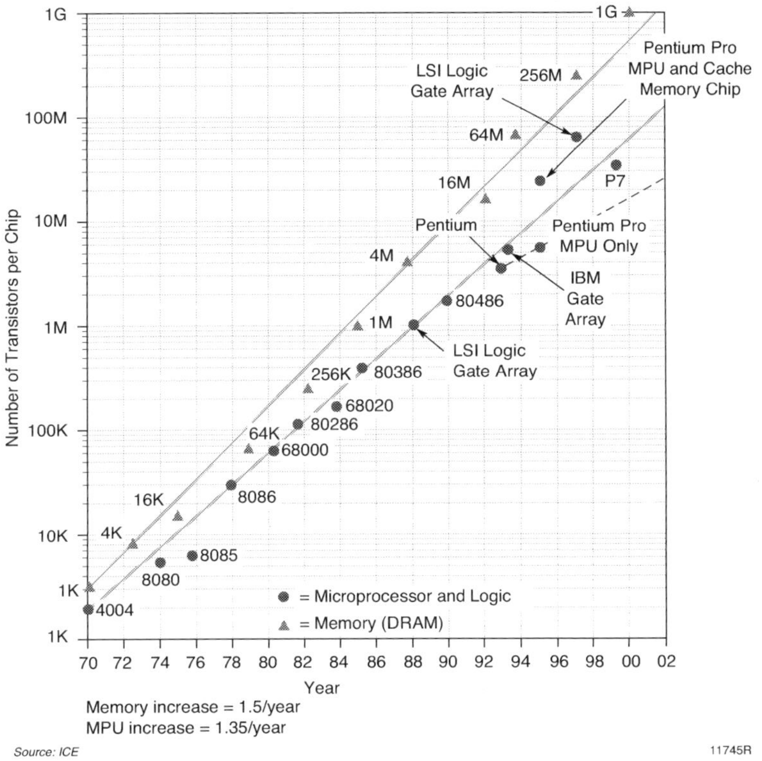

Figure 1-12. Moore's Law, showing the doubling of the number of transistors on a chip every 18 months, for almost 30 years of technology evolution.

Within each of these technology paths, there has been substantial growth in the functionality they have been able to provide. It is the revolutionary changes that have allowed the growth rates to continue, seemingly unabated. We are perhaps most aware of the rate of change from Moore's Law. This relates the observation by Gordon Moore, in the early 1970s, that the number of transistors on the leading edge integrated circuits is doubling roughly every 18 months. As shown in Figure 1-12, Moore's Law seems to have been upheld for almost 30 years.

A doubling every 18 months, like every exponential rise, will always appear to have an escalating growth rate in the most recent part of the curve. The nature of exponential growth is that the rate of change will always seem to be increasing in the current era.

Bob Lucky, a VP at Lucent Technologies, suggests that all technology growth is at an exponential rate. It just happens that we have one metric- the number of transistors on a chip- that can be tracked and measured over such a long period of time that we notice it in this instance. In fact, no single technology can support an exponential rate for extended periods. When practical limits are reached, new, revolutionary tracks are started, which are more able to sustain this growth rate. For example, air speed records have been steadily increasing, but it was the revolutionary introduction of the jet engine, over the propeller engine, that allowed speeds over 400 miles per hour to be reached.

Likewise, the current generation of packaging technologies is not sufficient to maintain the growth in smaller form factor, faster clock frequency, lower cost, lower power consumption, and faster time to market products that meet the exponential growth of the expectations of the electronics industry. Revolutionary changes are needed and are in the process of becoming the new, established technologies of choice. The nine most significant revolutionary changes affecting the packaging and interconnect industry are summarized in Figure 1-13.

One metric of the growth and relative maturity of some of these technologies is in the number of publications listed in the more popular information databases. The number of publications is a rough measure of the interest level, the number of designs and the amount of infrastructure developed.

NINE SIGNIFICANT REVOLUTIONS CURRENTLY ROCKING THE PACKAGING INDUSTRY

FROM	TO
Wire bonded peripheral chip I/O	Flip chip array I/O
Peripheral leaded packages	Area array BGA (ball grid array) packages
Large, low packaging efficiency packages	High packaging efficiency chip scale packages (CSP)
Packaged die mounted on boards	Multiple bare die on a board or substrate as in COB, DCA, and multichipackage
Mechanically drilled holes in circuit boards	Microvias produced by plasma, laser and photoimageable materials
Discrete passive components	Integrated and integral passives
Vertically integrated companies that design, market, develop, manufacture and assembly products	Out–sourced contract manufacturers of silicon, package assembly, board assembly, and box assembly
Interconnects transparent to signals	Packages, substrates, and components specially designed for acceptable signal integrity and EMI
CAD (Computer Aided Design)	Computer Aided Engineering (CAE) and Electronic Design Automation (EDA) for concurrent engineering

Source: Bogatin Enterprises 24671

Figure 1-13.

The following specific databases from the Dialog Corp, were searched:

2: INSPEC (1969- present)
6: NTIS - National Technical Information Service
8: Ei Compendex®
34: SciSearch® - a Cited Reference Science Database - 1990-
35: Dissertation Abstracts Online
64: Global Mobility Database®
65: Inside Conferences
77: Conference Papers Index
92: IHS International Standards and Specifications
94: JICST-EPlus - Japanese Science & Technology
99: Wilson Applied Science & Technology Abstracts
103: Energy Science and Technology
108: Aerospace Database
144: PASCAL
202: Information Science Abstracts
233: Microcomputer Abstracts(TM)
238: Abstracts in New Technologies and Engineering (ANTE)
239: MathSci®
275: IAC(SM) Computer Database(TM)
434: SciSearch® - a Cited Reference Science Database - 1974-1989
647: CMP Computer Fulltext
674: Computer News Fulltext
696: DIALOG Telecommunications Newsletters

These databases include all the important technical and trade publications for the packaging industry. From these databases, the number of unique entries under the following key words were searched:

- ball grid array
- chip scale package
- multi chip module
- microvia

The number of entries per year are shown in Figure 1-14.

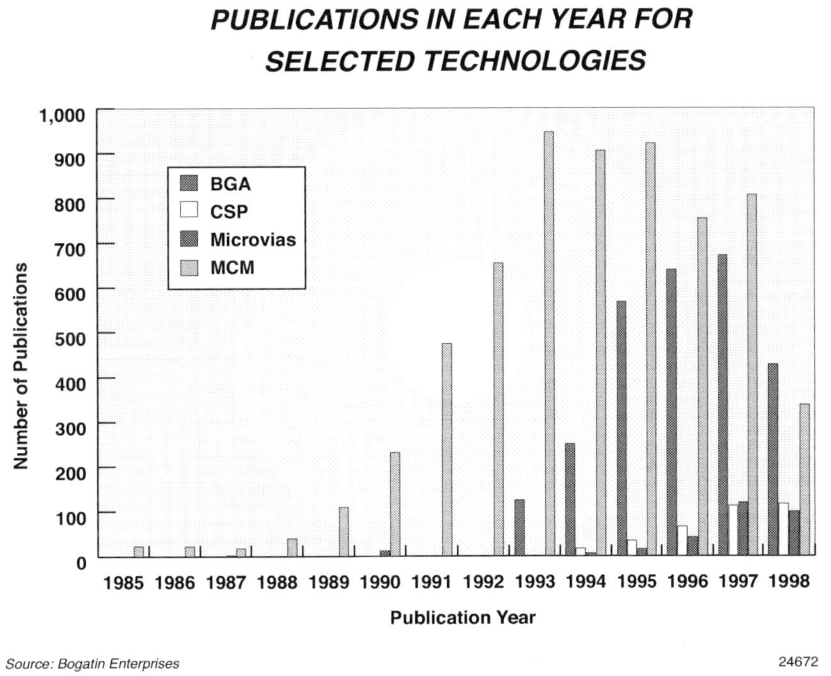

Figure 1-14. Publications in each year for new selected technologies. The low numbers in 1998 are due to the time delay for entries to be listed at the end of the year. This is a rough measure of the growth rate of a new technology.

From this distribution, it can be seen that MCM technology has at least been discussed in the literature for over 10 years. BGA technology has been popular for the last four years, while chip scale packages and microvia technology are just in their early phase of development.

What distinguishes an established technology is the infrastructure available to implement the approach and the number and variety of vendors in place with experience to provide the materials and service to manufacture with the technology. In the following chapters, the infrastructure for the new, revolutionary packaging technologies and selected vendors is reviewed.

A Perspective on the Future

Even when the new packaging and interconnect technologies are implemented and in full volume production, the older technologies, such as PGAs, DIPs and QFPs, will still have a large market share. Though the DIP package is almost 30 years old, there were over 8 billion DIPs used in production in 1998, and will be over 6 billion units used a few years from now. The predictions from Electronic Trends Publications for the unit volumes of various package designs are summarized in Figure 1-15.

Though many of the new technologies listed earlier are still evolving, and their niches are still being defined, some trends for the future seem clear.

Flip chip will be used for all ICs that are either performance driven or have I/O counts larger than about 600. In addition, low pin count chips will use flip chip I/O when direct chip attached to circuit boards for low cost applications. These will be limited to less than 100 I/O, so as not to tax the substrate interconnect density.

BGAs will be used for all single chip packages with pin counts over 200. This form factor offers the smallest size, using conventional assembly and board technology. It is the only way of cost effectively implementing high pin count packages, and has already dwarfed the use of pin grid arrays.

PREDICTIONS OF THE UNIT VOLUME OF PACKAGES

UNITS (MILLIONS)	1997	1998	1999	2000	2001	2002	CAGR
DIP (dual in–line package)	11,108	9,465	8,705	7,884	7,202	6,631	-9.80%
SO (small outline)	32,937	34,572	39,159	42,968	47,396	52,144	9.62%
CC (chip carrier)	3,801	3,762	4,032	4,249	4,413	4,711	4.39%
QFP (quad flat pack)	6,036	7,063	8,183	9,314	10,722	12,438	15.56%
PGA (pin grid array)	293	284	273	267	273	282	-0.77%
BGA (ball grid array)	930	1,651	2,720	3,914	5,243	6,755	48.67%
CSP (chip–scale package)	158	554	1,494	2,869	4,430	6,144	107.98%
DCA (direct chip attach)	3,074	3,523	4,160	4,747	5,308	5,814	13.59%
Total	58,337	60,875	68,725	76,212	84,989	94,919	10.23%

Source: Electronic Trends Publication

24673

Figure 1-15.

CSPs will be used for low pin count where performance, as either speed or small size, is important. The choice between BGA or CSP or leaded packages will depend on the cost/performance trade off for each application. If it can be implemented in a leaded package and meet the performance spec, it will always be the lowest cost solution. If it needs to be dense, or very fast, it will probably go CSP.

Microvia substrates will be used for high performance, high pin count packages or MCMs and small, high density boards, where functional density is important. High pin count DCA (Direct Chip Attach) and CSPs will require the use of microvia substrates.

MCMs, and in particular, few chip packages (FCPs) or multichip packages (MCPs), will play a role in providing a practical solution for "system on a chip" (SOC). This form factor allows mixed technologies, such as logic and memory, and more importantly, mixed vendors. It can also be ramped into production more quickly than SOC integration might be implemented.

This perspective on the future choices for single chip packages is summarized in Figure 1-16.

THE SINGLE CHIP PACKAGE SOLUTION MATRIX FOR THE FUTURE

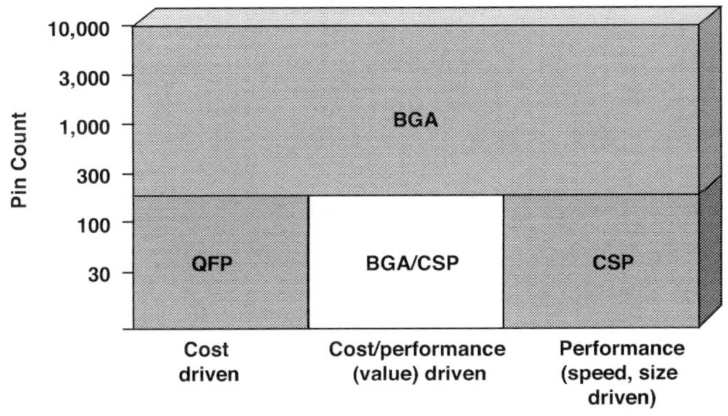

Source: Bogatin Enterprises 24674

Figure 1-16. The single chip package solution matrix for the future. Low pin count and lowest cost will be with leaded packages, such as QFPs. High pin count options will be BGA. Low pin count, performance driven will be with CSP. BGA and CSP will be possible choices for value driven applications.

2 Executive Summary of the Nine Revolutions Rocking the Packaging Industry

This chapter provides a brief introduction to the nine revolutions in the packaging and interconnect industry. In each summary, a description is presented of **what** the trend is. The **why**, including motivation, driving forces and advantages are then listed. A few examples of **how** this technology is being implemented are introduced. Finally, some of the players **who** are active in these technologies, both users and vendors, are listed.

The ensuing chapters review more details on each of these trends. The nine revolutions reviewed throughout this book are listed in Figure 2-1.

NINE SIGNIFICANT REVOLUTIONS CURRENTLY ROCKING THE PACKAGING INDUSTRY

FROM		TO
Wire bonded peripheral chip I/O	→	Flip chip array I/O
Peripheral leaded packages	→	Area array BGA (ball grid array) packages
Large, low packaging efficiency packages	→	High packaging efficiency chip scale packages (CSP)
Packaged die mounted on boards	→	Multiple bare die on a board or substrate as in COB, DCA, and multichipackage
Mechanically drilled holes in circuit boards	→	Microvias produced by plasma, laser and photoimageable materials
Discrete passive components	→	Integrated and integral passives
Vertically integrated companies that design, market, develop, manufacture and assembly products	→	Out–sourced contract manufacturers of silicon, package assembly, board assembly, and box assembly
Interconnects transparent to signals	→	Packages, substrates, and components specially designed for acceptable signal integrity and EMI
CAD (Computer Aided Design)	→	Computer Aided Engineering (CAE) and Electronic Design Automation (EDA) for concurrent engineering

Source: Bogatin Enterprises 24671

Figure 2-1. The nine revolutions rocking the packaging and interconnect industry.

REVOLUTION #1:

Flip Chip Area Array Off the Chip

What

The pads on a chip have traditionally been placed on the periphery of the chip to facilitate wire bonding to the row of pads on the package or substrate. On a flip chip, area array die, the pads are distributed on a grid, typically as fine as 8-10 mils (0.2mm to 0.25mm) pitch. An example of a peripheral I/O and an area array I/O chip is shown in Figure 2-2.

Who

All the leading semiconductor companies currently are in production with area array flip chip designs. In addition, there are three vendors who will apply the redistribution layers to wafers with peripheral I/O and add solder bumps. These are Aptos, Unitive and Flip Chip Technologies.

Why

Three forces drive the move to flip chip area array I/O: lower cost, smaller form factor and higher speed performance. In pad limited designs, the silicon die must be increased in size above what is required just to fit the gates to have enough perimeter to fit the pads. For high pin count, the time required to wire bond all the pads can be expensive. The cross over point is about 500-600 I/O. With area array, and the opportunity for more I/O, many extra power and ground connections can be added. When pushing the high speed limit, the inductance of a wire bond can contribute to excessive switching noise. A flip chip solder ball can have an inductance less than 1/10 the value of a comparable wire bond. This combined with the many more ground connections possible can dramatically reduce switching noise for a flip chip area array die.

How

The area array form factor can be provided in two ways. First, it can be designed in from the beginning, as is the case for most high end ASICs and microprocessors. Or, if the die is designed for peripheral I/O, a redistribution layer can be added to fan-in to an area array. Solder is the most common attach method, but adhesives are also used.

TYPICAL WIRE BOND PATTERN WITH FAN OUT FROM THE CHIP PERIPHERY TO THE PACKAGE BONDING SHELF

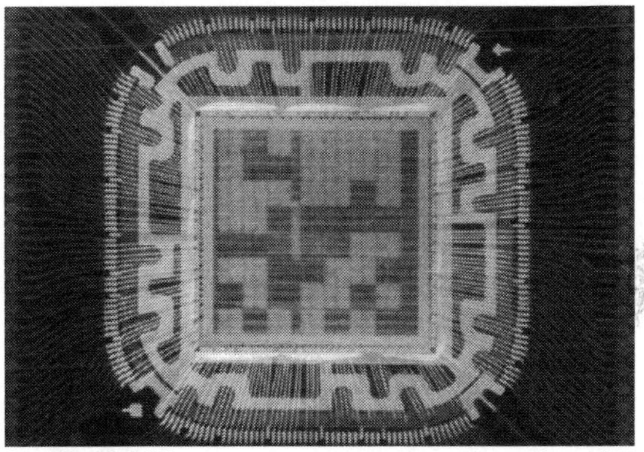

Source: Electronic Design/ICE 22409

SOLDER BALL FLIP CHIP ASIC

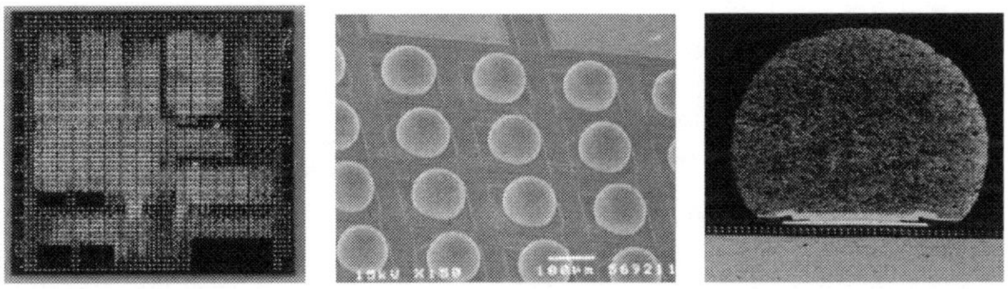

900 Ball Flip Chip ASIC | Close Up of the 5mil Diameter Solder Balls on the ASIC | Cross Section of Solder Ball Showing the UBM on the ASIC

Source: Fujitsu Computer Packaging Technology/ICE 22552

Figure 2-2. Trend #1-the use of area array I/O off the chip, rather than peripheral pads.

REVOLUTION #2:

Ball Grid Array Packages (BGA)

What

The BGA is a form factor for a package that has an array of balls on one side for reflow solder attach to a matched set of pads on the substrate. The solder ball pitch ranges from a typical pitch as large as 70 mils (1.78mm) down to 40mils (1.0mm). The BGA package is at the large pitch end of the continuum of grid array packages. When the pitch is below 40mils (1mm), the package type is usually called either chip scale or near chip scale. An example of a variety of BGA packages is shown in Figure 2-3.

Why

BGAs offer a smaller package body size and higher assembly yield over conventional peripheral leaded packages. As I/O count of a package increases, its body size with peripheral I/O will increase rapidly, taking up valuable real estate. Reducing the lead pitch to decrease the body size will increase the board cost and assembly difficulty. The grid array format allows a smaller body size for the same number of I/O. This cross over is at about 208 pins. The assembly defect rate of BGA packages can be less than 10% the defect rate of high pin count leaded packages.

WIDE VARIETY OF BGA TYPE PACKAGES

Source: Abpac 24712

Figure 2-3. Variety of BGA styles in production.

How

BGAs can be fabricated with either tape, ceramic or laminate substrates, with either peripheral pads on the die or area array pads. They can be as simple as a single layer of interconnect, or up to 10 layers for high performance chips. In its simplest form, a BGA is a small circuit board with gold pads on the top surface for the chip attach and solder balls on the other side for board attach. After assembly, the chip can be over molded to protect it from the environment. This configuration, called Over Molded Pad Array Carrier (OMPAC), was the first BGA in high volume.

Who

All large semiconductor suppliers ship product in BGAs for pin counts typically higher than 208. There are vendors of just the bare package, assemblers of the chip into the package and assemblers of the final BGA package to circuit boards. The leading package vendors are Ibiden, Kyocera, NTK, Shinko, Hadco, Via Systems and SMI. Many of the large semiconductor houses have their own captive package assembly lines. Contract package assemblers include Amkor, Abpac and ChipPAC. All the top ten CEMs (Contract Electronic Manufactures) are able to assembly BGAs to circuit boards, such as SCI, Solectron, Celestica, Jabil, Avex and Flextronics.

REVOLUTION #3:

Chip scale packages

What

Traditionally, Chip Scale Packages (CSP) referred to any package style where the resulting package was less than 20% greater in area than the silicon it packaged. This is a packaging efficiency of greater than 80%. There is some ambiguity in the industry as to whether the 20% increase is of the package area or package linear dimension. Recently, CSP has also come to refer to any package with an area array footprint having a ball pitch less than or equal to 0.8mm (32mils). CSPs are often referred to as microBGAs, however, this term is a registered name of the specific CSPs offered by Tessera. An example of Tessera CSPs is shown in Figure 2-4.

MICROBGA STYLE CSP's FROM TESSERA

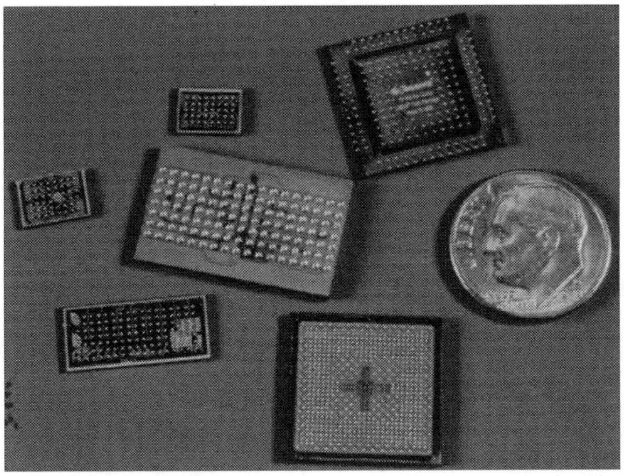

Source: Courtesy of Tessera 24678

Figure 2-4. Example of CSPs available from Tessera.

Why

A CSP is a compromise between the small size of a bare die, with the robustness of a package. The small size and high packaging efficiency means that devices can be placed closer together on a substrate and a higher functional density achieved. The package allows automated handling, high speed assembly, standard test fixtures, possible rework after assembly, reliable long term operation and a clean interface between the semiconductor vendor and the board assembler.

How

CSPs have two form factors, peripheral leads, as in lead over chip (LOC), or as an area array of solder balls, as in a miniature BGA. There are over 30 different CSP styles, each optimized by its proponent to provide some differentiation with the others. The two most popular styles use a BGA footprint on 0.8 to 0.5mm (32mil to 20mils) pitch. One approach is to use a rigid substrate, either BT laminate or cofired ceramic, with pads on one side to match the chip wire bond or flip chip pads. Routing traces in the substrate connect these pads to the bottom side of the CSP which has solder balls on a pitch to match the PCB the CSP will be mounted to. In the microBGA CSPs from Tessera, a flex film containing the solder ball array is laminated to the top of the die with a layer of compliant silicone. Wire bond like tabs are bonded to the die pads, which fan out to the solder ball array.

Who

Virtually all of the package suppliers and contract package assembly vendors offer a version of a CSP. These include Amkor, Abpac, ChipPAC, Kyocera, NTK, Shinko and Fujitsu. They are currently in use by many of the semiconductor vendors, such as Intel, AMD, TI, Motorola, LSI and VLSI.

REVOLUTION #4:

Bare die

What

Though most shipped products use the conventional approach of a collection of single chip packages mounted to a common substrate, there are alternatives that forego the package and use bare die. These include hybrids, MultiChip Modules (MCMs), Chip on Board (COB) and Direct Chip Attach (DCA). The emerging application that is moving to high volume use is the Multi Chip Package (MCP), or sometimes termed Few Chip Package (FCP). After encapsulation, it looks like a single chip package, but really contains multiple bare die on a common substrate. An example of a FCP is shown in Figure 2-5.

Why

The motivation for the use of bare die, as distinct from packaged die, is either to achieve a very small form factor, or to avoid the added cost of the package. When bare die are used, there is always the issue of Known Good Die (KGD). The added cost of testing and sorting die to be KGD can easily add more cost than an equivalent package. In the lowest cost applications, only die that are mature and have a very low post wafer sort drop out can be used to reap the cost savings advantage of bare die integration.

How

In cost driven applications, the bare die are tested on wafer and assembled onto the substrate either with wire bonding or flip chip. They are then glob top or under fill encapsulated and the board is processed and handled normally. In the case of small modules, the die are tested on wafer, and assembled to the small form factor substrate by wire bond or flip chip. The module is then tested and rework performed as needed. The module is then encapsulated and subsequently handled as though it was a single chip package. High performance and high cost applications might use die that have been through a KGD test to minimize the need for rework. Because of the close proximity of the die, a high interconnect density in the substrate is often needed. This has driven the development of very fine line substrates, using either cofired ceramic (MCM-C), laminate (MCM-L), or deposited thin film (MCM-D).

Who

Most package assembly vendors also assemble few chip modules, using ceramic or laminate substrates, such as Amkor, Abpac, ChipPAC, Shinko and Fujitsu. Most board assembly vendors also assemble chip on board, such as SCI, Jabil, Solectron and Celestica. Only a few semiconductor vendors offer a KGD program, notably TI and Intel. Other vendors will provide bare die with on wafer testing.

FEW CHIP PACKAGE IN CQFP FORM FACTOR USING LTCC SUBSTRATE

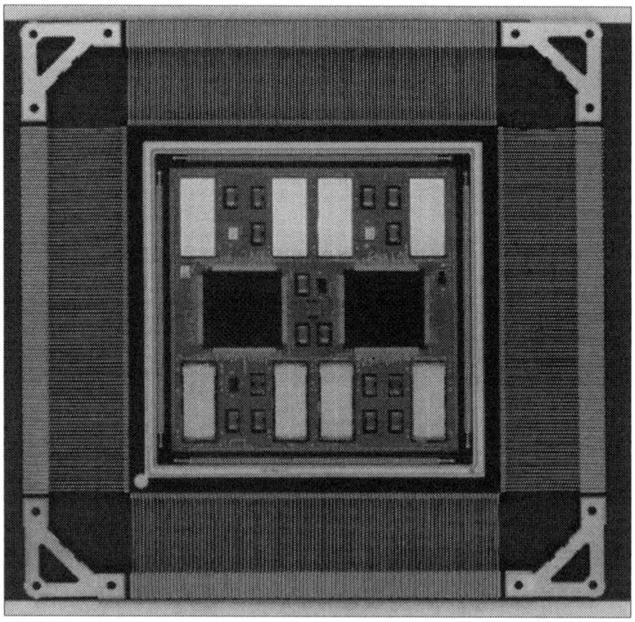

Source: CTS Microelectronics 24679

Figure 2-5. Example of a few chip module using a Low Temperature Cofired Ceramic (LTCC) substrate and flip TAB and wire bonded die, mounted in a ceramic quad flat pack (CQFP).

REVOLUTION #5:

Microvias

What

Microvias are vias produced in a non-mechanically drilled process. This usually means one of the four traditional methods of laser, plasma etched, chemically etched or using photo imageable dielectric. Since the manufacturing process typically involves fabricating one layer at a time, these substrates are often referred to as Build Up Multilayer (BUM) or Sequential Build Up (SBU). A close up of a board with microvias and conventional vias is shown in Figure 2-6.

PHOTO IMAGEABLE DIELECTRIC MICROVIAS

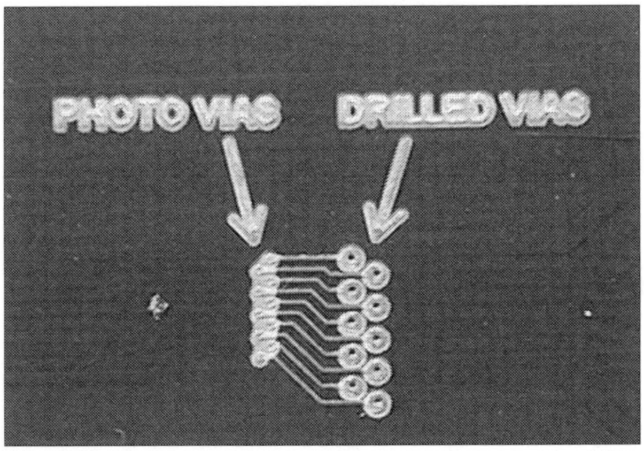

Source: Microvia Inc. 24677

Figure 2-6. Close up of microvias fabricated with a photo imageable dielectric and mechanically drilled.

Why

The use of microvias less than 5mils in diameter means that vias can be routed within the line width of traditional boards. This dramatically frees up routing density and requires fewer layers for the same functionality as dense boards. A 12 layer mechanically drilled board can be converted into a 6 layer microvia board. Secondly, when used with fine line lithography, of line widths on the order of 1-2mils (25-500microns), microvia substrates can provide a high surface pad density and interconnect density. This density can support the requirements of fine feature chip attach methods such as flip chip DCA, for use in single chip BGAs, and for fine pitch chip scale packages on small daughter cards and PC card formats.

How

Each layer in a microvia substrate is typically fabricated sequentially, built up on a substrate or a multilayer board representing the core. A layer of pure resin with no weave reinforcement is laminated to the prior layer and lithography used to define the holes. The holes are etched either individually with a laser, or en masse with chemical, plasma or optical etching, exposing the copper at the bottom of the hole. Standard additive plating processes are used to build the next layer of metalization and pattern it. In the next step, a new layer is added and the process repeats until all the layers are fabricated.

Who

All the leading edge PCB substrate and package manufacturers currently are in development or production with microvia substrates, using one or more of the above mentioned technologies. In the US, these include Hadco, Via Systems, Microvia Inc., Johnson Matthey and W.L Gore. In Japan, these include Ibiden, NTK and Kyocera.

REVOLUTION #6:

Integrated Passives

What

Passive components, such as resistors, capacitors and inductors, make up the largest component part counts in typical products. When mounted on the circuit board as individual units, they are called discretes. When multiple units are fabricated in a common substrate, they are called integrated passive devices (IPDs). When the discretes are fabricated as part of the substrate, they are called integral passives. Some examples of integrated passives are shown in Figure 2-7.

IPD ARRAY IN SOIC AND CSP PACKAGES

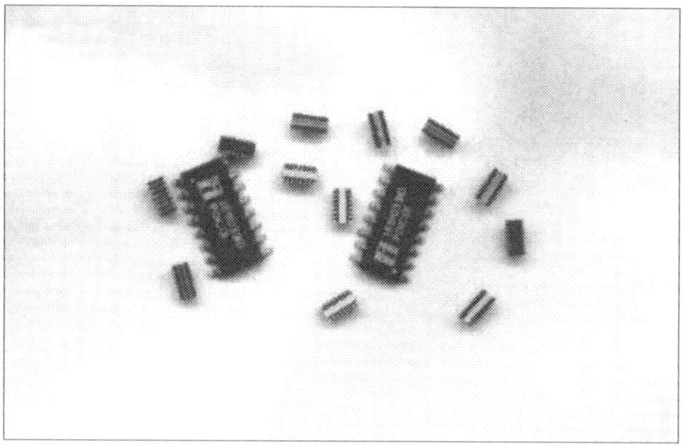

Source: Intarsia Corp 24682

Figure 2-7. Integrated Passive Devices (IPDs) from Intarsia, packaged in SOIC and CSP styles.

Why

When multiple discrete passives are combined together into integrated or integral passives there is a savings of board real estate, potential savings in total cost of ownership (TCO) and potentially higher performance. The smaller size of the integrated passives means the electrical properties can be more tightly controlled, and their bandwidth for acceptable performance increased.

How

There are a variety of fabrication technologies for integrated passives, some of which are merely extensions of discrete fabrication and others are taken from MCM substrate fabrication. Integral (embedded) components can be fabricated as part of the interconnect in LTCC (low temperature cofired ceramic) substrates using special inks. Resistor arrays can be fabricated in thin film metalization on ceramic substrates.

Who

All the discrete passive vendors also provide integrated passives. In addition, there are new companies, such as Intarsia, focused exclusively on integrated passives. There are three new integral passive vendors. Hadco holds the license for integral capacitance layers built into printed circuit boards. Ohmega Technologies holds the license for building resistors integral to PCBs. For cofired ceramic substrates, many of the ink suppliers, such as Dupont and Ferro, provide materials that can be used to fabricate resistor, inductor and capacitor structures in cofired ceramic substrates

REVOLUTION #7:

Outsourcing

What

In the manufacturing process flow, the main operations are: wafer fab, package fabrication, package assembly, board assembly and final box assembly. For each activity, there are multiple vendors that are dedicated to performing the function. A company wishing to design, manufacture, market and sell a product no longer needs to have the additional over head of manufacture, but can out source this function to vendors who can leverage the economies of scale by manufacturing 10x to 50x, the volume of any one company. It is possible for a small, $10 M company to leverage the manufacturing might of a billion dollar company by just providing the design database and have delivered back, fully fabricated and assembled parts. The manufacturing line of a typical assembly Contract Electronic Manufacturing (CEM) is shown in Figure 2-8.

PACKAGE FINAL ASSEMBLY LINE IN THE PHOENIX ABPAC FACILITY

Source: Abpac Corp. 24681

Figure 2-8. Overview of the highly automated package assembly line at the Abpac facility in Phoenix, Az.

Why

The availability of CEM services has changed the cost structure for manufacturing and the opportunities for small companies. It can often be much cheaper to contract specialized assembly operations than carry the overhead in equipment and skilled personal. When the product changes, and new technology needs to be introduced, the time normally required to build up the internal infrastructure can be eliminated by leveraging a CEM with this technology already in place.

How

In the past five years, many of the large, vertically integrated companies have sold off their internal manufacturing lines to independent CEMs. This has contributed to the growth of capacity and the security of the outsourcing business model. Most semiconductor and OEMs (original equipment manufacturers) have committed to outsourcing some portion of their manufacturing. In 1997, the outsourcing of assembly manufacturing was over $25 Billion, combined package and board level. And the success of the CEM business model has lead to the more than 20% growth rate in the sales of CEMs in 1998.

Who

Package assembly vendors are Amkor, Abpac, ChipPAC, IPAC, Shinko and Fujitsu. Board assemblers are SCI, Solectron, Celestica, Jabil, AVEX, and Flextronics.

REVOLUTION #8:

Designing for Speed

What

There are four high speed effects by which the interconnects can influence performance. They are typically grouped under the general category of signal integrity. If these effects are not accounted for, high speed products will fail. These effects are: signal quality in one net and its return path, cross talk between two or more nets, noise in the power and ground distribution, typically termed ground bounce, switching noise or delta noise, and EMI (Electro Magnetic Interference). The increasing role of the interconnect on the electrical effects of the system are illustrated in Figure 2-9.

Why

With on chip clocks at 500MHz and on board clocks at 100MHz and higher, the interconnects are no longer transparent. If commonly used designs from older generation products were used, the higher speed products would fail. One of the signal integrity effects would exceed the allocated noise budget and false triggering would occur. To minimize each noise source requires designing to a set of rules so the physical interconnects do not disturb the electrical signals beyond an acceptable level. In addition, new materials, components and technologies can enhance high speed performance.

How

Each of the four signal integrity effects have their own set of design rules that must be followed to minimize them. Signal quality is maintained by using a controlled impedance environment, which means keeping the characteristic impedance of the path for every signal as constant as possible. Cross talk can be controlled by keeping the separation between traces to no closer than a minimum value. Switching noise is minimized by keeping the inductance in the power and ground distribution to a minimum. This typically means using planes for transporting the power and ground, and where this is not possible, keeping the leads short. EMI can be minimized by careful control of the bandwidth of the signals, keeping common mode currents to a minimum in the circuit board and shielding potential radiators. When the design is complete, it should be simulated to verify acceptable performance before committing to hardware.

Who

There are two approaches to designing in acceptable signal integrity: develop the in house expertise, or contract out to signal integrity specialists. There is an increasing popularity in training courses for signal integrity, offered, for example, from the Technical Proficiency Institute. Also, many conferences have SI tutorial sessions, such as the PCB Design East and West, IPC Expo and DesignCon. Among the small firms that do signal integrity analysis are SIQual, NESA, GigaTest Labs and TriCN.

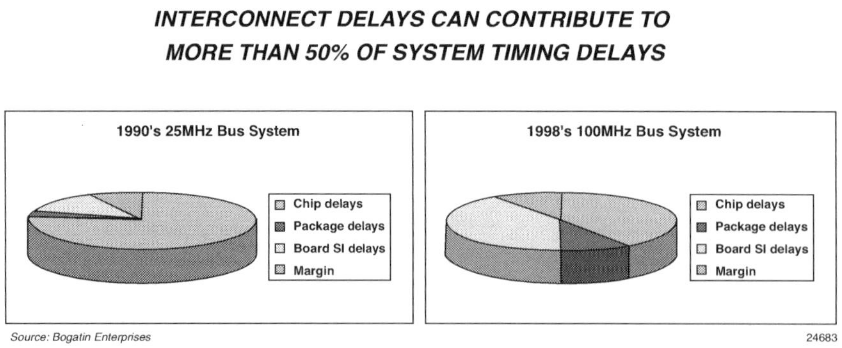

Figure 2-9. Increasing importance of the role of the packaging and interconnect in system performance.

REVOLUTION #9:

CAE

What

Computer aided engineering (CAE) adds intelligence, automation and analysis to traditional drafting tools. CAE is often grouped in the area of EDA (Electronic Design Automation). In packaging applications, CAE tools include the ability to automate many of the specific tasks such as net list creation, wire bond pad positioning and autorouting. After the design is complete, the features can be checked for manufacturability and performance. Electrical models can be extracted for the interconnect elements and simulations performed. An example of the complex designs that can be performed by a CAE tool is shown in Figure 2-10.

HIGH PIN COUNT BGA DESIGNED WITH XYNETIX ENCORE

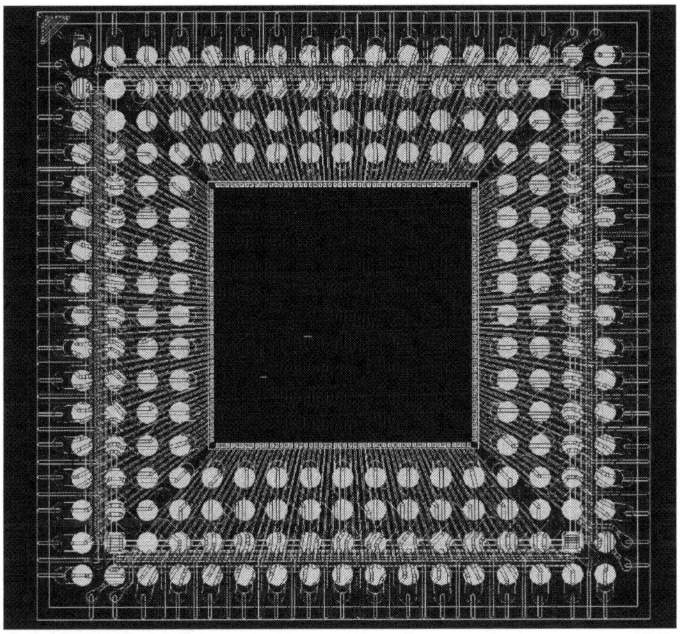

Source: Courtesy of Xynetix Corp 24680

Figure 2-10. Example of complex BGA designed with an automated EDA tool that generated the wire bonds, routing and netlist automatically.

Why

With time to market critical, the ability to design a product quickly is a competitive advantage. EDA tools which automate design of complex packages can cut the design cycle in half. In addition to completing the design, performing design rule checks and simulations of virtual prototypes will assure the success of the first article before release to hardware.

How

CAE tools add intelligence to traditional CAD tools. Specialized processes unique to package design, such as wire bond pad generation, solder ball pad generation and netlist creation are available. The database associated with the final layout can be compared against a predefined set of rules for schematic, test and manufacture. The physical design features of a virtual prototype can be translated into an equivalent electrical model by using either analytic approximations or by using a 2D or a 3D field solver. From the electrical models, the performance of the part with sources and loads can be simulated with SPICE or an IBIS based simulator.

Who

For package EDA design, there are four main vendors, Cadence, Xynetix, PADs and CAD Design Software. For package electrical analysis, there are many small vendors, such as Ansoft, ApSim, Pacific Numerix and OptEM Engineering.

3 Flip Chip Approaches

DRIVER FOR FLIP CHIP: HIGHER PERFORMANCE

The two most important trends in chip evolution are the move to higher pin count and the move to higher frequency operation. Both of these chip needs can be satisfied by the transition to flip chip bonding, while offering the possibility of lower total cost of ownership for the packaging solution.

Flip chip refers to mounting the die flipped over with the active side in near contact with the next level of package. A comparison of flip chip and traditional, active side up mounting as with wire bonding, is shown in Figure 3-1.

This shorter connection length can have a dramatic impact on performance. The most important package related limitation to the high speed operation of the chip is the inductance associated with the off-chip I/O. High inductance in the power and ground connections will increase switching noise and ground bounce. To first order, inductance scales with the length of the connection. A shorter length will have less inductance and contribute to lower ground bounce.

The partial self inductance, in nH, of a cylindrical rod of radius r, and length l, with l in cm, is approximated by:

$$L_{self} = 2xl\left[\ln\left(\frac{2l}{r}\right) - 0.75\right] \text{ nH}$$

Using this relationship, the partial self inductance of a wire bond, with radius of 0.5mils (13micron), and a solder ball, with approximate radius of 2mils (50microns) can be estimated. This estimate is shown in Figure 3-2.

CLOSE UP OF FLIPPED DIE ON FLEX SUBSTRATE

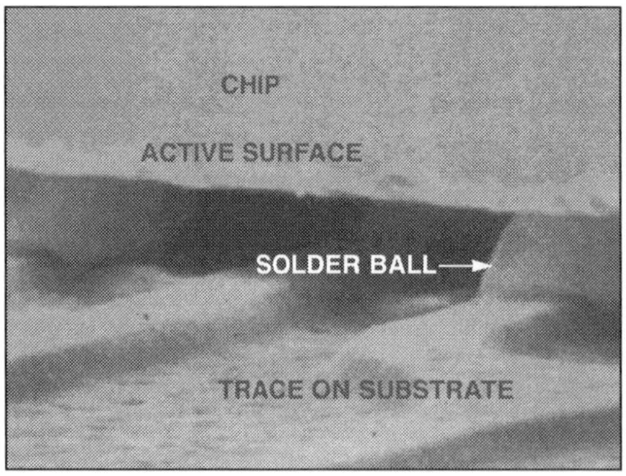

Source: FCT

ULTRA FINE PITCH WIRE BOND TEST CHIP IN LEADED PACKAGE

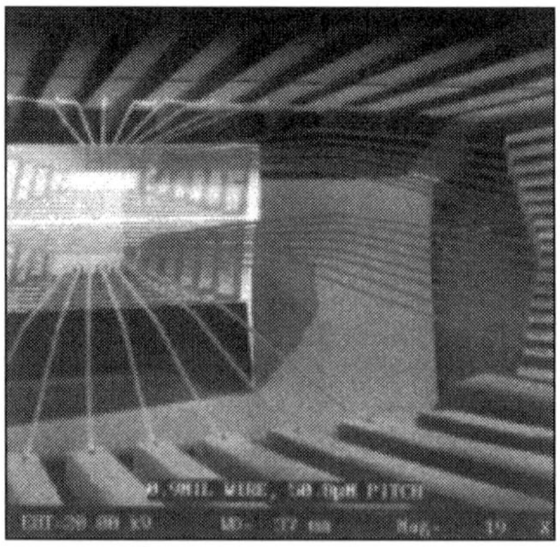

Source: ASM

24667

Figure 3-1. Mounting a die as a flip chip dramatically shortens the I/O length from the chip to the substrate. Left: Flip chip solder attached die on laminate substrate. Right: Fine pitch wire bonded die in lead frame package.

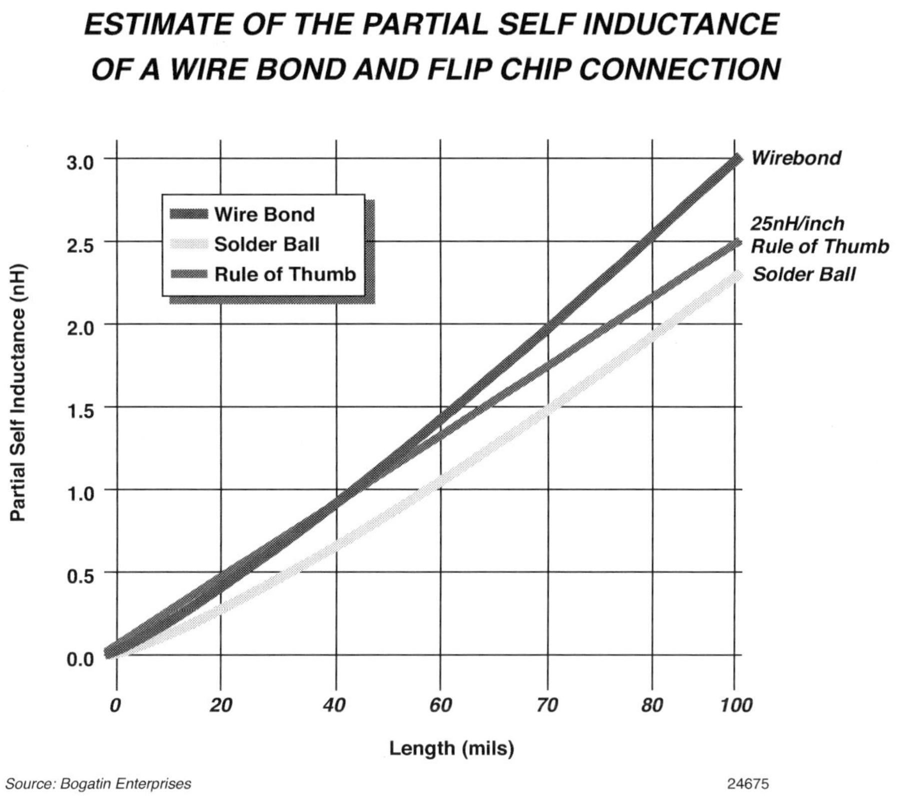

Figure 3-2. Estimated partial self inductance of a wire bond and solder ball, compared with the commonly used rule of thumb of 25nH/inch.

A wire bond 100mils long will have an inductance of about 3nH, while a solder ball, approximately 5mils long, will have an inductance of about 0.05nH. This is confirmed by measurements of the loop inductance of two solder balls in series, which should be approximately twice the self inductance of one, shown in Figure 3-3.

The lower inductance of the short flip chip connection will dramatically cut down the switching noise or ground bounce, provided, of course, that the power and ground distribution in the package is low inductance as well. This is shown in Figure 3-3.

Driver for Flip Chip: Form Factor

The pattern of I/O off the die can be exactly the same perimeter I/O pads used for wire bonding, or they can be distributed as a full area array and anything in between. An example of the three common configurations for ASICs is shown in Figure 3-4.

The first term that determines the pattern is the pitch that the next level of interconnect can handle and the number of I/O that need to come off. If perimeter I/O can handle the requirements, it will always be the lowest cost, and no changes need to be made to the die in transitioning from a wire bond to a flip chip design. An example of a low cost flip chip perimeter I/O chip is shown in Figure 3-5.

When the needed I/Os cannot be fit around the perimeter, they can be distributed across the area. This is accomplished by either designing the area array I/O connections in the early stage of the chip layout, or by redistributing the fine pitch peripheral pads to area array pads with one or two additional routing layers. These redistribution layers (RDL)can be added to the wafer as a post fab operation. An example of the fabrication of a redistribution layer is illustrated in Figure 3-6.

MEASURED LOOP INDUCTANCE OF A FLIP CHIP CONNECTION

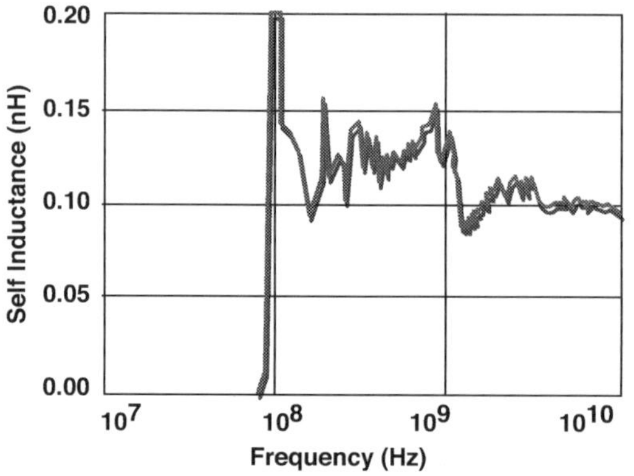

SIMULATED SWITCHING NOISE WITH FLIP CHIP AND TAB

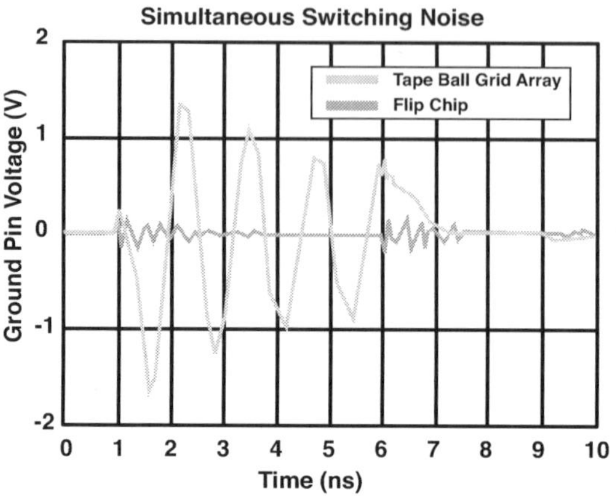

Source: Unitive Electronics Inc. 24676

Figure 3-3. Performance of flip chip connections. Left: Measured loop inductance of two flip chip solder ball connections, as approximately 0.1nH. Right: Simulation of the ground bounce expected from a TAB connection with inductance of 5.1nH and this flip chip connection.

SOLDER BALL ARRAY PATTERNS RECOMMENDED BY IBM

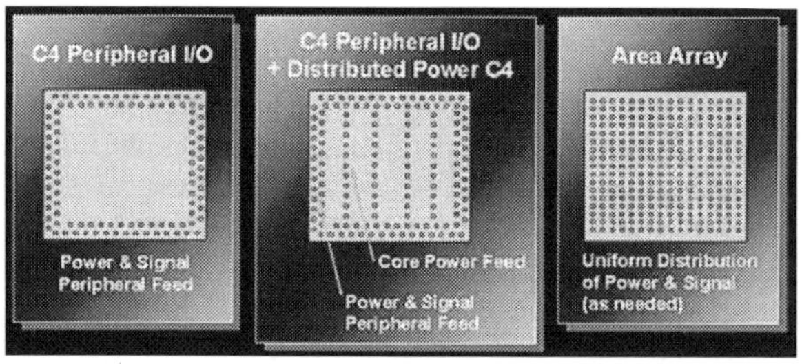

Source: IBM 24684

Figure 3-4. Range of I/O form factors for flip chip die, from perimeter, to full array.

The use of the entire area of the die for I/O can dramatically increase the number of pads that can come off the die. Using the tightest pitch area array currently in production of 200micron pitch, there is the potential of as many as 8,000I/O from an 18mm square die. In contrast, a state of the art wire bond die, at 75micron pitch, can provide only 1000I/O off this die. There are ASIC chips in production today with over 2000I/O. These I/Os can only be fit by an area array distribution. Even smaller die, only 10mm on a side, can accommodate over 2000I/O. This comparison is shown in Figure 3-7.

SMALL FLIP CHIP WITH PERIMETER PADS

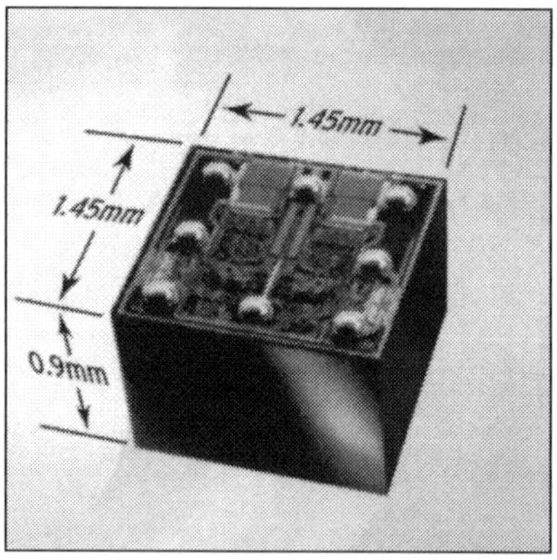

Source: National Semi 24685

Figure 3-5. Small analog chip with perimeter I/O and flip chip connections, with a pitch of about 500microns (20mils), easily accommodated with conventional circuit board substrates.

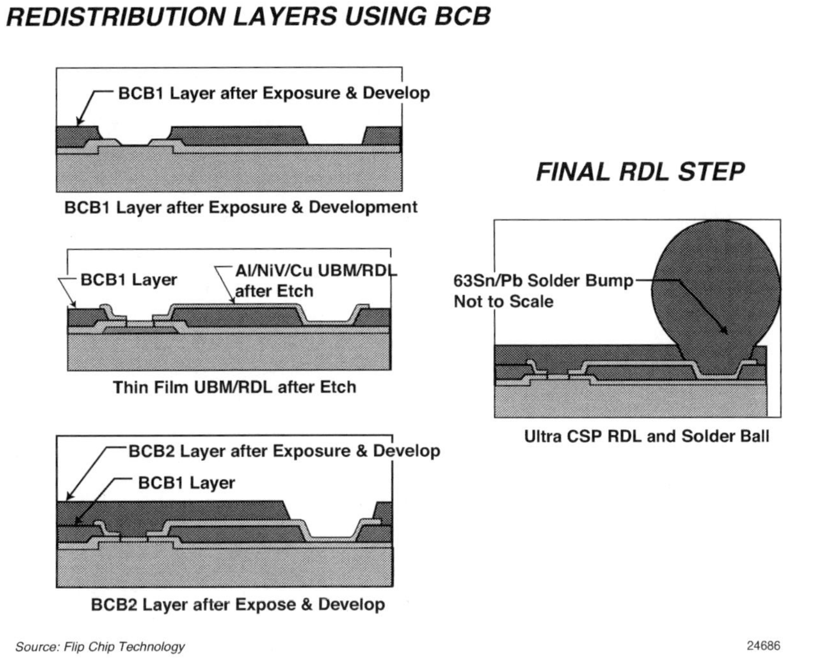

Figure 3-6. Schematic of the construction of redistribution layers on top of the die that connect peripheral pads to multiple rows. Due to the masked steps, adding redistribution layers can be expensive.

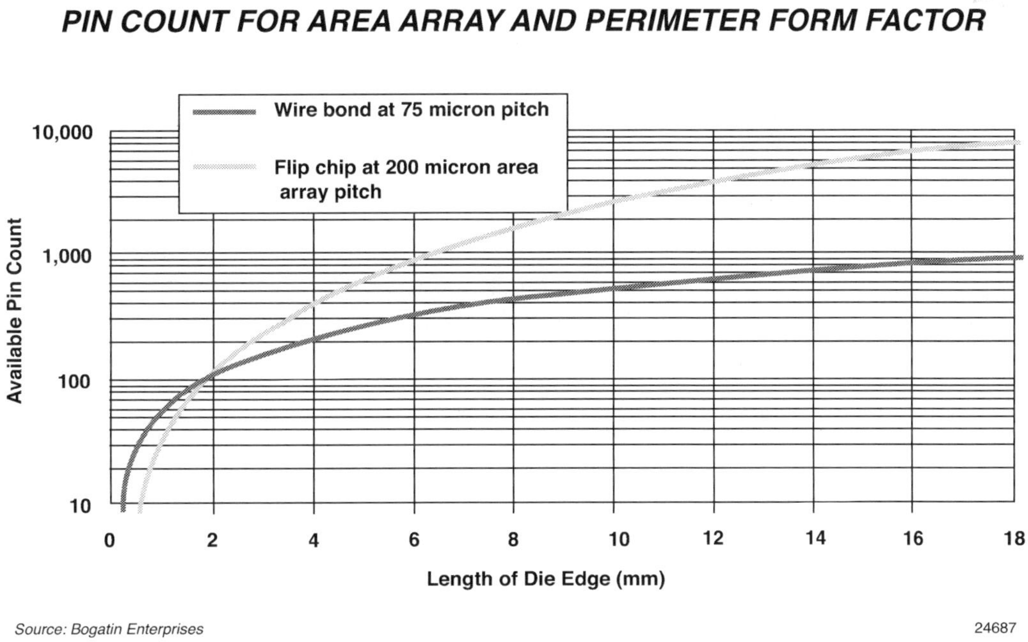

Figure 3-7. Comparison of available off chip pads with state of the art, 75micron wire bond pitch and state of the art 200micron area array pitch.

Designing the I/O locations to be distributed across the surface of the die will make dramatic improvements in electrical performance. In addition to the previously mentioned lower inductance, the resistance feeding the on-chip power and ground distribution network will be less. For example, if the top metal, 1micron thick aluminum, has stripes, 0.1mm (4mils) wide to distribute power, the resistance of a 5mm section is about 1Ohm. If pads were distributed on 250micron centers (10mils), the maximum resistance could be kept to as low as 0.1Ohm, resulting in much lower IR drops to the center of the die.

Applications and Markets

Flip chip assembly had its origins in the early 1960s with IBM and AT&T. IBM adopted an early version of the currently used solder ball attach, while AT&T introduced a type of flip TAB (Tape Automated Bonding), they termed beam lead. In the 1970's solder ball based flip chip was adopted by Delco Electronics for automotive applications. Since these early days, flip chip has diversified and spread into low end and high end applications.

There are two generic form factors for substrates where flip chip attach is used, flip chip on board (FCOB) and flip chip in package (FCIP). FCOB is when the bare die is mounted onto a large area substrate, typically in low cost, high volume consumer applications, such as watches, hard disk drives and flat panel displays. Historically, this configuration has been termed Direct Chip Attach (DCA).

FCIP is when the bare die is mounted on a single chip or multichip package substrate. These are typically high pin count, high performance and lower volume applications. An example of each is shown in Figure 3-8.

FCOB APPLICATION FOR HARD DISK DRIVE CONTROLLER

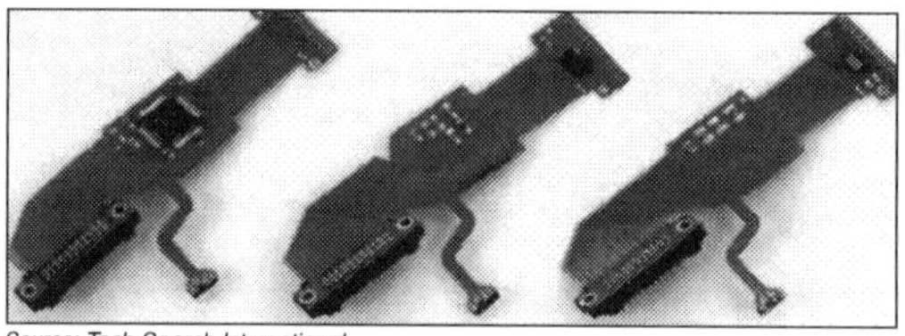

Source: Tech Search International

EXAMPLE OF A FCIP ASIC

Source: Fujitsu Microelectronics 24688

Figure 3-8. Examples of the two form factors where flip chip attach is used. Top: Flip chip on board (FCOB) used in a hard disk drive application. This illustrates the evolution from leaded package, wire bonded chip on board (COB), and the smaller, lighter form factor of flip chip. Bottom: Flip chip in package (FCIP) used for a high pin count ASIC.

The largest application market by far is for low end FCOB products. Citizen alone ships over 1 Million watches a day with FCOB components. In addition, automotive and consumer applications make up the largest volume of FCOB use. However, the high end Xeon processor from Intel and the K6 processor from AMD are shipping as FCIP. Many chip scale packages (CSPs) with 50 to 200 leads, in consumer applications, use a die that is flip chip attached to a small interposer substrate. As these mainstream, high end applications increase, the percentage of FCIP will increase. Tech Search International estimates that by 2001, over 20% of the flip chip applications will be FCIP. Their prediction is shown in Figure 3-9.

The distribution of flip chip usage by application, as reported by Prismark Partners, is shown in Figure 3-10.

Future of Wire Bonding

Though flip chip applications will proliferate at the low end and the high end, wire bonding will always play a dominant role. Wire bonding allows the ultimate in flexibility and the capital expense to set up volume production for wire bond assembly is less than $50k per station. It is the low risk path, with many established and local suppliers. If the performance hit from the wire bonds is not limiting performance, and the I/Os can fit along the perimeter, wire bonding may be the right choice.

In 1996, there were about 20 billion chips fabricated for wire bond assembly, with a total of about 1.2 trillion pads. If these were all wire bonded with a bond length of 70mils (2.0mm), a total of about 2 million miles of wire bond would have been used. This is enough gold and aluminum wire to make almost five round trips from the Earth to the Moon! Wire bonding will always have a role to play.

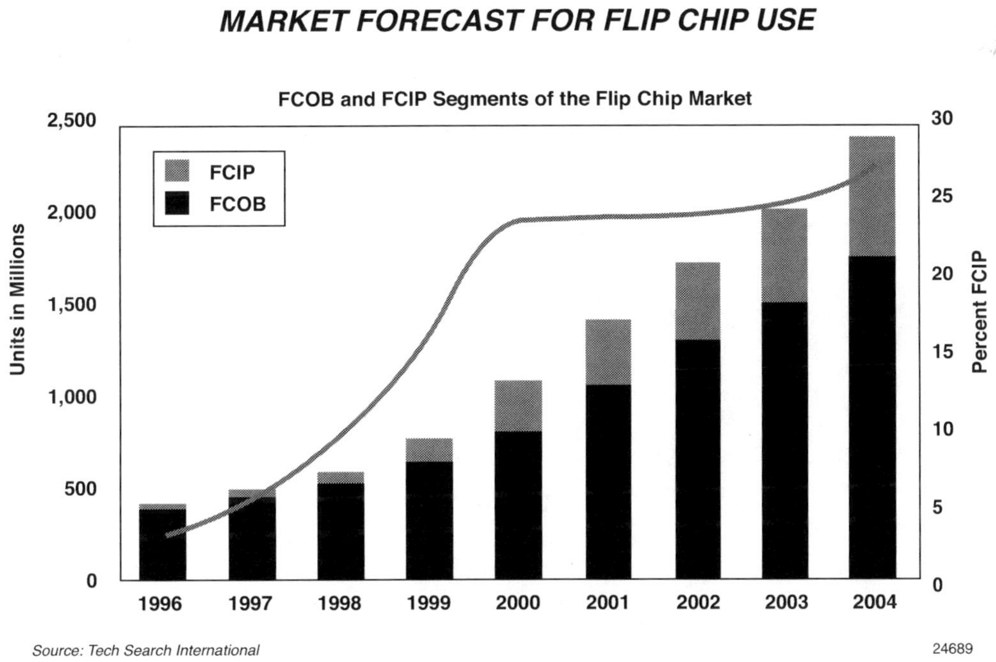

Figure 3-9. Predicted unit volume shipment of flip chip devices and distribution among FCIP and FCOB.

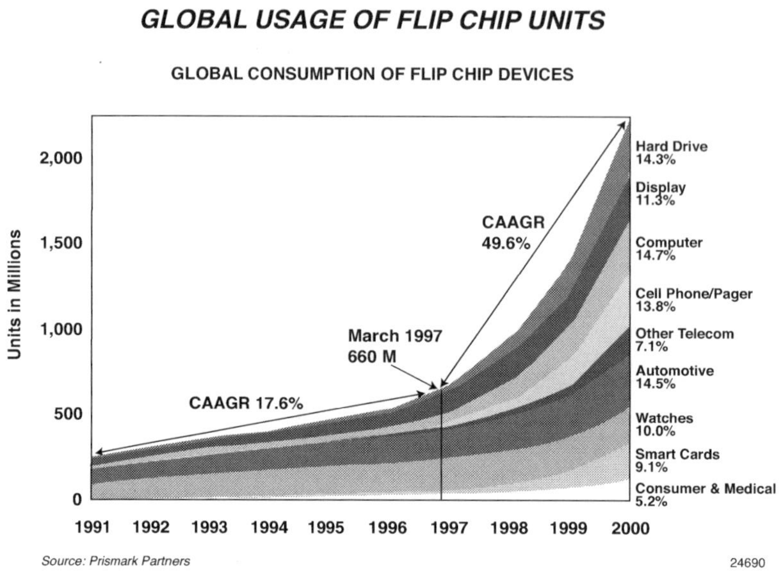

Figure 3-10. Applications for flip chip devices, both FCOB and FCIP.

As flip chip technology advances, so will the capabilities of wire bonding. Though 70micron pad centers is the finest pitch in volume production in 1999, 50micron pitch on one row has been demonstrated. By using two staggered rows, each on 100micron centers, 50micron effective pitch can be implemented now, though there may be a yield loss for such a large number of wire bonds. Figure 3-11 shows examples of these two, leading edge wire bonding capabilities.

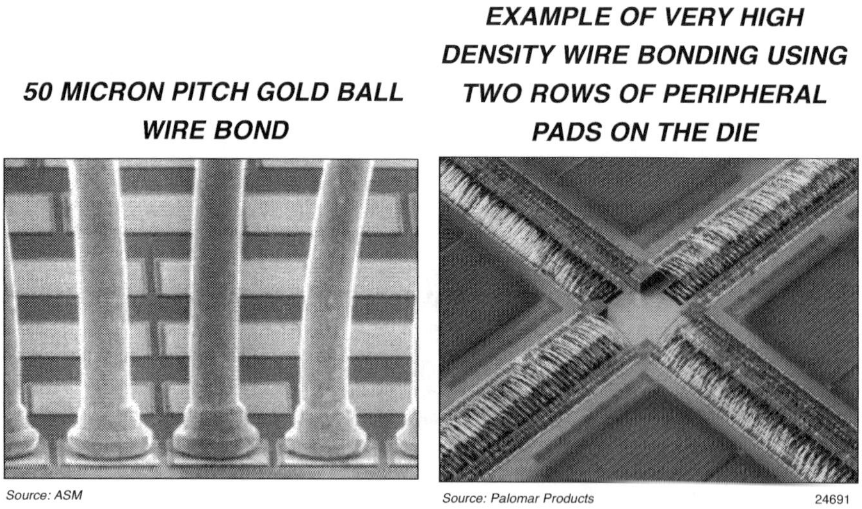

Figure 3-11. Achieving 50micron pitch with wire bond. Left: Ultra fine pitch gold ball bonding at 50micron pitch, using 23micron diameter gold wire, demonstrated by ASM. Right: Two rows of pads, each at 100micron centers. Most of the bonds in this example are between adjacent die, though some go to the underlying laminate substrate.

IBM has announced the production availability of an ultra fine pitch BGA package that is capable of handling a die with 60micron single row on-chip pad pitch and 45micron effective pitch using two staggered rows on the die at 90microns pitch on each row. The package has two bonding shelves, each with a pad pitch of 180microns (7mils). The effective pitch with the two rows is 90microns (3.5mils). These chip and package features, shown in Figure 3-12, probably represent the limit of what will ever be used by wire bonding. The die that would need these pitches on chip or on package, probably are high pin count and high speed. It would have a significant enough performance advantage if implemented as flip chip that it would probably never be designed for wire bond.

FLIP CHIP IMPLEMENTATION

As with many new packaging approaches, there is a rich variety in the reported implementations of flip chip devices. This wealth of options has contributed to the slow adoption of flip chip attach- there have been too many options for new users to decide on. Until recently, there hasn't been anything standard about the flip chip process. There are five basic steps in all the variations:

Under Bump Metalization (UBM)

This step involves the preparation of the aluminum pad into a bump. Typically a glue metal such as Cr or Ti is first deposited. Then a barrier or solderable metal such as Cu or Ni is applied.

Bump Build Up

On top of the UBM, a bump is built up. It can be solid that does not re-melt, or made of a solder that will reflow during assembly.

Attach Material

The bumped chip is attached to the substrate by either solder or a conductive adhesive. Typically adhesives are used for low temperature environments such as RF ID tags, smart cards, LCD flat panel displays, and sensor applications.

Substrate Attach

Die can be attached to single chip packages, including chip scale packages, multichip module substrates or boards.

ULTRA FINE PITCH BGA PACKAGE | **60 MICRON PITCH WIRE BOND**

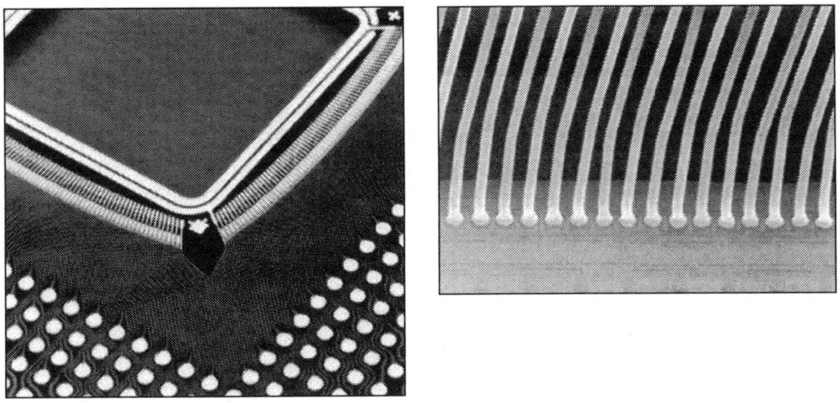

Source: IBM

24692

Figure 3-12. Ultimate limits to wire bonding, available from IBM. Right: Close up of on chip wire bonds at 60micron pitch. Left: BGA package with two staggered bonding shelves with 180micron pitch on each row.

Underfill

A low viscosity polymer is injected under the die to provide environmental protection of the active surface and stress relieving the solder joint to increase the reliability of the joint.

There are four primary processes that are currently in high volume production and will play a dominant role in the future:

- The IBM C4 process
- The maskless zincate process
- A ministud bumping with ACF
- Gold ball bonding and conductive epoxy

IBM PROCESS

The process originally developed by IBM and still in use is illustrated in Figure 3-13.

High temperature solder was originally used because evaporation was the process to deposit the solder. Eutectic solder cannot be evaporated due to the large difference in vapor pressures between the lead and tin. This process has been termed Controlled Collapse Chip Connection, or C4. The term C4 is generally applied to all flip chip solder ball connections.

Variations on this method include the use of Ti or Ni as the glue metal layer, and sputtering the metalization, and the electroplating of eutectic solder or screening of solder paste to build up the ball. With eutectic solder, conventional reflow ovens can be used for the reflow and die attach.

Flip Chip Technologies currently uses a modification of this process, illustrated in Figure 3-14.

A cross section of the solder ball attached to a plated pad on a substrate is shown in Figure 3-15.

MASKLESS ZINCATE PROCESS

The next generation process that has the potential of being the lowest cost bumping process is completely maskless. It uses the exposed aluminum bonding pads on the chip as catalytic surfaces to first Zincate, and then electrolessly plate Ni. As a final step, a flash of electroless gold is plated on the Ni to preserve its solderability. This process is illustrated in Figure 3-16.

STEPS IN IBM C4 PROCESS

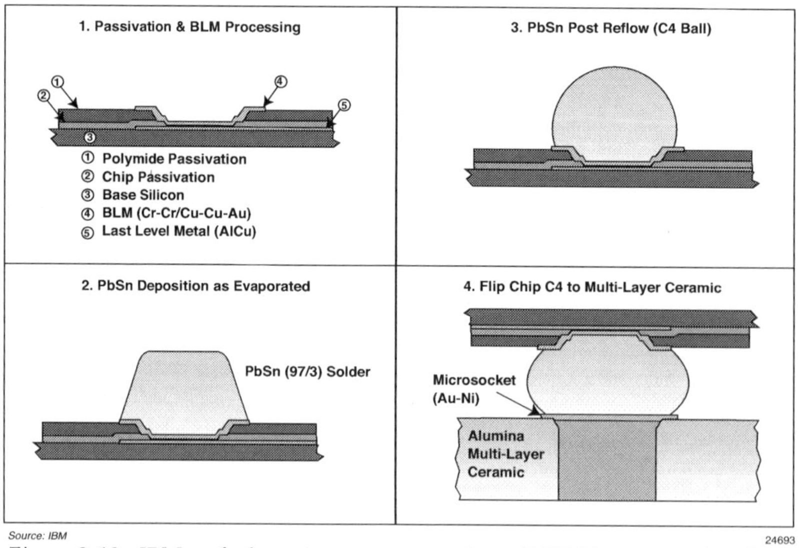

Figure 3-13. IBM wafer bumping process: creation of UBM by evaporation, high temperature solder deposition through a shadow mask, reflow of the solder bump and high temperature solder reflow to a ceramic substrate.

CLOSE UP OF SOLDER BALL AND UMB PAD

BUMPING PROCESS BY SCREENING SOLDER PASTE

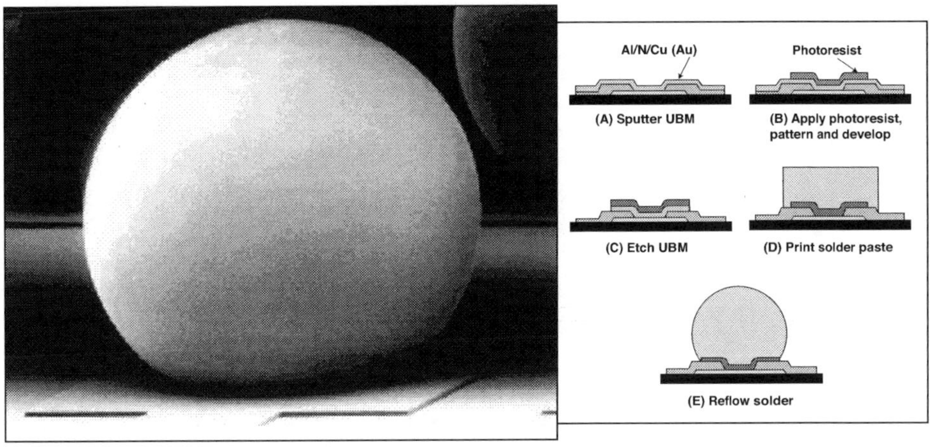

Source: FCT 24694

Figure 3-14. FCT bumping process and resulting solder ball after reflow. Note the oversized UBM pad encapsulating the Al pad and chip passivation.

CROSS SECTION OF SOLDER BALL UNDER FLIP CHIP

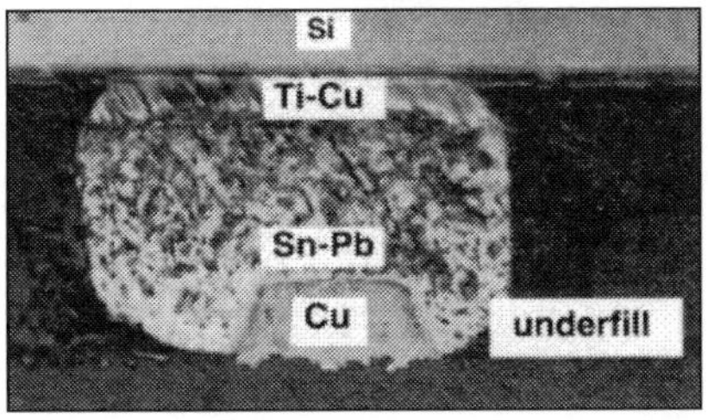

Source: Express Packaging System 24695

Figure 3-15. Cross section of conventional flip chip solder ball attached to a substrate.

After the UBM is deposited, solder can be screen printed over the bumps and reflowed. Figure 3-17 shows these steps.

Because there is no mask involved, all of the lithography steps are eliminated. This process has the potential of being extremely low cost. It will be used by PacTech GmbH, Unitive and Flip Chip Technologies.

The precise UBM selected has a strong impact on the reliability of the resulting solder bump. Too much stress in the UBM will either crack the silicon or stress it so that in a ball shear test, the silicon will crater. A good shear test will leave the solder ball sheared in half. Examples of failed and passed ball shear tests are shown in Figure 3-18.

MINISTUD BUMPING AND ACF

There are two non-solder approaches for flip chip attach, currently in volume production. The first uses an anisotropic conductive film (ACF). Once the UBM is applied, a small bump is plated up, and covered with gold, as for example, with the zincate process. This surface is mounted to pads on a matching substrate with a layer of ACF between them. The adhesive film contains a low density of small conductive particles, far enough apart so they do not touch, but close enough together, so there is a high probability of having at least 5-10 of them on every die pad.

SCHEMATIC OF THE ELECTROLESS ZINCATE BUMPING PROCESS

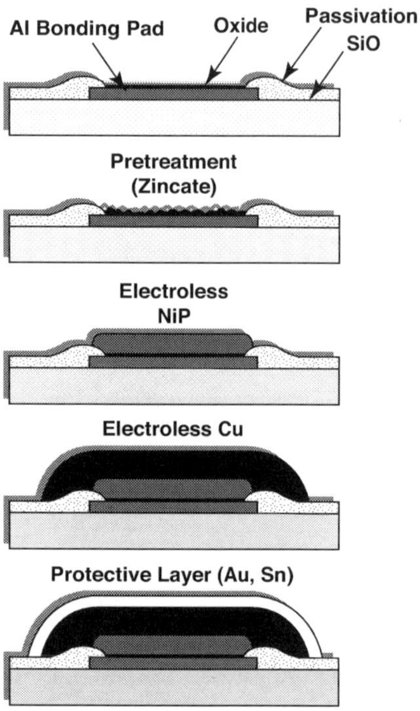

Source: IEEE Transactions on Components 22128

Figure 3-16. Zincate process for the maskless bumping of a wafer.

This technique is commonly used when the substrate is very flat, as with the glass surface of flat panel displays. This attach method is sometimes called chip on glass (COG). Figure 3-19 illustrates the assembly process, and a cross section of an assembled chip. One limitation of ACF for general use is it's high contact resitance from 0.1Ω to 1Ω.

ADHESIVE ATTACH

An alternative polymer attach method uses isotropically conductive adhesive, and non-plated bumps. When a polymer based attach is used, it is possible to keep the process temperatures low enough so delicate substrate materials can be used. In the bonded interconnect technology (BIT) approach from Fujitsu, gold ball bond studs are attached to the aluminum pads of the die using a modified wire bonder. After the gold stud is formed, it is dipped in conductive epoxy and then flip mounted to the substrate. This approach does not require any special treatment of the die and can be implemented in conventional assembly lines. For low pin count chips, this is a simple, low risk, low cost process. A similar process is used by Matsushita, termed Stud Bump Bonding (SBB). Both processes are in high volume use in consumer applications in Japan. This process is illustrated in Figure 3-20.

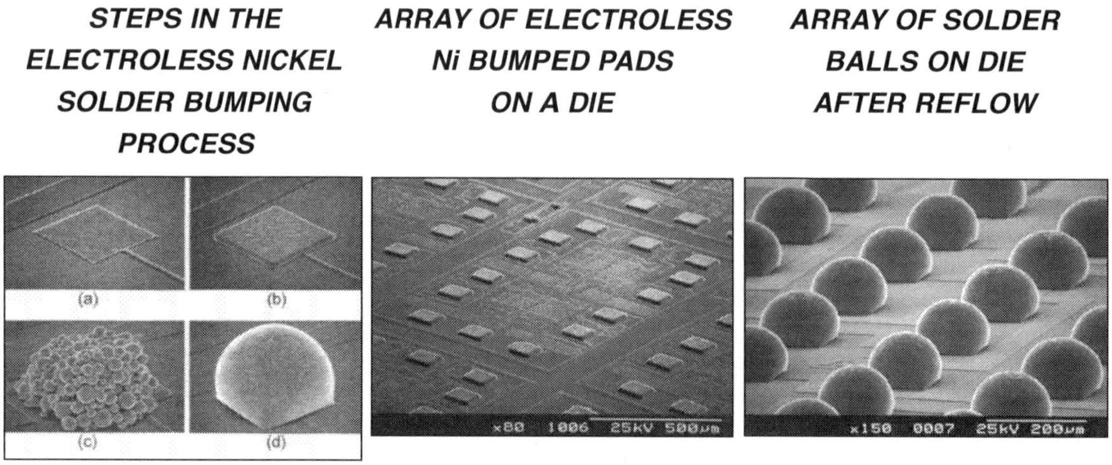

Source: Pac Tech GmbH 24697

Figure 3-17. Left: SEMs of the bare aluminum pad, after the maskless electroless deposition of the UBM, after screen printing solder paste, and after reflow. Center: An array of pads after UBM deposition. Right: Same array of pads after solder deposition and reflow.

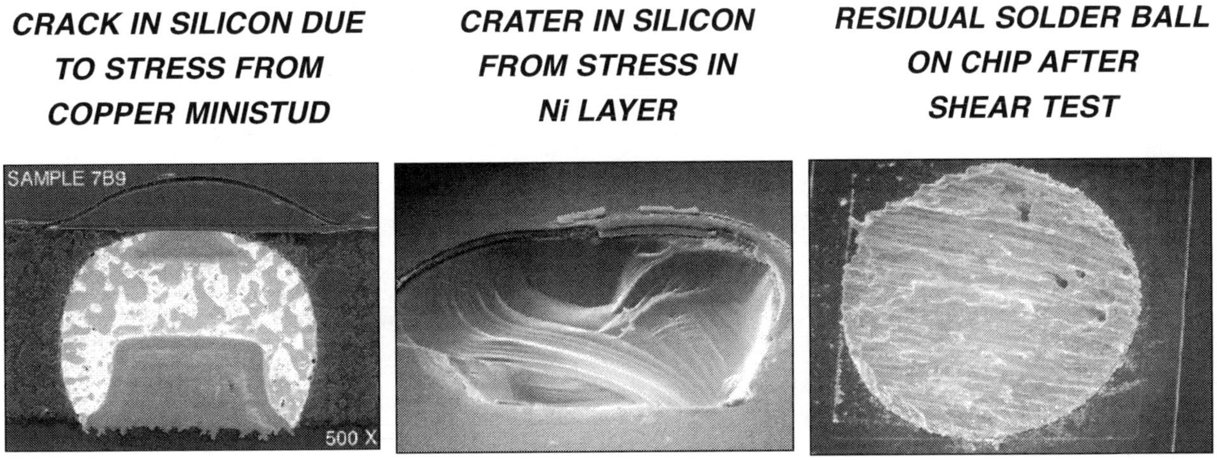

Source: FCT 24698

Figure 3-18. Left: Cracked silicon due to stress in the UBM. Center: Crated silicon after ball shear test. Right: Result of ball shear test showing residual solder ball on die pad.

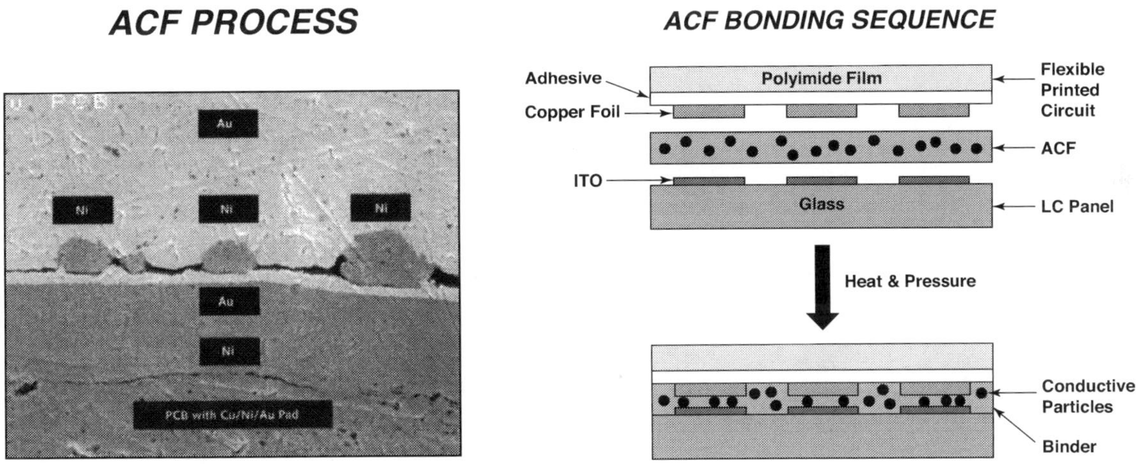

Source: Express Packaging Systems 24699

Source: SST/ICE 20964

Figure 3-19. Schematic of the ACF assembly process, with a cross section of a gold bumped ball in contact with a gold plated substrate bump. Note the compression of the nickel particles into the gold bump.

SINGLE-BUMP GOLD BALL BOND PROCESS

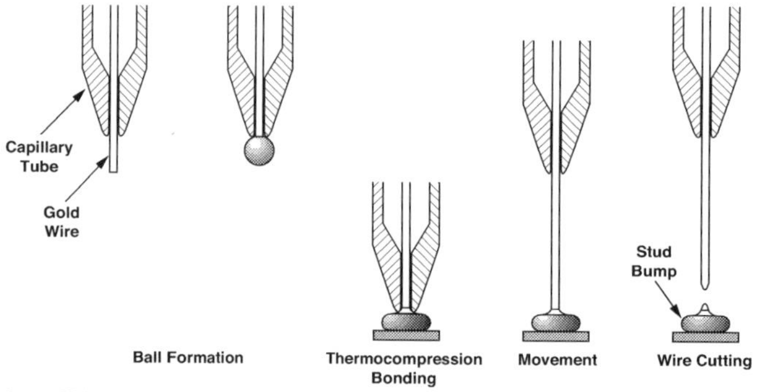

Source: ICEMM Proceedings '93/ICE

19377

CLOSE UP OF MATSUSHITA STUD BUMP BONDING (SBB)

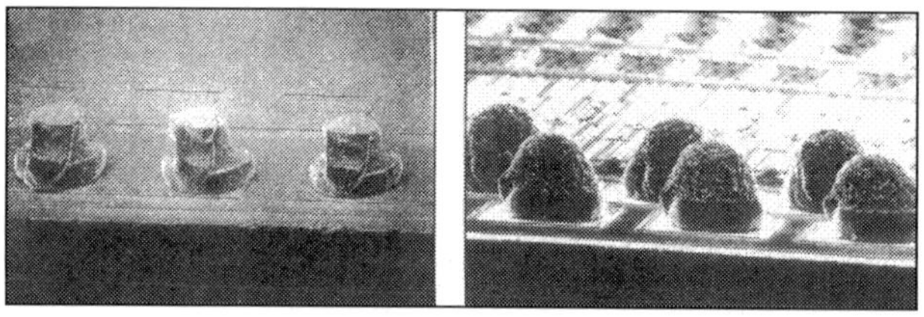

Source: Express Packaging System

24700

Figure 3-20. Schematic of the SBB stud bump bonding process and examples of the as fabricated gold studs and after coated with conductive epoxy, ready for flip chip assembly to a substrate.

In addition to the gold wire bond stud bump, a polymer bump can be used. This has the advantage of being potentially low cost because the polymer can be screen printed over the whole wafer. An UBM layer is required to provide a noble surface. A thermoplastic, silver filled epoxy is screen printed leaving a polymer bump. The chip can be flip chip mounted to the substrate and heated to re-melt the thermoplastic. As these operations only involve maskless electroless plating and screen printing, they have the potential of being very low cost as well. A dielectric protection layer can also be screen printed, keeping the pads open. Polymer Flip Chip, a division of Epoxy Technology is a pioneer in this technology. Examples of polymer flip chip bumps are shown in Figure 3-21.

POLYMER BUMP ON Pd PLATED PAD **EPOXY PADS ON SUBSTRATE**

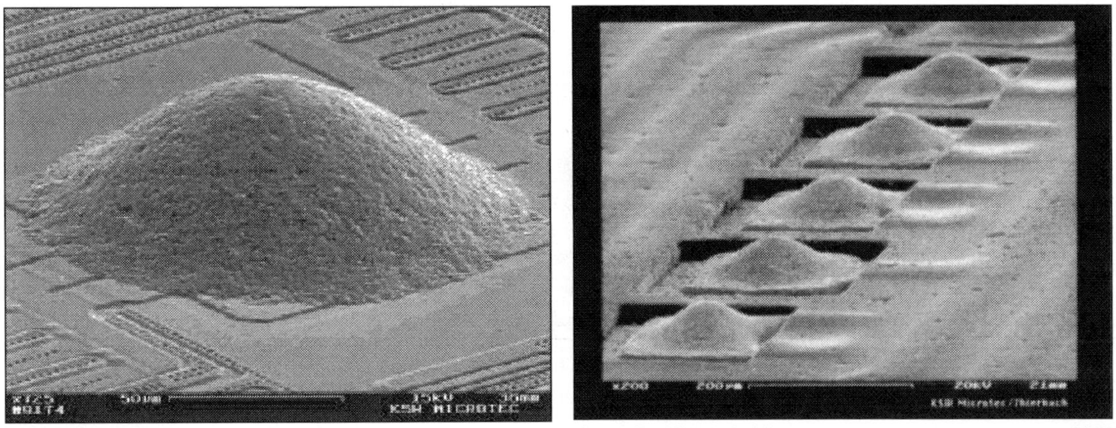

Source: Polymer Flip Chip   Source: Ksw Microtec GmbH   24701

Figure 3-21. A single conductive polymer bump screen printed on a gold pad on a chip, and multiple pads with a dielectric protection layer.

4 Ball Grid Array (BGA) Packages

PACKAGING OPTIONS IN PERSPECTIVE

The packaging industry acts much like a collective pack rat in never throwing anything out. Once the effort has been put into establishing the manufacturing infrastructure, the assembly infrastructure, reliability testing, field failure correlation and resource investment in moving up the experience learning curve, OEMs who have built up confidence (i.e., established low risk) in a packaging approach are reluctant to change. That's why the venerable DIP package is still with us and is being produced at the rate of over 8 billion units per year.

Though rarely is a package option removed, new alternatives have been added to the list. The driving force on the package form factor has always been the same: enabling increasing I/O in a smaller surface area. This means increasing the packaging efficiency, or the area of the silicon to the area of the package footprint:

Packaging efficiency = Silicon area / package area

There have been three revolutions in the nature of the form factor that have allowed ever increasing capability and many evolutions within these three tracks. These three revolutionary paths are: through hole, SMT (surface mount technology) peripheral and SMT area array. This is shown in Figure 4-1.

The end result in each revolutionary track is a higher packaging efficiency package. For example, the dual inline package (DIP) style has rapidly moved to the Small Outline IC (SOIC), shown in Figure 4-2. Its variants are the highest unit volume package in production, driven mostly by their extensive use in memory applications.

THREE REVOLUTIONS IN PACKAGE FORM FACTOR

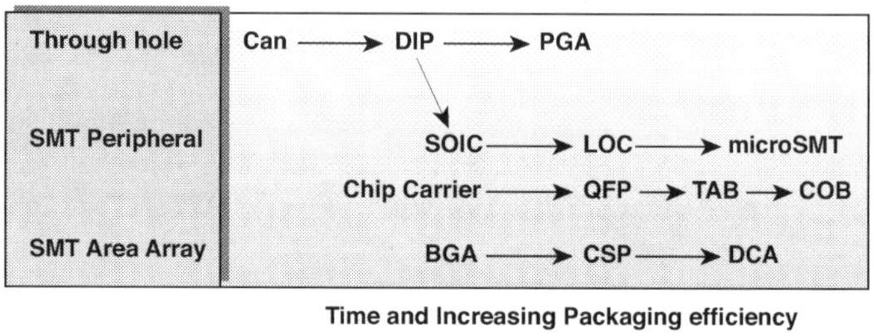

Source: Bogatin Enterprises 24705

Figure 4-1. Three revolutions in package form factor

EVOLUTION OF THE DIP INTO THE SOIC

Source: Microchip Corp. 24706

Figure 4-2. Evolution of the DIP into the SOIC.

The transition from one revolutionary track to another: through hole DIP to peripheral SMT, to area array SMT, can best be illustrated by looking at projected unit volumes of usage, as shown in Figure 4-3. Though the exact numbers may vary with analyst, the trend is the same- we are now firmly in the peripheral SMT generation with the next revolution of area array SMT packages, such as BGA, CSP and DCA, growing at a rapid rate.

FUTURE VOLUME ESTIMATES FOR THE THREE REVOLUTIONARY PACKAGE STYLES

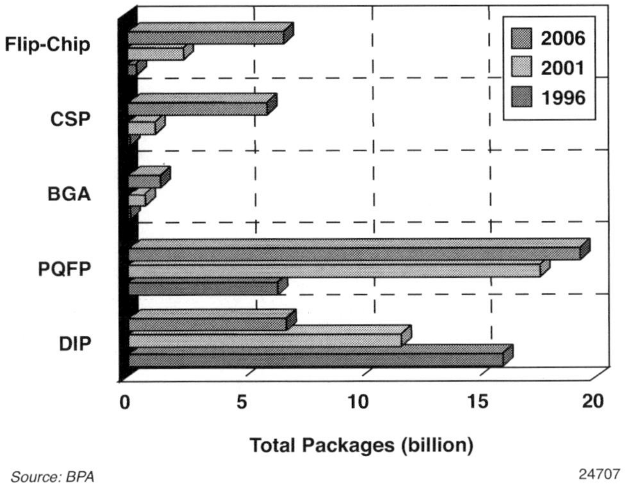

Figure 4-3. Unit volume estimates for package styles in the three generic families.

Each time an alternative package style is offered, there is a decision tree that each end user goes through in determining which is the one for them. It has been suggested by Tom Gregorich, ASIC Products Manager of Advanced Packaging at Qualcom, that there are "Ten Commandments of IC Package Development" on which a mainstream package selection is based. They are:

Commandment 1: Customers will select a package which fits their application and has the largest terminal pitch (for easy assembly), the smallest number of terminal rows (for easy routing) and the lowest cost (more important than any other items).

Commandment 2: The lowest cost package is the package with the highest production volume.

Commandment 3: As terminal pitch decreases, the effective volume occupied by the package, including the package thickness and printed circuit board fan out must also decrease.

Commandment 4: Package fan out requirements must not exceed the customer's PCB routing capabilities or require extra PCB layers.

Commandment 5: Packaging should not require special handling for moisture control.

Commandment 6: Package reliability must not adversely affect the reliability of the customers' product.

Commandment 7: Designers must provide continuous, measurable improvements in packaging that contribute to reducing the total cost of the customers' products.

Commandment 8: Customers tend to utilize known, familiar packages unless forced to change.

Commandment 9: Customers do not know what type of packaging they will need in the future, but they are always right.

Commandment 10: The right packaging at the wrong time is still the wrong package.

As the transition is made from peripheral surface mount to one of the three new area array SMT options, some combination of these commandments will be used by each customer to decide which will be the successful, high volume variants. The next three chapters outline the current issues with each of the new SMT area array technologies, and the criteria associated with their success.

AREA ARRAY

The key element that adds value to the area array form factor is the ability to pack more I/O per unit area than with a peripheral leaded fan out. This form factor is being applied to more than just single chip packages. It is appearing in multichip package applications and connector applications. Figure 4-4 is an example of a SMT connector from Berg with an area array form factor.

A secondary benefit is the higher yield and associated lower assembly costs for the coarser pitch area packages compared with finer pitch peripheral packages.

The details of the driving forces on the increasing use of BGA packages is summarized in the companion ICE publication, **Roadmaps of Packaging Technology**. The two important features, higher I/O density and higher assembly yield, are illustrated in Figure 4-5 and Figure 4-6.

HIGH DENSITY CONNECTOR WITH BGA FOOTPRINT

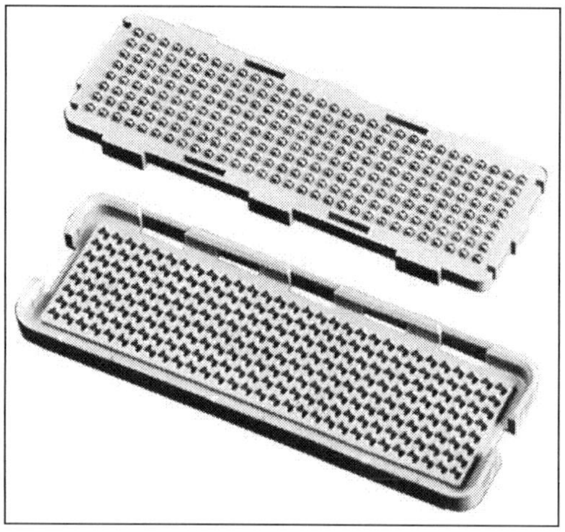

Source: Berg 24708

Figure 4-4. Area Array form factor applied to connectors.

BODY SIZE COMPARISON OF BGA AND QFP

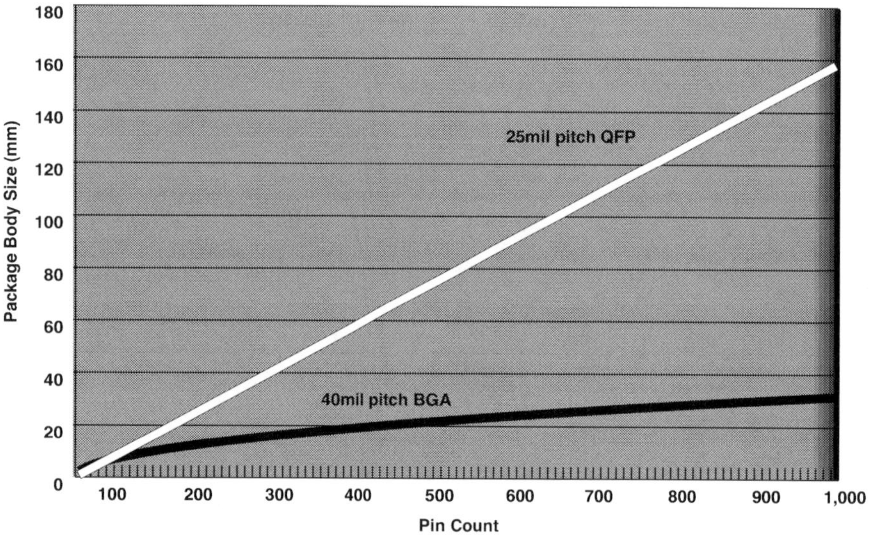

Source: Bogatin Enterprises 24709

Figure 4-5. I/O density for 25mil (0.625mm) pitch QFP package and 1.0mm (40mil) pitch BGA package.

With an area array format, there is a continuum in pitch, from 1.5mm (60mils), down to 0.1mm (4mil) pitch. As the pad pitch decreases from the coarse end, the type of package changes. This includes the name of the family, the fabrication technology and processes, the materials, the intended application and the thickness. The map of these different families is shown in Figure 4-7, which includes the BGA, near chip scale package (NCSP), chip scale package (CSP) and direct chip attach (DCA).

A BGA is defined and registered with JEDEC as having a ball pitch of 1.50mm (60mils), 1.27mm (50mil) or 1.0mm (40mil). The minimum body size registered is 7mm on a side. For a pitch of 1.5mm, this would result in 16 balls. The maximum body size currently registered is 50mm on a side. The range of BGA ball counts supported by JEDEC specs encompasses total ball counts of from 16 up to 2401 in a filled array at the tightest ball pitch of 1.0mm. Within this broad family of BGA, there is an incredible proliferation of styles, sizes and pin counts.

Some of this variety is shown in Figure 4-8.

In delineating the various BGA types, as well as CSP families, there are two ways of categorizing the package families: by the fabrication technology and by the application focus. By fabrication technology, there are four main distinguishing features: the nature of the chip attach, how the chip is assembled to the package, the material of the package, and the method of protection. In following each of the multiple forks, it is clear that there are numerous combinations for a final BGA, and all of them are currently in production. This wide variety of compositions for a final BGA style is illustrated in Figure 4-9. As each combination has a different name, it is easy to see why there is a confusion of package styles.

ELECTRONIC CARD ASSEMBLY AND SOLDER DEFECTS FOR BGA AND FINE PITCH PQFP

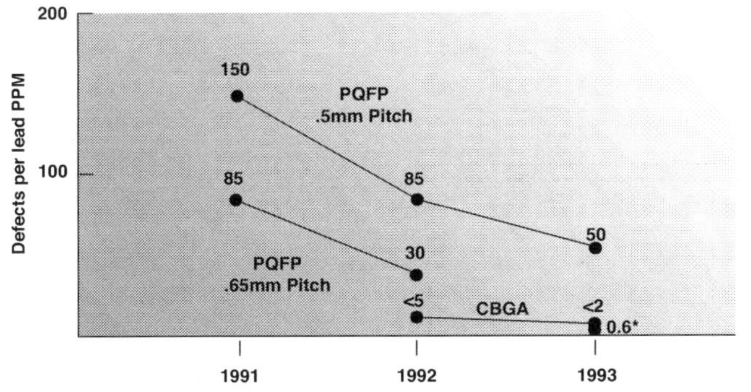

Source: IBM Austin 24710

Figure 4-6. Assembly defect rate for fine pitch peripheral and BGA.

AREA ARRAY PACKAGE FAMILIES BY BALL PITCH

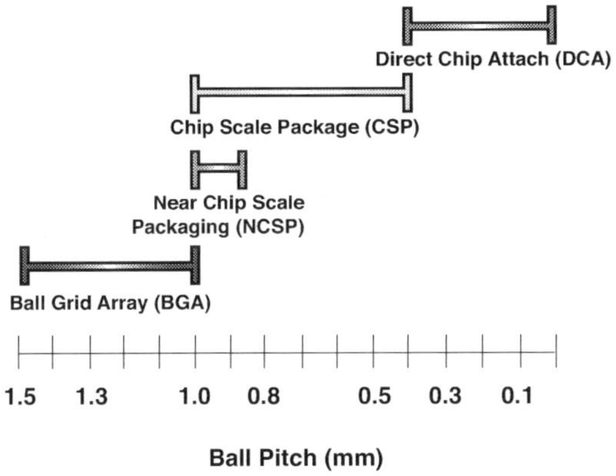

Source: Bogatin Enterprises 24711

Figure 4-7. Continuum of ball pitch and the associated package family.

Given this complexity in the types of BGAs in use, there is a simplified description, based on the nature of the substrate, into three categories: Tape (TBGA), Ceramic (CBGA) and Plastic (laminate) (PBGA). Examples of each of these are shown in Figure 4-10.

This rich variety of BGA types has been fueled by many vendors seeking a differentiator for their technology, sometimes to get around the patent protections of other designs so as to avoid licensing fees or the possibility of optimizing the cost for specialized applications.

Based on application, there are three functional categories:

cost driven
value driven
performance driven

WIDE VARIETY OF BGA TYPE PACKAGES

Source: Abpac 24712

Figure 4-8. Variety of BGA styles in production.

MATRIX OF POSSIBLE BGA OR CSP COMPOSITIONS

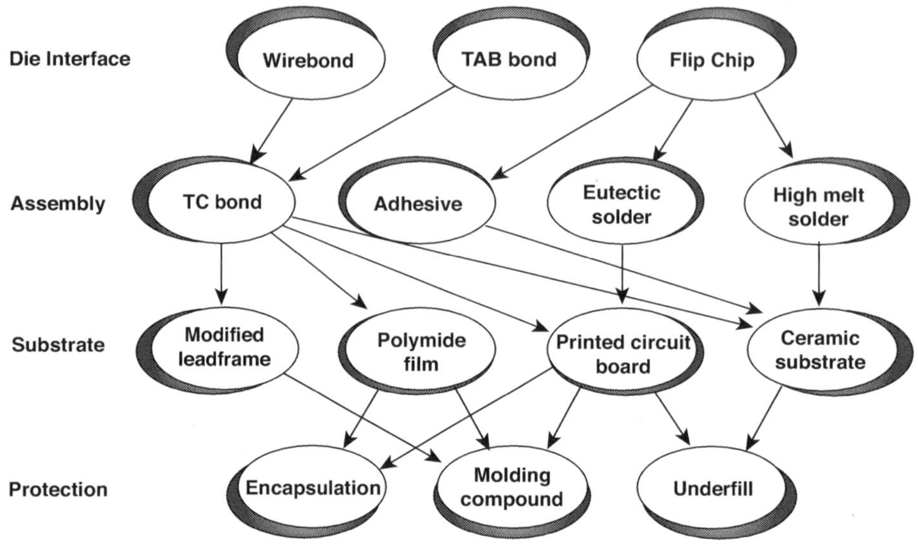

Source: Advanced Packaging Magazine 24713

Figure 4-9. Matrix of possible BGA or CSP compositions.

EXAMPLES OF THE THREE TYPES OF BGA SUBSTRATES: TAPE, CERAMIC, AND PLASTIC

Source: IBM 24714

Figure 4-10. The three generic varieties of BGAs based on the nature of the substrate.

COST DRIVEN APPLICATIONS

For low pin count, under 208 leads, when performance is not a primary issue, the lowest cost package is generally a leaded package. Typical costs of a leaded package are $0.005 per pin, compared with $0.005-$0.01 for the lowest cost plastic BGA packages. In the low pin count regime, a pad pitch for BGA packages less than 1.0mm is routine. This finer pad pitch will result in a smaller body size and hence lower cost package and still allow the use of conventional printed circuit boards for routing.

In this pitch range the packages are categorized as chip scale packages (CSPs). Examples of BGA-like, low pin count CSPs are shown in Figure 4-11. This package style, and its use in low pin count applications, is discussed in the next chapter.

For pin counts in the 200-500 range, the lowest cost is obtained with the fewest number of layers, typically one or two. The lowest cost BGAs are those in the highest production volume. They are composed of a double sided core of PCB laminate, with metallization on both sides for cavity up applications. This is the original style first proposed by Motorola as the Over Molded Pad Array Carrier (OMPAC). An example is shown in Figure 4-12.

A novel approach for low cost, recently introduced by Siemens, replaces the solder balls with molded plastic columns to provide the compliant standoffs. The entire substrate, cavity and bumps are molded all in one shot. The entire surface of the molded package is then electrolessly plated with copper and then electroplated with tin. A high speed laser system is used to direct-write remove the tin where the copper should be etched. The remaining tin is used as an etch mask to remove the copper. The laser direct-write approach is used to provide the patterning of the tin over the 3D surfaces of the cavity.

EXAMPLES OF LOW PIN COUNT, FINE PITCH BGAs CLASSIFIED AS CHIP SCALE PACKAGE

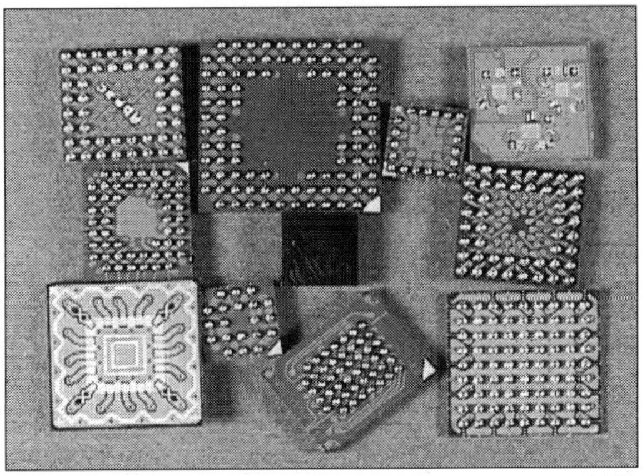

Source: Abpac 24715

Figure 4-11. Low pin count chip scale packages with a form factor identical to high pin count BGAs.

A 50mm x 50mm area can be patterned with 25micron lines in under 16 seconds. An example of this Polymer Stud Grid Array package (PSGA) is shown in Figure 4-13. It has the potential of low cost, as the entire molded part can be manufactured for a few cents. However, its suitability will probably be for low pin count and low performance, as its electrical performance will not be high.

As pin count increases, the total cost of ownership for leaded packages increases dramatically due to part cost and yield impact. In general, higher pin count chips are higher performance chips and the increasingly worse electrical performance of leaded packages make them unsuitable for these chips, at any cost.

THE FIRST PBGA: THE OMPAC (OVER MOLDED PAD ARRAY CARRIER)

Source: Motorola/ICE 22238A

TYPICAL PBGA CROSS SECTION

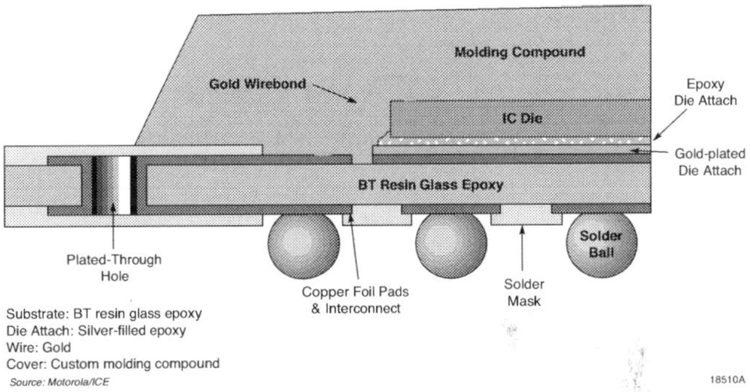

Source: Motorola/ICE 18510A

Figure 4-12. Top and bottom view and cross section of two layer OMPAC style BGA.

The tape BGA or TBGA style is inherently limited to one or at most two metal layers. It is basically a flex film of Polyimide, 50microns (2mils) thick with pads in the center for either flip chip attach or fine pitch wire bond, and a fan out to a ball grid array pattern. A metal backing can act as a stiffener or as a heat spreader. An example of a TBGA package is shown in Figure 4-14. With few vendors, this is a low volume package style. Though the performance can be enhanced with two metal layers, it is no longer a low cost package.

POLYMER STUD GRID ARRAY (PSGA) PACKAGE TYPE

Source: Siemens 24716

Figure 4-13. Example of the Siemens Polymer Stud Grid Array package (PSGA).

One advantage of the TBGA is the ability to provide very fine lines in the die attach cavity for flip chip fan out or fine pitch wire bonding. In the Sheldahl ViaThin process, for example, the Polyimide vias are laser drilled, and the traces are 15micron (0.6mil) thick copper. The typical line width/spacing is 50microns (2mils) and 37.5micron (1.5mil), for a minimum pad pitch of 87.5micron (3.5mil). This is close to the minimum IC bond pitch in production. An example of a Sheldahl ViaThin package is shown in Figure 4-15.

CELERON PROCESSOR FOR PORTABLE APPLICATIONS PACKAGED IN A FLIP CHIP TBGA PACKAGE

TBGA STYLE PACKAGE

Source: Intel

Source: Amkor

24717

Figure 4-14. TBGA examples.

VALUE DRIVEN: COST/ PERFORMANCE

The performance limits of the low cost BGA styles are set by the uncontrolled impedance of the signal traces and the high inductance in the power and ground distribution. The larger the physical size of the package, i.e., the higher the pin count, the worse the performance. This is a generic feature in the use of just two metal layers. This can be slightly compensated by using one of the metal layers as a ground plane. This will enable controlled impedance traces, and slightly lower power and ground inductance. For low pin count, cost driven packages can be used in excess of 100MHz. For higher pin counts, over 200, and clock frequencies of over 100MHz, low cost two layer packages may not be suitable. An example of the cross section of a two metal layer BGA from Amkor, the SuperBGA® (SBGA), is shown in Figure 4-16.

To enhance the electrical performance of BGAs, more layers are added to the substrate. The next level of expense, and performance, is a four layer substrate. The construction is signal, power, ground and signal. The signals can all be controlled impedance, typically 50 Ohm, and the power and ground planes can provide low impedance and integrated decoupling capacitance. These packages are typically used with wire bond die attach. The largest volume, high pin count BGAs are fabricated in this configuration, typically for ASICs and FPGAs. Performance can be added as needed, by adding more layers for either more power planes or higher signal density than can be routed in two layers. An example is shown in Figure 4-17.

SIDE VIEW OF THE VIATHIN TBGA PACKAGE STYLE

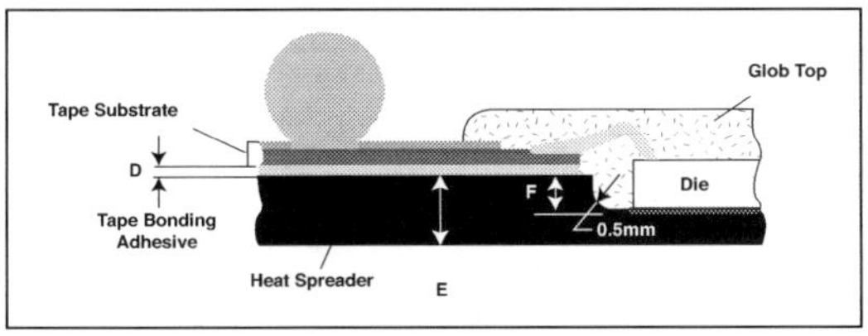

TOP VIEW OF THE VIATHIN TBGA PACKAGE STYLE

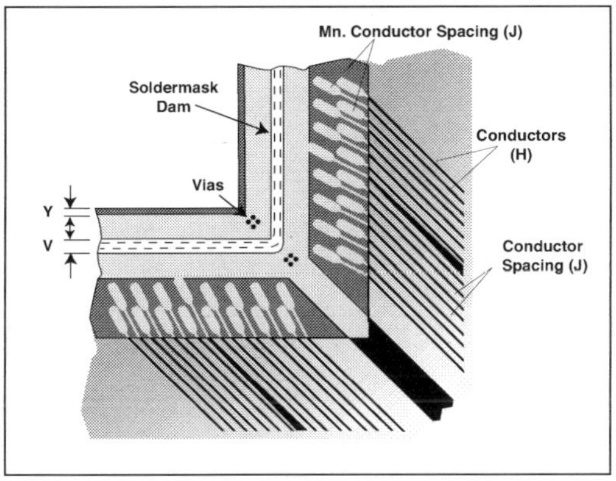

Source: Sheldahl 24718

Figure 4-15. Sheldahl ViaThin Package example. Top: cross section of two metal layer TBGA with heat spreader. Bottom: top view sketch of the fan out showing a ground ring and peripheral wire bond pads on 87micron (3.5mil) pitch.

PERFORMANCE DRIVEN BGAS

High pin count, over 500 pins, is a generic feature of most high performance BGAs, such as for use with processors, DSPs (Digital Signal Processors) and ASICs. Though the unit volumes are not as high as the low pin count packages the ASPs (Average Sales Price) are higher, because the pin count is greater and the price per pin is in the $0.02-$0.04 range. The higher cost is due to features added to support signal integrity requirements for the higher frequencies. There are predominately four features in the highest performance packages, suitable for clock frequencies above the 300MHz range:

- Fine pitch wire bond cavity with multiple bond shelves or pads for flip chip attach
- Multiple power and ground planes, with as thin a dielectric as possible
- Multiple signal routing layers using low dielectric constant materials
- Surface pads for low inductance decoupling capacitors

The most popular technology to implement high performance BGAs historically has been the ceramic BGA. CBGAs have two important features for flip chip applications. The ceramic TCE, at about 5ppm/°C, matches pretty closely the silicon's at 3.5ppm/°C. This ensures a very reliable chip attach solder joint in flip chip assemblies. Secondly, vias as

CROSS SECTION OF THE SBGA

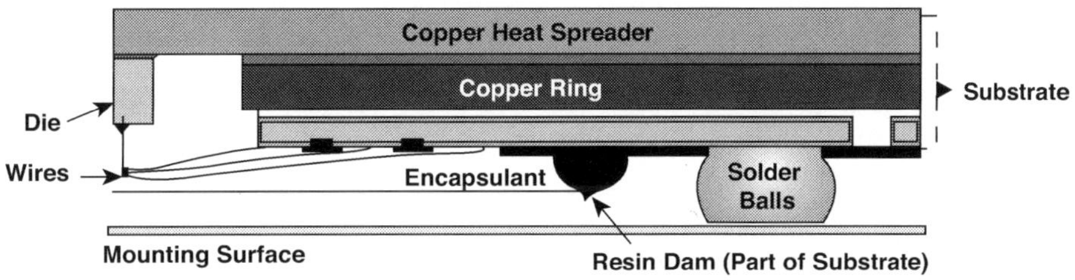

Source: Amkor 24719

Figure 4-16. SuperBGA from Amkor, with two layer laminate mounted on a copper base and copper heat spreader. This is a compromise between low cost and good electrical and thermal performance.

small as 4mil (0.1mm) in diameter and as many as 10-20 layers for power and ground distribution and signal routing, has meant the fine pitch flip chip pads could be routed.

TYPICAL HIGH PIN COUNT BGA USED IN THE AGP CHIP SET

Source: Intel 24720

Figure 4-17. Typical BGA used for high pin count ASICs.

One of the limitations of the ceramic BGA has been the high dielectric constant of the ceramic, at 9-10 and the high resistivity of the tungsten-molybdenum metallization (~20 microOhm-cm). Recently IBM introduced a glass-ceramic BGA that gets around these limitations. The glass ceramic material is a cordierite ceramic with a dielectric constant of 5. The lower firing temperature of 900°C allows the use of copper metallization.

Though the low TCE of glass ceramic is ideal for flip chip solder connections, it causes a new set of problems for large packages mounted to laminate substrates. Without special attention, normal solder balls farther than 1cm from the neutral point will crack under just a few thermal cycles. To increase the lifetime during thermal cycling, large standoffs must be added to the package, rather than the typical 30mil diameter high temperature solder balls. IBM offers a solution using high melting point solder columns. These Ceramic Column Grid Array (CCGA) packages are used for some very high pin count ASICs, offered exclusively through IBM. Some examples of these packages are shown in Figure 4-18.

Laminate substrates for use in high end applications have traditionally been limited to wire bond chip attach. An example of a high performance BGA, in its LGA format, before solder ball attach, is shown in Figure 4-19. This Intel processor uses an eight layer package with three wire bond shelves.

The cross section construction of a comparable high performance BGA (HPBGA), from Amkor, is shown in Figure 4-20.

In general, high performance chips run at high clock frequency and have a large number of pin outs. To meet the performance goals, there is an increasing trend for these chips to be attached by flip chip solder balls. The next generation high performance PBGAs will be with flip chip attach.

CERAMIC COLUMN GRID ARRAY (CCGA) PACKAGE FEATURES

Source: IBM 24741

Figure 4-18. CCGA packages from IBM.

HIGH PERFORMANCE WIRE BONDED PBGA

Source: Intel and Business Week 24722

Figure 4-19. Eight layer high performance PBGA, without the solder balls attached with three bonding shelves with an Intel microprocessor.

Two new technology features have open up this opportunity for laminate packages in the very high performance end: underfill polymers and microvia substrates. If the BGA substrate the flip chip is assembled to has a high TCE, such as 12-16 ppm/°C, typical of FR4 and BT laminate, the chip to package solder joints will fail after only a few thermal cycles. If, however, the typical 5 mil gap under the die is filled with a low modulus polymer, the stress from the TCE mismatch will be distributed over the surface of the die and the solder balls will last orders of magnitude longer. This is reviewed in the ICE companion publication, **Roadmaps of Packaging Technology**.

The second feature that has enabled the use of laminate high performance BGAs is the introduction of microvia substrates. These are substrates with via connections from one layer to another that can be as small as 1mil (25microns), and with fine lines, as narrow as 1mil line and space. Microvia substrates are reviewed in detail in a following chapter. The close pitch vias and high routing density are critical to provide connections to the chip's solder balls, which are typically on a 200micron – 250micron (8mil – 10mil) grid. An example of the Pentium III processor, flip chip attached on a microvia substrate with polymer underfill, is shown in Figure 4-21.

CROSS SECTION OF A HIGH PERFORMANCE PBGA

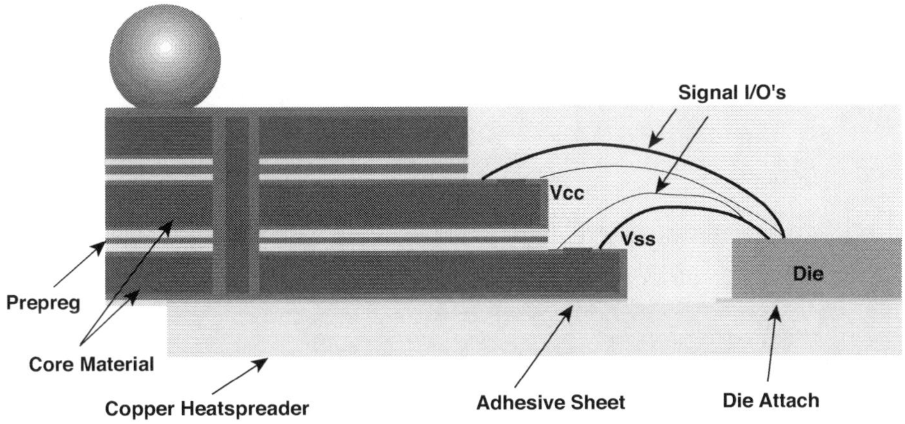

Source: Amkor 24723

Figure 4-20. Cross section of typical high performance BGA.

PENTIUM III PBGA WITH FLIP CHIP AND MICRO VIA SUBSTRATE

Source: Intel 24724

Figure 4-21. Intel Pentium III high performance BGA using flip chip attach and a microvia substrate.

In addition to the micro via laminate suppliers for BGA substrates, such as Fujitsu, Ibiden, Kyocera, NTK, Toppan, ASTI, NEC, Samsung, Hadco, Merix, Johnson Matthey Electronics (JME) and Sheldahl, reviewed in a following chapter, W.L. Gore has introduced a new substrate technology specifically for high performance BGA packages. It uses their Gore-Tex expanded PTFE (polytetrafluoroethylene) foam dielectric, trademarked MICROLAM™ dielectric and fine line traces with laser drilled microvias. This technology, termed Via on Chip Pitch™, offers excellent electrical performance. An example of prototype packages, with metal reinforcement stiffeners is shown in Figure 4-22.

The expanded PTFE acts as a reinforcing web for a thermoset polymer. Without glass weave, it is an ideal material for laser drilling of vias. A solid copper core provides the mechanical support on which copper clad polymer layers are laminated. After each lamination, traces are patterned and vias are laser drilled. Typical via pitch is 150microns (6mils) and line width/spacing is 25microns (1mil)/45microns (1.75mils), for a pitch of 70microns (2.75mils). These feature sizes can easily accommodate the most advanced flip chip attach. An example of the cross section of a seven layer structure is shown in Figure 4-23. This technology has recently been licensed to NTK.

VIA ON CHIP PITCH HIGH PERFORMANCE BGAs

Source: W. L. Gore 24725

Figure 4-22. Examples of Via on Chip Pitch™ PTFE based BGA packages from W. L. Gore.

CROSS SECTION OF THE MICROLAM SUBSTRATE USED FOR BGA PACKAGE

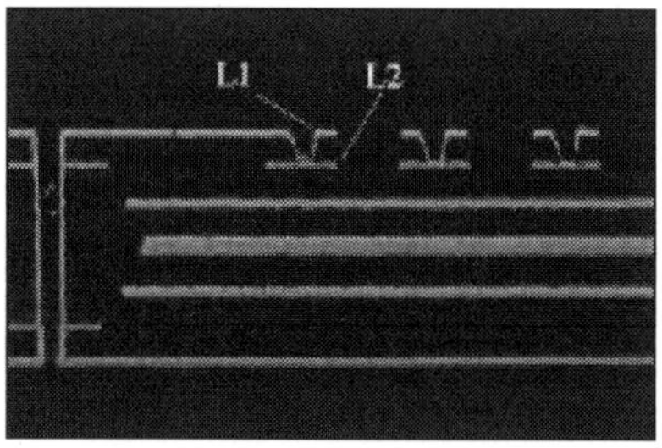

Source: W. L. Gore 24726

Figure 4-23. Cross section of a seven layer Microlam™ substrate with 25micron line widths.

The Gore BGAs have a combination of features for excellent electrical performance:

- Thin dielectric layers between power and ground for low inductance
- Low dielectric constant in signal layers for low delay
- Short vias from the chip pads to the power and ground planes
- Fine lines and tight vias pitches for controlled impedance high density routing

ASSEMBLY

The assembly infrastructure for BGAs has been well documented in the ICE companion publication, **Roadmaps of Packaging Technology**. One of the recent innovations in assembly of the BGA package involves the use of a controlled atmosphere reflow oven for solder ball attach, which eliminates the need for solder flux.

All laminate BGAs use eutectic solder balls, which reflow during assembly.

The typical BGA package assembly process is:

- Fabricate laminate substrate as land grid array (LGA) package
- Die attach, either wire bond or flip chip
- Overmold or glob top encapsulate
- Ball attach
- Singulate/test

Typical ball attach processes involve:

- solder fluxing the substrate
- placing the solder balls
- reflow attach the solder balls
- clean the flux residue

With the growing Green movement and concern for minimizing water waste generation steps, a new process has been offered from Scientific Sealing Technology (SST) that does not require solder flux or cleaning. They offer a vacuum furnace which can batch process the reflow operation of either solder ball attach to a package, to a wafer, or the reflow of a flip chip to a package or the assembly of a BGA package to a board. Figure 4-24 is an example of the furnace.

The components with solder balls resting on the surface are placed on a custom machined graphite plate that acts as the heating electrode. This is mounted inside the vacuum chamber.

An example of the graphite plate with BGA's is shown in Figure 4-25.

CONTROLLED ATMOSPHERE SEALING CHAMBER FOR FLUXLESS SOLDER BALL REFLOW

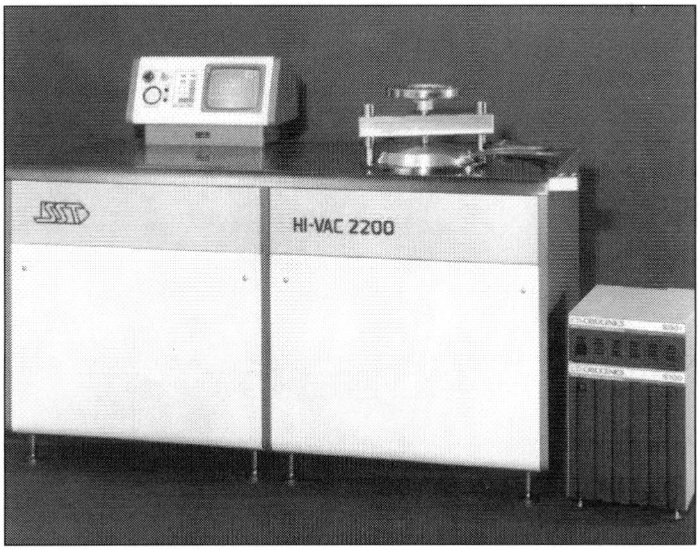

Source: Scientific Sealing Technology 24727

Figure 4-24. Vacuum furnace from SST.

GRAPHITE BGA FIXTURE

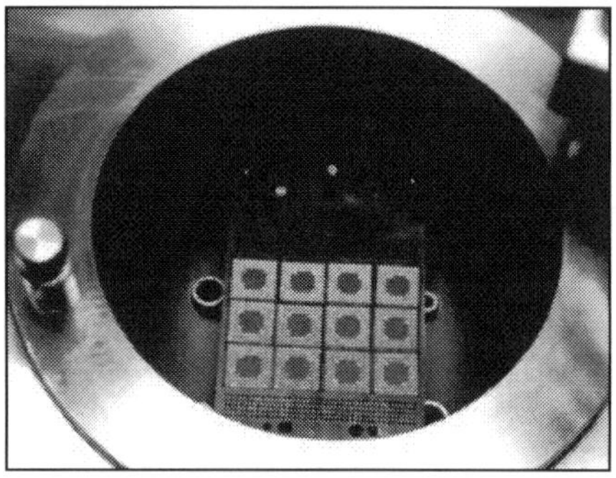

Source: Scientific Sealing Technology 24955

Figure 4-25. Example of graphite heating element fixture in which solder balls reflow on a BGA.

Once the parts are mounted, the chamber is pumped down and purged with either dry nitrogen or forming gas. With no oxygen present, no flux is needed to assure good solder joints. The entire cycle time can be less than 10 minutes, and chambers are available with a usable surface area of over 10 square feet. Under some conditions, the use of the vacuum furnace can cut the assembly time down for flip chip attach and solder ball attach to BGAs.

In addition to eliminating a water cleaning step, no flux results in no voids in the solder balls. An example of solder balls reflowed both on chip and on a BGA package are shown in Figure 4-26.

REFLOWED SOLDER BALLS ON A PBGA PROCESSED WITHOUT FLUX AND WITHOUT A CLEANING STEP

SOLDER BALLS ON A FLIP CHIP REFLOWED IN VACUUM FURNACE WITHOUT THE NEED OF A POST CLEAN STEP

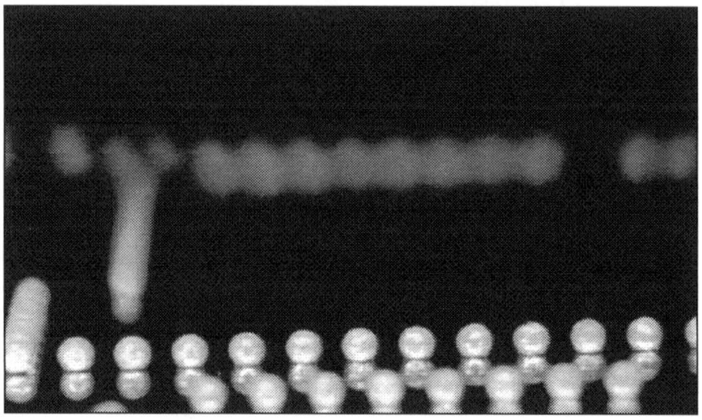

Source: Scientific Sealing Technology 24728

Figure 4-26. Solder balls reflowed with no flux, on a BGA package and on a chip.

5 Chip Scale Packages (CSP)

It is sometimes misleading paying too much attention to the various published roadmaps of package needs for the future. For example, the SIA road map predicts that by the year 2003, the pin count need for high performance packages will be 2200 leads. With packages currently in production in 1999 with over 1500 pins (in BGA format), even this number of 2200 seems overly conservative. With the excitement of ever more complex chips looming in the future, it is easy to loose sight of where the real volume is- at the bottom.

Figure 5-1 is a prediction from Prismark Partners of the volume demands for various pin count packages. Almost 40 billion packages will have less than 16 leads in the year 2002! Over 85 billion packages, more than 90% of all produced packages in 2002, will be of 120 pins or less. To paraphrase Richard Feynman, speaking of the yet to be invented field of micro machining, "...there is plenty of room at the bottom".

With the accelerating design and production of personal and portable products, smaller form factor is critical. The convergence of smaller form factor and high volume production for the lowest pin count devices has resulted in the recent introduction of chip scale packages. Some examples of these ultra small packages are shown in Figure 5-2.

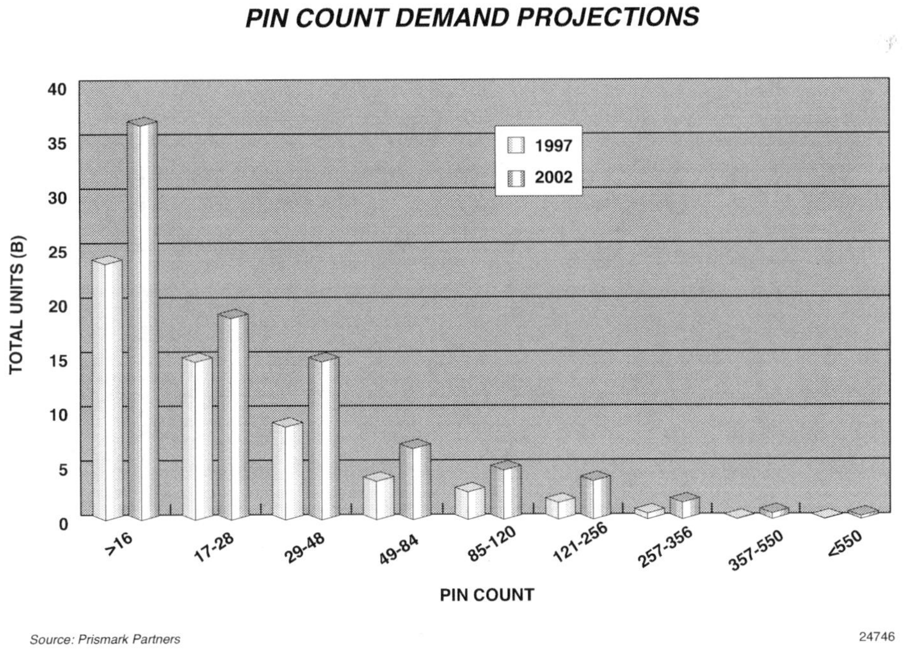

Figure 5-1. Pin count demand estimates in 1997 and 2002.

EXAMPLES OF CSP FORMATS

Source: EP&P 24747

Figure 5-2. CSPs in peripheral and area array format. Note that the background object is a penny.

WHAT IS A CHIP SCALE PACKAGE?

On August 26, 1994, an ad hoc group from the Surface Mount Council met at the Surface Mount International conference and arbitrarily decided to define a chip scale package as a package whose dimension was less than 1.2 x the dimension of the chip. This results in a packaging efficiency of 70% or higher. This definition is only a starting place. It covers some of the low end parts, but becomes ambiguous in cases where a package has a fixed form factor, due to a pre defined pin layout, and the die shrinks. This may cause the packaging efficiency to drop below 70%, but it should still be classified as a CSP.

To account for the more general case, CSP has also come to include any package with an area array ball pitch less than 1.0mm (40mils).

The key feature for all CSPs is their extremely small size, not much larger than the chip itself. This is the chief aspect that provides value. The physical size can be almost as small as a grain of sand, as with the One Wire chip from Dallas Semiconductor, to almost 20mm on a side, as for example a high pin count CSP from Tessera. Figure 5-3 shows examples of these two extremes.

By whatever description, chip scale packages will play a significant role in future portable products. Though there are many predictions for the future growth of CSPs, they all point to a growth rate of almost 100% per year, with current volume estimates of almost 1 billion units shipped in 1999. The various predictions for CSP product volumes as summarized by Tessera, are shown in Figure 5-4.

THIMBLE FULL OF ONE WIRE CHIPS IN CSP FORMAT

Source: Dallas Semiconductor

HIGH PIN COUNT CSP COMPARED TO QFP

Source: Tessera 24748

Figure 5-3. Chip scale packages can range from less than 1mm to over 20mm in body size. Left: One wire chip from Dallas Semiconductor. Right: High pin count CSP compared to a 28mm QFP, from Tessera.

SUMMARY OF ANALYSTS' ESTIMATES OF CSP UNIT VOLUME GROWTH

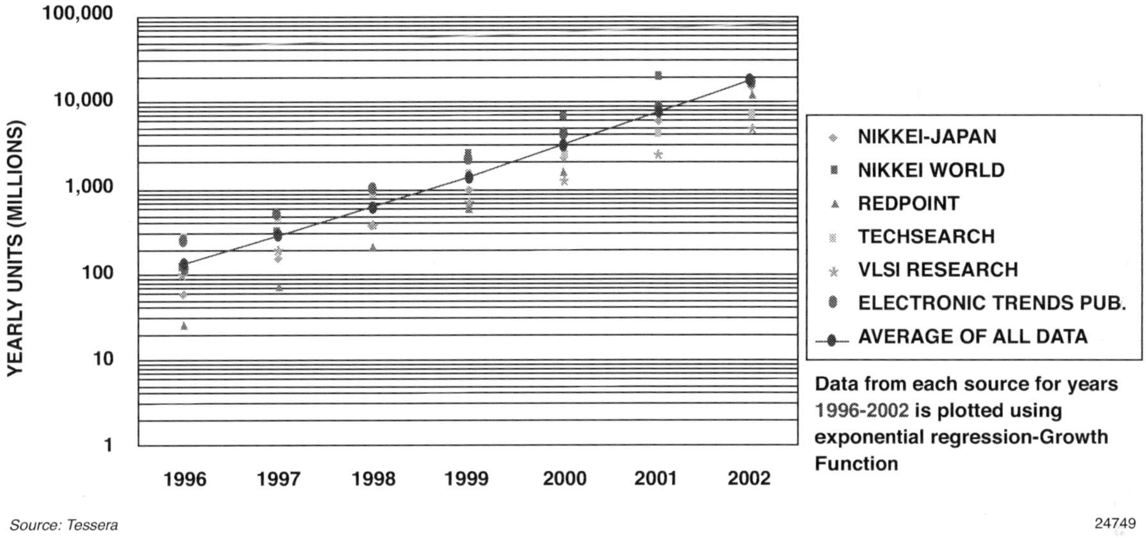

Figure 5-4. Summary of six analysts' estimates of the predicted production rates for CSP devices, with an average value of 100% growth per year.

In mid 1999, there were over 100 published types of CSPs, developed by semiconductor vendors, package assembly contractors, board level assembly contractors and OEMs. This diversity is due, in part, to the many niches of small pin count parts- analog, RF, digital glue logic, memory and clock distribution chips, to name a few. In addition, each vendor and user is looking for a way of differentiating their parts or their services, or to get around having to pay a patent royalty.

There are two ways of categorizing this vast array of CSPs: by the form factor they present to the assembly equipment and the next level substrate, or by their manufacturing technology, which ultimately will relate to their unit cost.

TWO FAMILIES OF CSPS: PERIPHERAL AND AREA ARRAY FORM FACTOR

In peripheral packages, there is no standard footprint, and they more closely fit the standard definition of CSP: package size less than 1.2 x the length of the chip. Though they resemble miniature leaded packages such as the QFP, but without the leads, the manufacturing processes are very different, and they are sometimes referred to by a term coined by Fujitsu as small outline non-leaded (SON) packages, to make this distinction clear. An example of a SON package is the MicroSMT package from ChipScale Inc, used for low pin count parts, shown in Figure 5-5.

Among the area array CSPs, there is a proliferation of styles, fabrication technologies and substrate materials. However, they all have the same form factor and there is the beginnings of JEDEC registrations for these new area array sizes. In the language of JEDEC, an area array CSP is a fine pitch BGA or FBGA. As seen in Figure 5-6, area array CSPs look very similar to BGAs, but have a tighter ball pitch of from 0.8mm to 0.4mm, as mentioned in the previous chapter.

MICROSMT CSPs COMPARED TO A CONVENTIONAL SOIC

Source: ChipScale Inc. 24750

Figure 5-5. Peripheral leadless CSPs from ChipScale Inc, compared to a conventional SOIC.

COMPARISON OF BGAs WITH CSPs

Source: SMT Magazine 24751

Figure 5-6. Comparison of BGA packages and CSPs showing similar form factor, but much tighter pitch of the CSPs.

The various area array CSP specs in current review by the JEDEC JC-11 committee classify the package by two categories: ball pitch and thickness. Body sizes can range from 4mm to 21mm. The registered ball pitches are:

- 0.80mm
- 0.75mm
- 0.65mm
- 0.50mm
- 0.40mm

The registered package thicknesses are labeled as:

- L = low 1.7mm max
- T = thin 1.2mm max
- V = very thin 1.0mm max
- W= very very thin 0.8mm max
- U = ultra thin 0.65mm max

The value in a registered and standardized footprint is to establish open tooling for test and handling equipment as well as facilitate board routing strategies. This is an important step in building the infrastructure for high volume production.

CSP FAMILIES BY TECHNOLOGY

These same 100 different CSPs can be parsed into four generic categories, differentiated by manufacturing technology, which are:

- flex circuit interposer
- rigid substrate
- lead frame
- waferscale

The general format and largest vendors or users for each family are summarized in Figure 5-7.

Rather than one approach winning out and all the others disappearing, it is likely that examples from each of these four families will maintain a significant market share into the future. The predicted volume production for each of these four families, as predicted by Electronic Trends Publications, is shown in Figure 5-8. The flex circuit interposer will probably dominate due to its high expected volume for memory applications, however, the other types will be about equally used.

FOUR GENERIC CSP FAMILIES

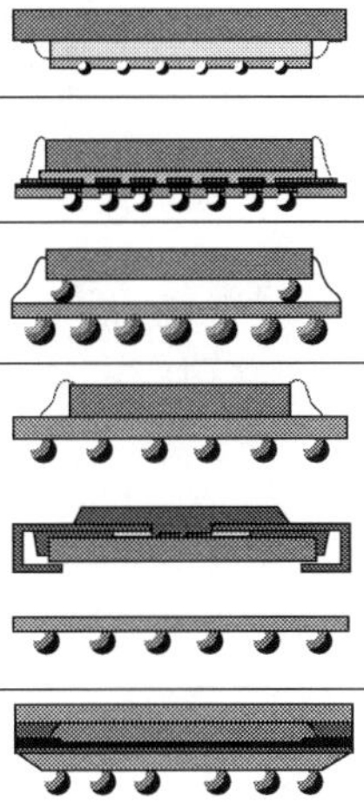

Category	Type	Example	Companies
Flex Circuit Interposer	TAB/Flip Chip		GE, IZM, KME, Mitsubishi, NEC, Rohm, Sony, Tessera and licensees
	Wire Bonding		Amkor/Anam, Fujitsu, Hitachi, LSI Logic, Mitsubishi, Sharp, TI Japan, Toshiba
Rigid Substrate	Flip Chip		Citizen Watch, Fujitsu, Matsushita, Motorola, Old Electric, Sony
	Wire Bonding		Amkor/Anam, Cypress, Fujitsu, LSI Logic, Motorola, National Semi, NEC, Rohm, Sony, Toshiba
Lead Frame	Wire Bonding		Amkor/Anam, Fujitsu, Hitachi Cable, LG Semicon, Matsushita, TI Japan, Toshiba
Wafer Level Assembly	Redistribution		ChipScale. EPIC, FCT, NEC, Sandia National Labs
	Substrate		ChipScale and licensees, ShellCase, Tessera, 3-D Plus

Source: TechSearch International Inc. 24752

Figure 5-7. Four main CSP families and largest supporters.

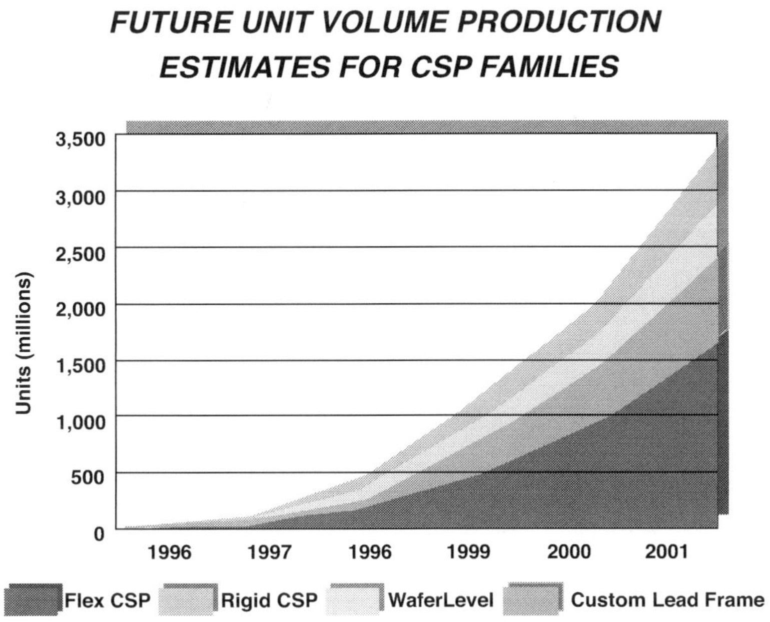

Source: Electronic Trends Publication 24753

Figure 5-8. Unit volume production rates for each of the four CSP family types.

Examples of each type of CSP family that are either currently in high volume production or likely to be in high volume production are reviewed in the following sections.

FLEX CIRCUIT INTERPOSER CSP

The flex circuit interposer type CSP is probably the highest volume design. TechSearch International estimates there will be over 850 million units sold in 2000, about half the total unit volume of CSPs. This design uses a thin layer of flex circuit, such as Polyimide, between the chip and the substrate. The use of a flex substrate allows the use of very fine line interconnects. It can match the pitch of the chip and provide the fan out to the solder ball pitch with just one metal layer.

On one side of the flex layer are

the solder balls. The chip is attached to the circuitry on the flex layer by either wire bond, TAB or flip chip. One advantage of this design is the high reliability of the solder ball connection between the flex and the substrate or chip. The most popular names and associated users are:

CSP name	User
Chip on Flex	GE
Flip chip BGA	Hitachi
JACS-Pak	Motorola, Schaumburg, Ill.
Fine Pitch BGA	NEC Corp
Resin Molded CSP	Nitto Denko Corp
F BGA	Sharp
microBGA	Tessera
microStar BGA	TI
fleXBGA	Amkor
E-CSP	3M

Tessera MicroBGA

The most widely know CSP is the microBGA®. The name is a registered trademark of Tessera, though has almost become the de facto name for any CSP with a fine pitch solder ball spacing. The microBGA is one of the oldest and most optimized CSP designs. A cross section is shown in Figure 5-9.

The microBGA starts as a strip of flex film bonded to a carrier frame so that as many as 40 CSPs can be processed at a time. The chips, with peripheral pads, are bonded to the film with an array of small silicone bumps. Windows in the film expose the chip bond pads and the gold TAB-like leads are single point bonded to the chip. The entire strip of 40 CSP sites is then encapsulated. After marking, the solder balls are attached and then the CSPs are singulated. A few of these steps are shown in Figure 5-10.

One of the chief advantages of this unique structure is the ability of the flexible TAB lead and the compliant elastomer under the die to take up any thermal expansion mismatch between the chip and the circuit board substrate.

This technology has been selected for the Rambus RDRAM chip, due for volume ramp beginning in the second half of 1999. It is also being used in many flash memory products by Intel. An example of the Rambus chip and flash products is shown in Figure 5-11.

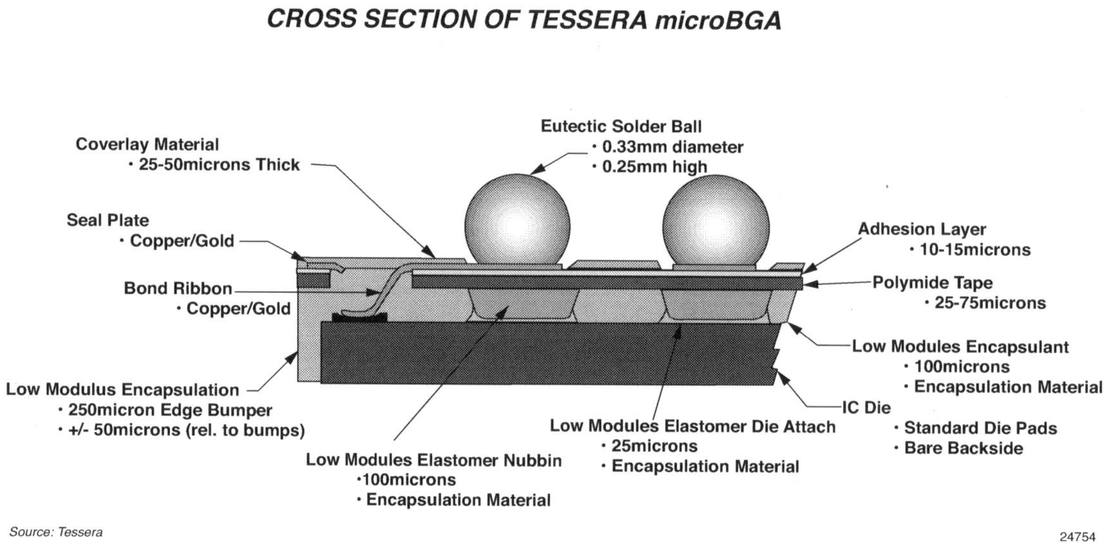

Figure 5-9. Cross section of the Tessera microBGA.

PANEL ASSEMBLY UNIT

CLOSE UP OF SINGLE POINT BONDED TAB LEADS

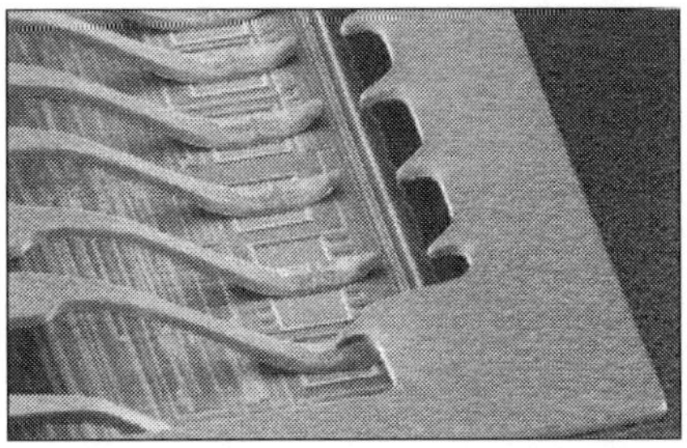

COMPLETED MICROBGA CSP

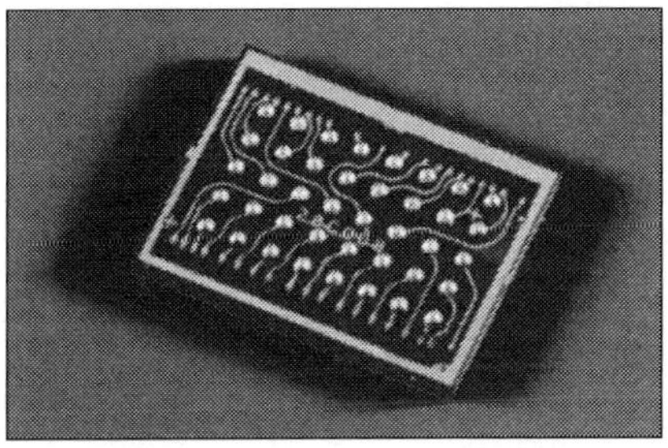

Source: Tessera 24755

Figure 5-10. Examples of the steps in the microBGA manufacture. Left: starting panel of up to 40 CSPs. Middle: single point bonding of the TAB leads to the peripheral chip bonding pads. Right: the final singulated CSP.

MICROBGA USED FOR RAMBUS AND FLASH

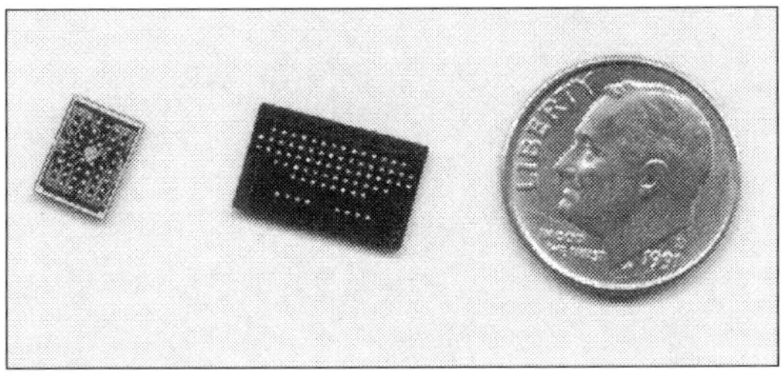

Source: Tessera

FLASH MEMORY PARTS PACKAGED IN MICROBGA CSP FORMAT

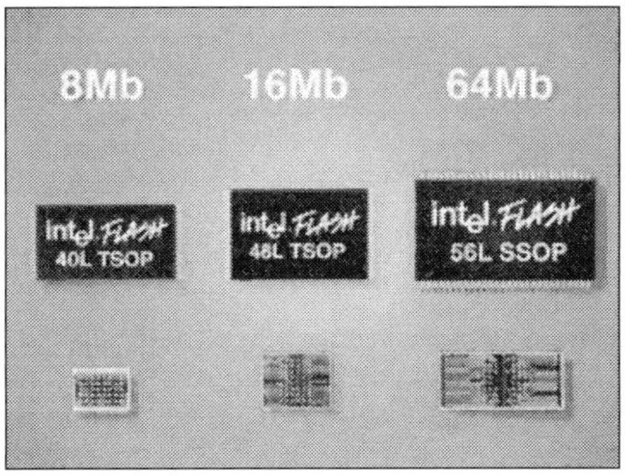

Source: Intel 24756

Figure 5-11. Memory product applications for the Tessera microBGA. Left: Rambus chip. Right: flash SRAM products from Intel.

It is broadly licensed to over 25 different users, including:

- AMD
- Intel
- Hitachi
- Hyundi
- LG Semicon
- Sharp
- Samsung
- SGS Thomson
- Siemens
- Sony
- TI
- Amkor
- ASE
- ChipPAC
- Shinko

Amkor fleXBGA

The fleXBGA is currently in high volume production at Amkor. It is one of the simplest and potentially lowest cost designs. The substrate is a single metal layer Polyimide film with gold bonding pads on the top surface to match the chip pads. Windows are opened in the Polyimide on the bottom side for solder ball attach to the copper traces. After the chip is attached and wire bonded, it is encapsulated with a filled molding compound. Then solder balls are attached to the bottom side. The ball pitch is currently at 0.8mm, however, the Polyimide flex fine lines can accommodate pitches down to 0.5mm. This CSP is in volume use by VLSI for RF products. An example of a cross section and top view is shown in Figure 5-12.

RIGID INTERPOSER SUBSTRATE CSP

The rigid interposer CSP is a natural extension of the BGA design. It is little more than a sheet of either ceramic or laminate, such as IBM's DryClad or BT resin. On one side are pads to match the chip, either wire bond or flip chip attach. On the other side are pads to attach solder balls, with routing and vias between the two surfaces. If flip chip is used, the die is underfilled after attach. The final CSP is typically encapsulated by a molding compound after chip attach and before the solder balls are attached. An example of ceramic based CSPs is shown in Figure 5-13.

CROSS SECTION OF THE FLEXBGA STYLE CSP

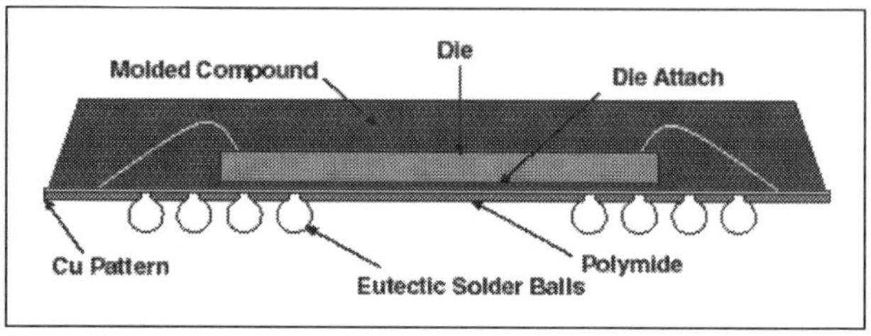

Source: VLSI

FLEXBGA

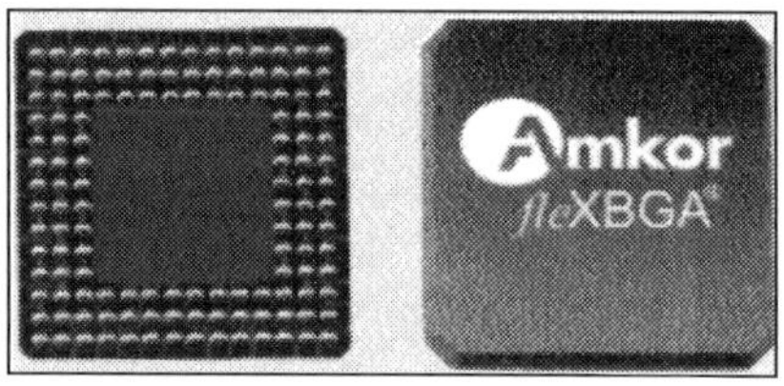

Source: Amkor 24757

Figure 5-12. FleXBGA from Amkor.

CERAMIC INTERPOSER CSPs

Source: Kyocera 24758

Figure 5-13. Ceramic rigid interposers with ball pitches from 0.8mm to 0.5mm.

Alternatively, a laminate substrate can be used as the interposer. This is commonly used for consumer product applications in Japan, for example. An example of a laminate CSP used in production by Xilinx for FPGA applications is shown in Figure 5-14.

The rigid interposer CSP design requires the least development and was the first type placed in high volume production in Japan for hand held Camcorders. There are numerous types currently in production, summarized below:

CSP Name	User
NUCSP	EPS
Ceramic Fine Pitch BGA	Fujitsu
Mini BGA	IBM
Small Form	LSI Logic
Stud Bump Bond	Matsushita
Slightly Larger than IC Carrier (SLICC)	Motorola
Flip Chip BGA	Sony
Chip Size Thin Package	Toshiba

CUSTOM LEAD FRAME CSP

For very low pin count packages, typically less than 68, all the leads can be fit around the perimeter of the package on 0.5mm (20mil) centers. This small size CSP can take the place of the single small outline package (SSOP), without the fragile leads of this package style. The various lead frame type CSPs and users are:

CSP Name	User
Small Outline Non-leaded (SON)	Fujitsu
Lead on Chip	Hitachi
MicroStud BGA	Hitachi
Bottom Lead Package	LG Semicon
Molded Bump	Mitsubishi
Very Small Peripheral Array	The Panda Project
Flip Tape Carrier	Rohm
Bump Chip Carrier	Fujitsu

Other lead frame type CSPs, but manufactured at the wafer scale, are listed in the next section.

The highest volume lead frame CSP is the bump chip carrier (BCC) from Fujitsu. It is currently in use for RF products in cell phones, pagers and other wireless products. For pin counts of 16 leads, the pitch is 0.65mm. For larger lead count, the pitch is 0.5mm (20mils). A close up of the BCC is shown in Figure 5-15.

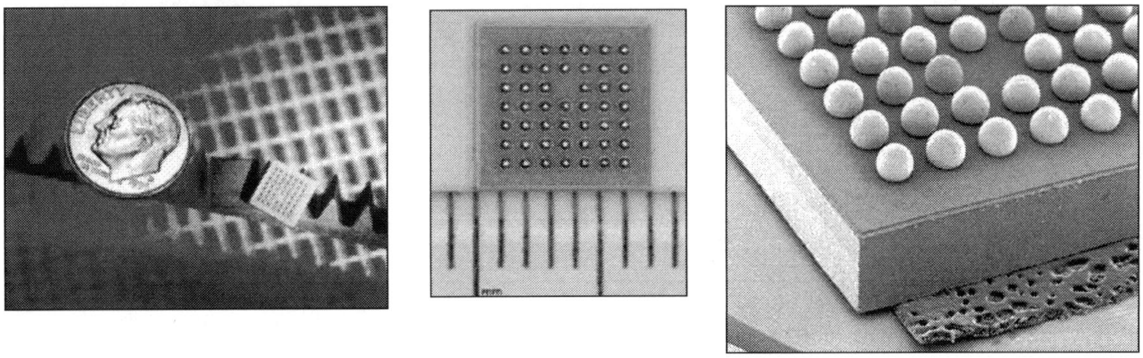

Figure 5-14. Laminate based rigid interposer CSP used by Xilinx. Left: size of the CSP compared to a dime. Middle: close up of the CSP from the ball side, on a 0.8mm pitch. Right: SEM of the solder balls.

There are two general approaches to achieving wafer level packaging, a modified flip chip technology and a custom construction. The more popular approaches for wafer level assembly are:

CSP Name	User
MicroSMT	ChipScale Inc
Shellcase	ShellCase Ltd
XBGA	Xicore
Mini BGA	Sandia
Ultra BGA	Flip Chip Technology
Super BGA	Fujitsu
WAVE	Tessera
MicroSMD	National Semiconductor

The general approaches for flip chip like WLA CSPs are very similar. Many of the vendors basically use the same process to build a CSP as for a solder bumped die, sometimes changing the solder ball diameter, or sometimes, just merely changing the name. In flip chip applications where the chip is to be mounted to a single chip package, the solder balls are typically on a 200micron–250micron (8mil-10mil) pitch, and the solder ball diameter is typically 125micron (5mil). In CSP applications, the solder ball pitch is usually set to match one of the JEDEC standards with a much larger solder ball. The solder ball sizes used by Flip Chip Technologies for their UltraCSP are:

Pitch	Bump Diameter
0.50mm	0.30mm
0.65	0.35
0.75	0.50
0.80	0.50

An example of the UltraCSP showing the redistribution layers and larger solder balls on an SRAM, is shown in Figure 5-17.

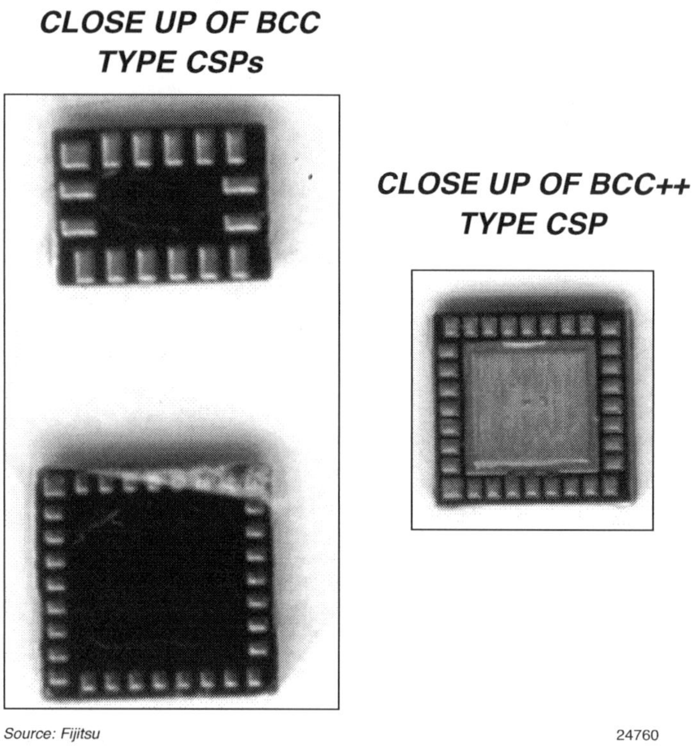

Figure 5-15. Close up of the Fujitsu BCC lead frame type CSP.

The construction cross section is shown in Figure 5-16. The die is mounted to a lead frame lithographically fabricated on a carrier. It is then wire bonded to the topside of the perimeter leads. In the case of the BCC++ package, wire bonds can also be made to a large central die paddle that can be attached to a ground pad on the circuit board. These multiple ground taps result in a low inductance path to the chip. After wire bonding, the chip is encapsulated and the surface of the leads are solder dipped.

WAFER LEVEL ASSEMBLY (WLA) CSP

It is generally agreed that to reach the lowest possible total cost of ownership, the design, fabrication and assembly of the CSP should move toward a wafer level technology. In this approach, the package is applied to the entire wafer and all the dice are packaged at the same time. After the wafer is diced, each chip is in packaged format, ready for test and assembly.

CROSS SECTION OF THE BCC CSP

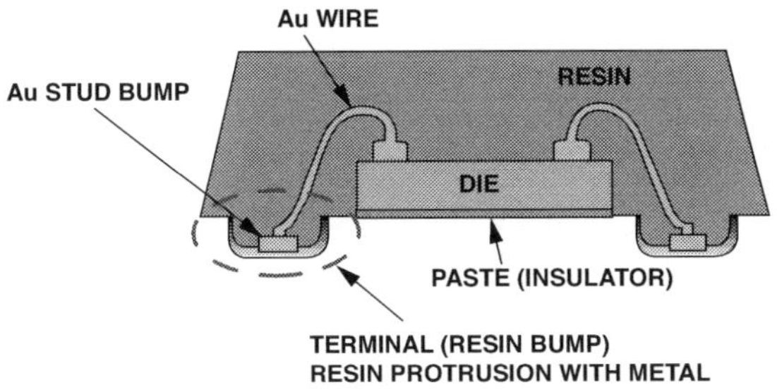

CUT AWAY VIEW OF THE BCC CSP

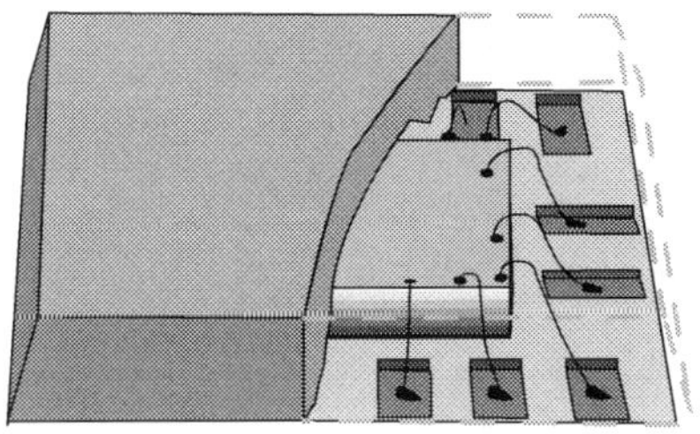

Source: Fujitsu 24761

Figure 5-16. Cross section of the BCC.

ULTRA CSP

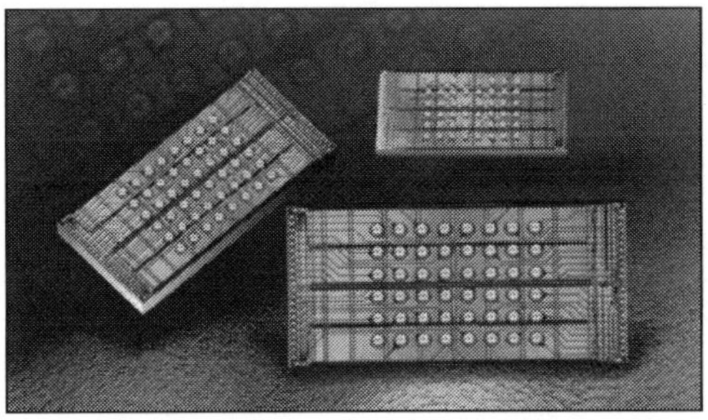

Source: Flip Chip Technology 24762

Figure 5-17. UltraCSP from Flip Chip Technologies packaging an SRAM.

Another example of a solder bumped die offered as a CSP is National Semiconductor's microSMD. The first products released in this package are very small op amps. The entire package is only 1.45mm on a side, with eight solder balls along the perimeter on 0.5mm centers. An example of the microSMD package is shown in Figure 5-18.

MICROSMD CSP OF THE LMC6035N DUAL OP AMP

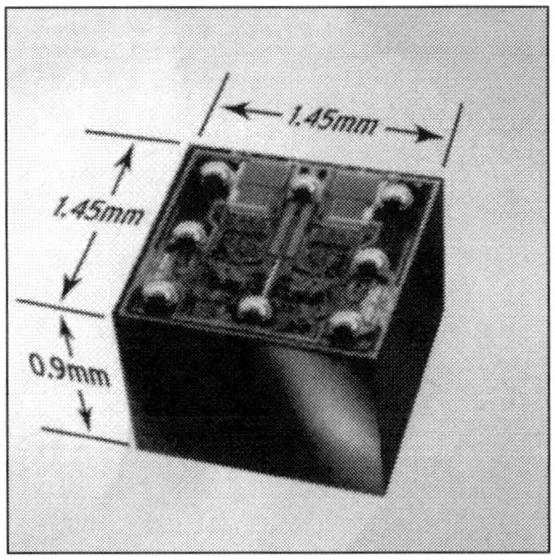

Source: National Semi 24685

Figure 5-18. MicroSMD package of the LMC6035 dual op amp.

There are three notable exceptions to the flip chip like WLA CSP approaches, from Fujitsu, Inc, ShellCase and ChipScale.

Fujitsu SuperCSP

On top of a finished wafer, a redistribution layer routes chip I/O pads to a JEDEC standard pad array, typically on 0.5mm – 0.8mm centers. On top of these new pads, copper columns are plated up about 90microns in height. These will be used as standoffs for solder balls. The entire wafer is encapsulated with a thermoset epoxy using a modified compression molding step. This is illustrated in Figure 5-19.

After compression molding, the top surface release sheet is peeled off. The copper studs are left exposed. On top of these studs, solder balls are placed and reflowed. The wafer is then diced into individually packaged chips. Figure 5-20 is an example of the final SCSP compared with the chip before encapsulation.

COMPRESSION MOLDING ENCAPSULATION OF SCSP

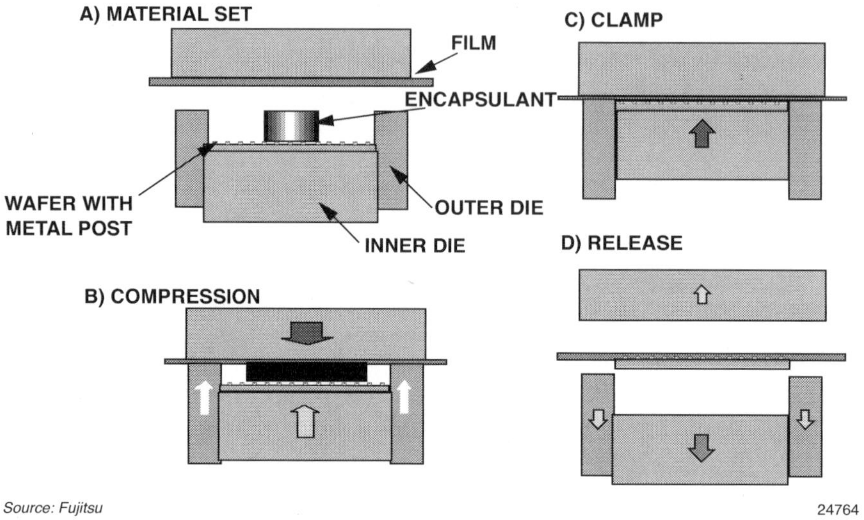

Figure 5-19. Compression molding to encapsulate the SCSP.

SUPERCSP BEFORE AND AFTER ENCAPSULATION

Source: Fujitsu 24765

Figure 5-20. Fujitsu Super CSP before encapsulation and after.

Shellcase CSP

ShellCase Ltd. uses a unique approach to WLA by sandwiching a thinned wafer between two glass plates and keeping a clear optical path to the surface of the die. This makes it ideal for optoelectronic applications such as image sensors and EPROMs that are UV erased.

An example of a ShellCase CSP and cross section, co-developed with Xicore and termed the XBGA, is shown in Figure 5-21.

The manufacturing steps for the ShellCase CSP are as follows:

- A thin protective glass layer is bonded to the active side of a silicon wafer with epoxy adhesive.
- The silicon material between the die (in the streets) is etched away from the backside, yielding individual IC's attached to the supporting glass layer.
- The grooves between the dies are filled with an inert material, and a second thin glass cover is bonded onto the silicon die's back side to achieve a complete protective enclosure for each die.
- An organic layer is applied and patterned to act as a compliant layer underneath the solder joints.

- Deep notches are sawn between the dies, revealing the cross-sections of the bond pads.
- A metal layer, patterned by lithography to individual leads, is deposited to contact the bond pads at their cross-sections. Soldering leads are formed on the upper surface of the package. Contacts are plated by nickel.
- A solder mask layer is applied.
- For BGA type devices, the bumps are screened and then reflowed at wafer level
- Wafer dicing yields individual packaged dies.

CLOSE UP OF SHELLCASE CSP

CROSS SECTION OF SHELLCASE CSP

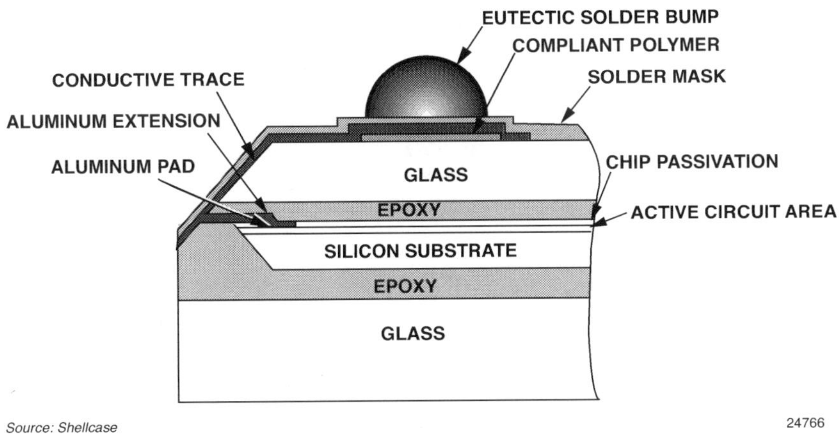

Figure 5-21. Shellcase CSP compared to a penny and the cross section of a XBGA co-developed between Xicore and ShellCase.

These process steps are diagrammed in Figure 5-22.

The ShellCase CSP is unique in providing a transparent surface for the die. When used for optical applications, the leads can be connected to the back side, leaving the upper surface of the die exposed. This configuration is called Shell-OP. An example of a Shell-OP CSP is shown in Figure 5-23.

ChipScale Inc.

The MicroSMT packages from ChipScale may be the oldest CSP technology. It was originally in production in 1990 for few pin count RF components and was licensed to Motorola for their RF components. In wafer form, gold leads are patterned from the peripheral pads to the center of the dicing street. From the back side, the streets are etched through, exposing the beams. Posts are build up and metallized bringing the surface connections to the back side. The die is then encapsulated leaving the bottom of the metallized posts exposed. A cut away view is shown in Figure 5-24.

The die is mounted faced up. Typical applications include RF devices, discretes and passive components. This package style is used by Intarsia for their integrated passive devices. Examples of MicroSMT CSP are shown in Figure 5-25.

THE IDEAL CHIP SCALE PACKAGE

It has been suggested by Unitive Electronics Inc that the ideal chip scale package should met the following specs:

- Finished part should be roughly the same size as the die
- Be cost competitive with the lowest cost alternative package
- Moisture insensitive
- Be reworkable at the board level
- Be compatible with standard suface mount processes and not require additional steps, such as underfill

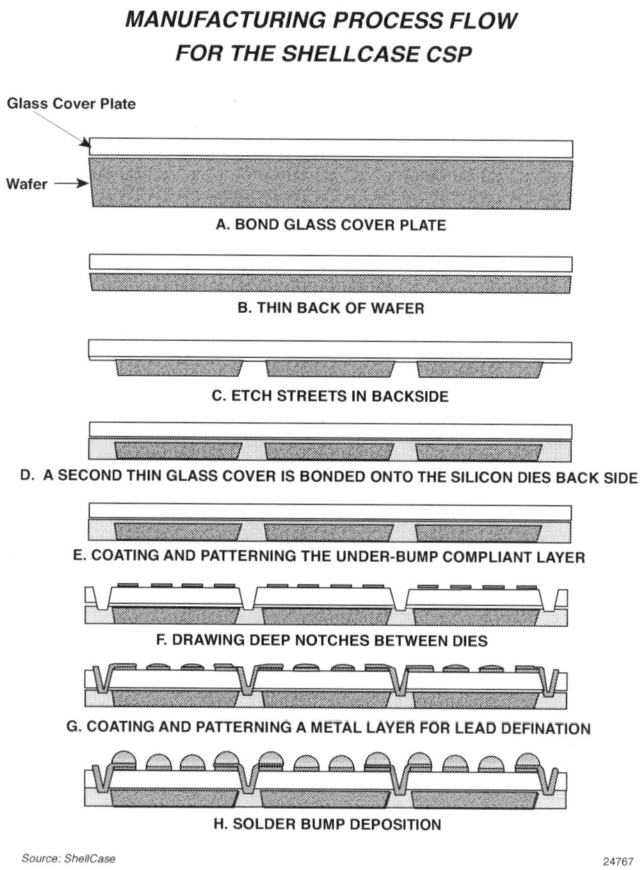

Figure 5-22. Process steps of the ShellCase CSP.

- Can be thermally enhanced by board assembler or end user
- Infrastructure should be able to keep pace with volume demand
- Be able to use existing IC die designs and wafer layouts currently on the shelf
- Proven reliability in the intended application
- Protect the die from alpha particle emissions
- Protect the board customers from the die manufacturer's stepping or shrinks
- Provide a robust form factor for handling, shipping testing and assembling the parts

There is a running debate in the industry over the relative merits of flip chip direct chip attach (DCA) for universal application vs. CSP. The ideal CSP will have many of the elements of DCA, such as wafer level fabrication and roughly chip size. However, there are three limitations of DCA for general application as a chip scale package:

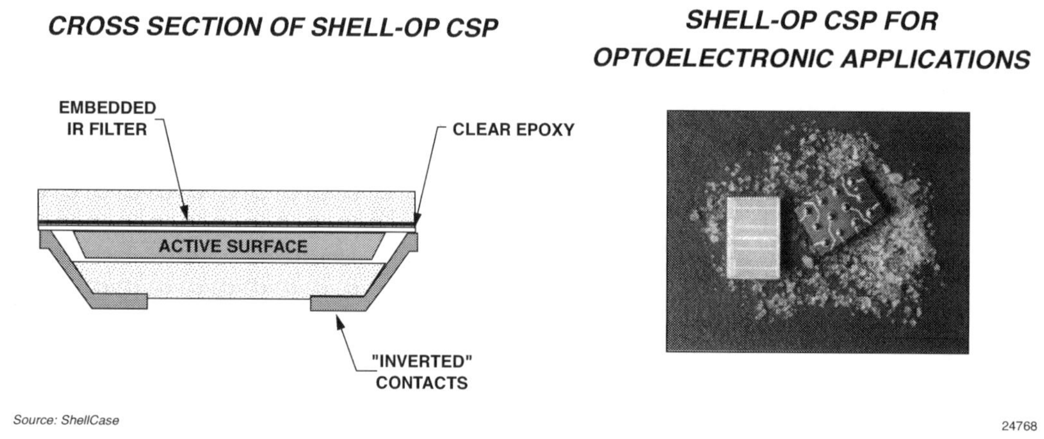

Figure 5-23. Shell-OP CSP from ShellCase.

CUT AWAY VIEW OF THE MICROSMT CSP

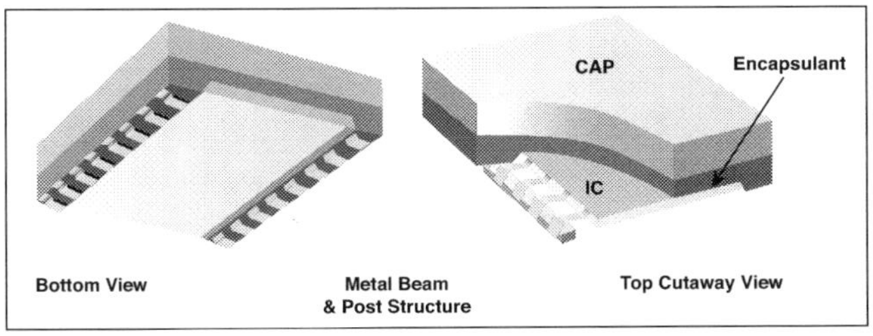

Parameter	MSMT	0.3 QFP	Flip Chip
Height (mm)	.5-.8	1.4	.5-.7
Inductance (nH)	0.1 to 0.2	1-7	0.1 to 0.2
Capacitance (pF)	0.02 to 0.03	0.5 to 1	0.3
Attachment	Solder	Solder	Solder and Underfill

Source: ChipScale Inc. 24769

Figure 5-24. MicroSMT from ChipScale Inc.

MICROSMT CSPs COMPARED TO A CONVENTIONAL SOIC

Source: CHipScale Inc. 24750

INTEGRATED PASSIVES FROM INTARSIA ASSEMBLED IN CHIPSCALE INC MICROSMT CSP PACKAGES

Source: ChipScale Inc. 24770

Figure 5-25. Examples of MicroSMT CSPs. Top: low pin count amplifiers compared to a standard SOIC version. Bottom: Integrated Passives from Intarsia.

- A rigid solder joint that is the only compliant element between the chip surface and the substrate surface will have potential reliability problems through thermal cycling due to the TCE mismatch, for higher pin count devices.

- The surface of the die must be protected from the environment, from alpha particles emitted from the radioactive lead isotopes and impurities in the solder, and from handling, shipping and testing.

- The solder ball size is on the order of 125microns (5mils) and would require a tight coplanarity spec for the mounting substrate, as well as be difficult to interface to routine test sockets.

Many of the various CSP options are designed to get around these limitations while not adding too much cost. Some merely make the flip chip solder balls larger, other approaches allow DCA with underfill to an interposer, similar to FCBGA.

Are CSPs merely "training wheels" in preparation to a migration to bare die DCA? The trend for the future will be to have CSP technology move toward wafer scale fabrication, at which point the notion of a "bare die" will disappear. This is further indicated by the development efforts of most CSP users toward wafer level assembly. Figure 5-26 is an example of the current WLA designs of Tessera, termed Wafer Area Vertical Expansion (WAVE) technology.

The distinction between DCA and CSP will probably end up being only in solder ball pitch, ball size and lead count.

As pointed out in the ICE companion publication, **Roadmaps of Packaging Technology**, conventionally drilled PCB substrates can route CSP devices when the lead count is low, on the order of 100-200 balls, depending on the body size.

For higher ball counts, more advanced (and more expensive) microvia substrates, discussed in a following chapter, are required. This routing restriction is a major reason that virtually all the CSP applications currently in high volume production are for low pin count devices, typically less than 100 leads. This includes discrete logic, RF devices and memory: DRAM, SRAM and flash. Along with the smaller size packages comes shorter leads which have lower inductance, an important performance feature for high speed and RF devices.

The routing density on the surface of the board can be optimized if the surface solder attach pads and CSP solder ball diameters are made smaller. This leaves more space between the surface pads for fan out traces. To take advantage of this routing, the smaller solder balls should not be the main compliant element. This is one of the important distinguishing features among the CSP alternatives. The Tessera CSP, for example, provides compliance in an elastomer coating and a flexible TAB lead, as illustrated in Figure 5-27.

Of the over 100 different CSP types, this feature will be an important element of the successful CSP technologies.

EARLY WLA PROTOTYPE OF THE TESSERA WAVE CSP

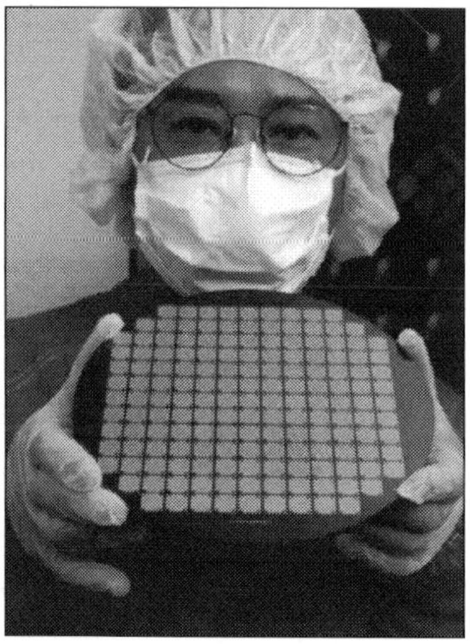

CROSS-SECTION OF THE TESSERA WAVE CSP

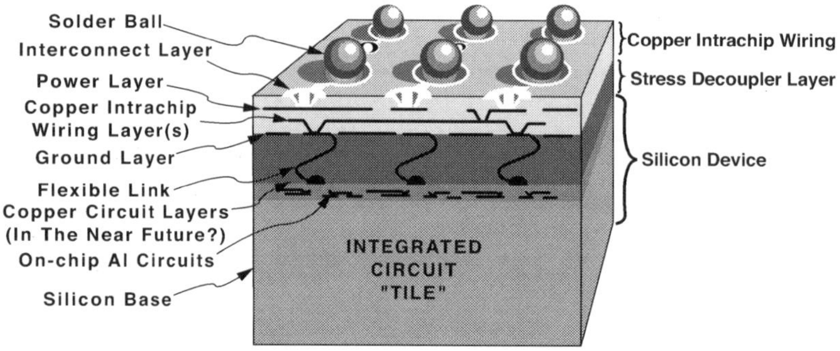

Source: Tessera

24771

Figure 5-26. Tessera WLA CSP technology. Bottom: Cross section of WAVE structure. Top: early prototype fabricated on wafer scale.

HOW THE TAB LEAD AND ELASTOMER PROVIDE HIGH RELIABLILTY COMPLIANCE IN THE TESSERA MICROBGA CSP

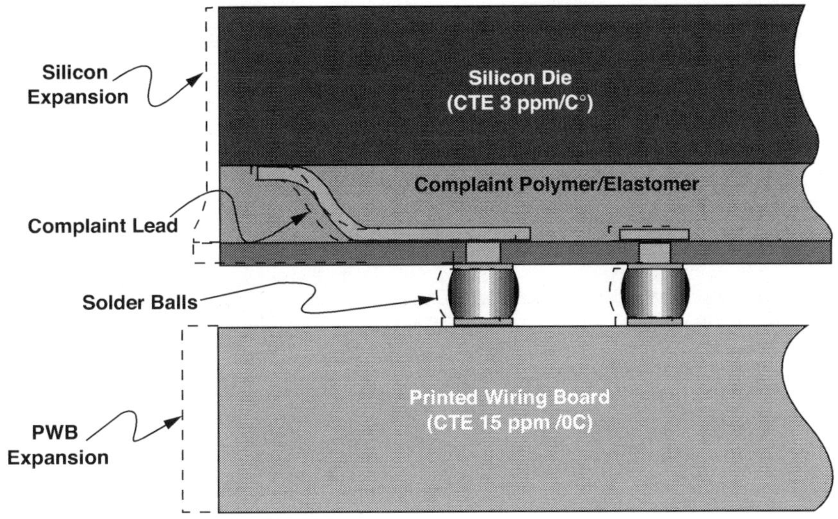

Source: Tessera 24772

Figure 5-27. Illustration of the compliance in the Tessera microBGA that allows for a TCE mismatch.

6 Bare Die Integration

WHAT EVER HAPPENED TO MCMS?

In the late 1980s and early 1990s, MCMs (Multi Chip Modules) were seen as the salvation of VLSI packaging. The MCM was viewed as the way to minimize the detrimental impact of the package- both the ballooning size of the package and the delay and noise related performance limitations. Many examples were fabricated to demonstrate the smaller size and higher performance of MCM implementations. An example is shown in Figure 6-1.

COMPARISON OF CONVENTIONAL AND MCM RISC MICROPROCESSOR CHIP SETS

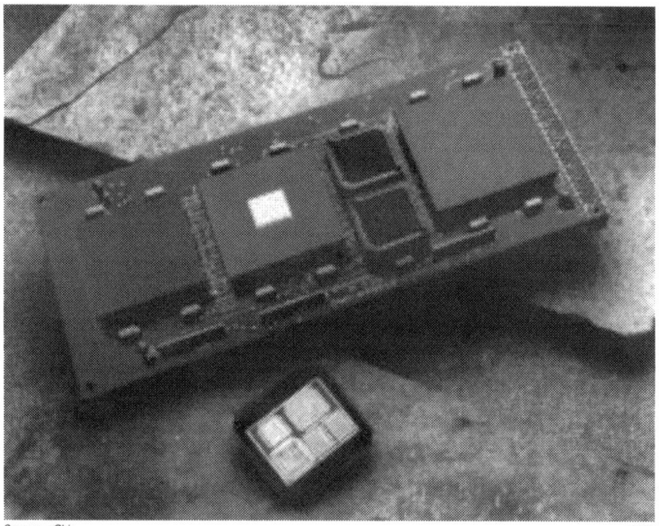

Source: nChip 15882

Figure 6-1. Comparison of a Sparc processor in conventional single chip packages on a circuit board and in an MCM format, fabricated by nCHIP.

The vision of MCMs in these early days was as a collection of high pin count bare die, extremely close together, mounted on a common, high density, multilayer thin film substrate. Thin film was seen as necessary in order to provide the interconnect density required by very high I/O bare die.

Ten years ago, for lead pitches over 250, the only alternative to a QFP was a pin grid array package. High pin count PGAs had been built with 1000 pins, but required circuit boards with many layers just for pin escapes. This dramatically increased the total cost of ownership, even if there was just one high pin count device in the system. The package mounting requirements, especially for leaded packages, never taxed the via density of the circuit boards. The chips had to be spread far apart due to the limitations of the packages. Faced with this situation, the alternative of using an MCM when high pin count chips were involved, was attractive.

Since then, the vision of MCMs has transformed considerably, primarily due to two changes: new single chip package alternatives and microvia laminate substrates. The BGA and more recently, the CSP, have a dramatically higher packaging efficiency than prior single chip packages. This is in contrast with the larger peripheral lead frame based packages such as the QFP.

With the use of microvia technology, described in the next chapter, and fine lines on 150micron (6mil) centers, the interconnect density available in laminate substrates can approach that from thin film, but at a cost of 10% to 50% of the thin film substrate cost.

When a module uses CSPs having a package footprint the same as the bare chip, but with the robustness and handling characteristics of a packaged die, mounted on a high density PCB substrate, it looks like an MCM. However, it is constructed using conventional, well established processes. An example of a conventional module, with the density of an MCM, is shown in Figure 6-2.

DIMM BOARD WITH CSP DRAMs

Source: Kingpin 24773

Figure 6-2. A memory module using CSPs and fine line substrate, with the density of an MCM.

Much of the early perceived benefit of an MCM has been achieved by other means that does not involve the use of fragile bare die. However, there are still well established niches where the use of an MCM, i.e., bare die integrated into systems, provides either performance, size, cost or time to market advantages over the conventional approach of individually packaged die on a PCB substrate.

THE NEW VISION OF AN MCM

As described in the ICE companion publication, **Roadmaps of Packaging Technology**, the term MCM is rather vague and ambiguous. There are four different approaches of integrating bare die into systems that have variously been grouped under the category of MCM:

- Chip on Board (COB) or direct chip attach (DCA)
- Hybrid
- High performance MCM
- Multi Chip Package (MCP) or Few Chip Package (FCP)

COB

Chip on Board is used to refer to the case where the bare die is attached to the substrate and wire bonded. When the chip is attached as flip chip, it is termed Direct Chip Attach (DCA). When the chip is attached to a glass panel, as for example, in LCD applications, it is termed Chip On Glass (COG).

The key element of COB applications is that they are very low cost. In all cases, the die is low pin count, 100 leads or less, and from a very mature product line where the wafer test yield is greater than 99%. When wire bonding is used, the die is glob top coated after assembly and test. The total board cost is low. If any rework is required, the board is typically thrown away. An example of a COB application using a low temperature cofired ceramic (LTCC) substrate is shown in Figure 6-3.

A very large niche for this technology is the attach of the drivers to LCD substrates, COG. There are three approaches to interface the LCD drivers: using a ribbon connection to a separate PCB substrate, using TAB or with flip chip COG. These approaches are illustrated in Figure 6-4.

VARIOUS COB COMPONENTS WITH A LTCC SUBSTRATE

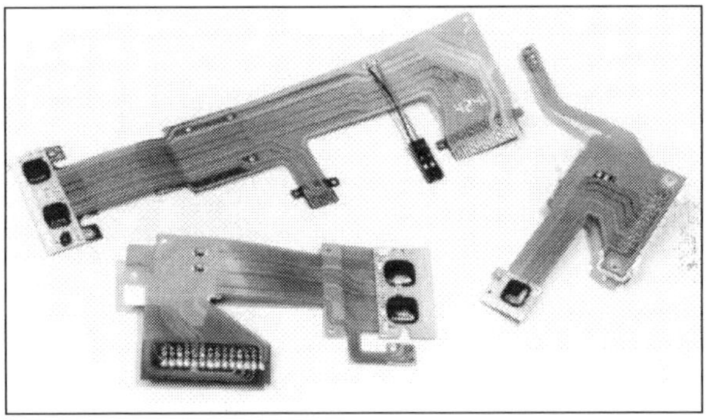

Source: CTS Microelectronics 24774

Figure 6-3. Example of COB technology.

The use of COG has been enabled by the use of Anisotropic Conductive Film (ACF). The ACF material has small conductive particles that make electrical contact between opposite conductor pads on the chip and the substrate. It works well under two conditions: flat mating surfaces and when high contact resistance (0.1-1Ohm) is not an issue. Both of these conditions are well met in LCD driver applications. The adhesive film acts as the encapsulant for the driver chips. The cross section of a COG chip mounted with ACF is diagrammed in Figure 6-5. An example of narrow sliver drivers mounted to an LCD element is shown in Figure 6-6.

Hybrids

One of the oldest approaches for MCMs, which is still in volume production, are hybrids. These are typically small, thick film ceramic substrates with a "hybrid" combination of bare chips and passives. The substrate has advanced to include laminate and thin film as well as low temperature cofired ceramic (LTCC). An example of a ceramic hybrid and laminate hybrid are shown in Figure 6-7 and Figure 6-8.

Hybrids had their start in low volume military applications and high volume telecom applications. They have been, and will continue to be, used for many specialized applications especially for mixed signal in communications.

High Performance MCMs

The original driver for high end MCMs was the mainframe computers starting with the IBM 3083. Though the first generation mainframes using MCMs were ECL based, these have evolved to CMOS based. The higher integration level with CMOS results in higher performance than the equivalent ECL technology. This is illustrated in Figure 6-9.

All four main frame computer vendors, IBM, Fujitsu, Hitachi and NEC, use a similar high density MCM technology with over 60 layers of cofired glass ceramic and up to 6 layers of thin film metal, Polyimide dielectric on top.

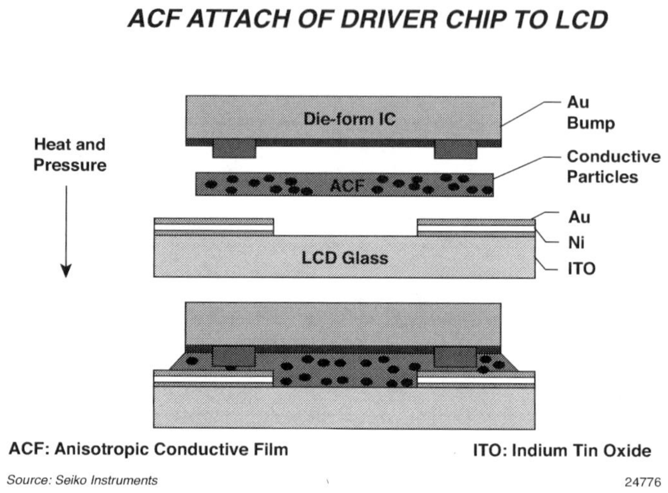

Figure 6-5. The use of Anisotropic Conductive Film (ACF) to electrically attach a driver chip to an LCD display.

Very few variations of this technology have migrated into commercial MCM use. One reason is that the thin film, high density substrate is very expensive. Not many applications except the mainframes and some high end avionics processors absolutely

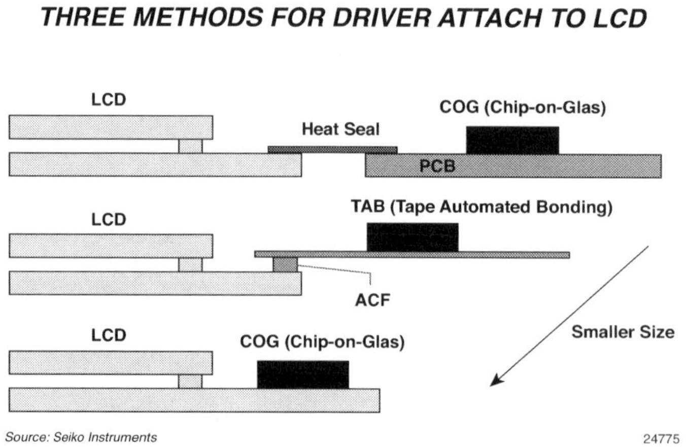

Figure 6-4. Three methods for interfacing the LCD driver chips.

requires the interconnect density of thin film. The performance increase or size and weight reduction for these applications can justified the cost. Many have understood the acronym, MCM, to stand for Mucho Cost Modules.

Numerous merchant vendors tried to create a business based on thin film substrates, notably nCHIP, Alcoa Microelectronics, Raychem's Advanced Packaging Systems, Honeywell, Pacific Microelectronics Center (PMC), TI, Micro Module Systems and Hughes.

LCD ELEMENT WITH DRIVER ACF ATTACHED (UPPER LEFT)

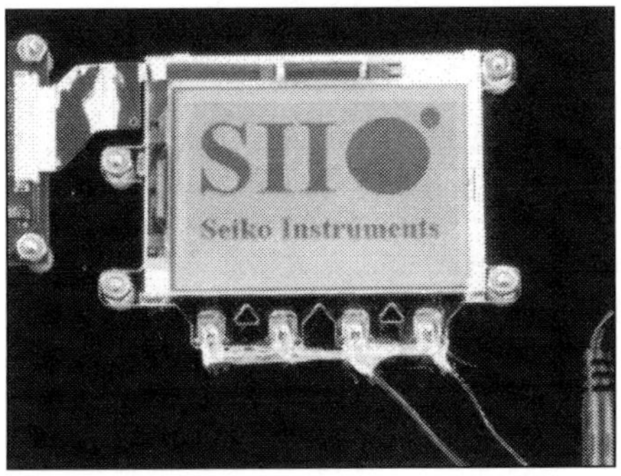

Source: Seiko Instruments 24777

Figure 6-6. Drivers mounted as COG to the upper left of a small LCD.

HYBRID MADE FROM LAMINATE SUBSTRATE

Source: Advanced Packaging Magazine 24779

Figure 6-8. Laminate substrate based hybrid. Contains bare die, passives and a transformer with a custom lead frame.

VARIOUS HYBRID MODULES USING CERAMIC SUBSTRATES

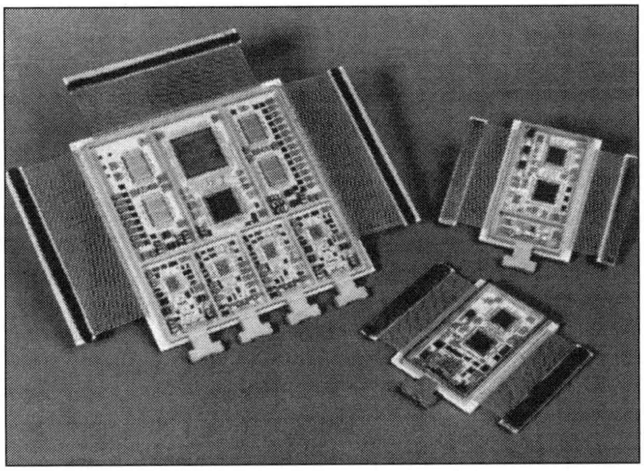

Source: CTS Microelectronics 24778

Figure 6-7. Conventional ceramic hybrid used for microwave applications. Lead frame is a custom configuration specific for the application. The substrate interconnects bare die and passive components.

To date, only Hughes currently still provides thin film MCM substrate and module services. One of the reasons the Hughes product line has survived is that many of their modules are designed into the avionics systems of current generation fighter aircraft with a production life of 10-20 years. An example of a thin film multilayer high performance MCM from Hughes is shown in Figure 6-10.

High performance MCMs will continue to be used by the captive mainframe vendors, but will find few other commercially viable opportunities in the short term. The projections for the merchant MCM market have been dropping.

Multi Chip Packages

After experimenting with many MCM technologies and applications, the industry has definitely found a strong and growing niche for MCMs when the final module has a form factor that matches a standard package size, either a QFP, PGA or BGA. These packages with MCMs inside, have been called Multi Chip Packages (MCP) or Few Chip Packages (FCP). An example of an MCP with a BGA footprint is shown in Figure 6-11.

PERFORMANCE MIGRATION FROM ECL TO CMOS FOR MAINFRAME COMPUTERS

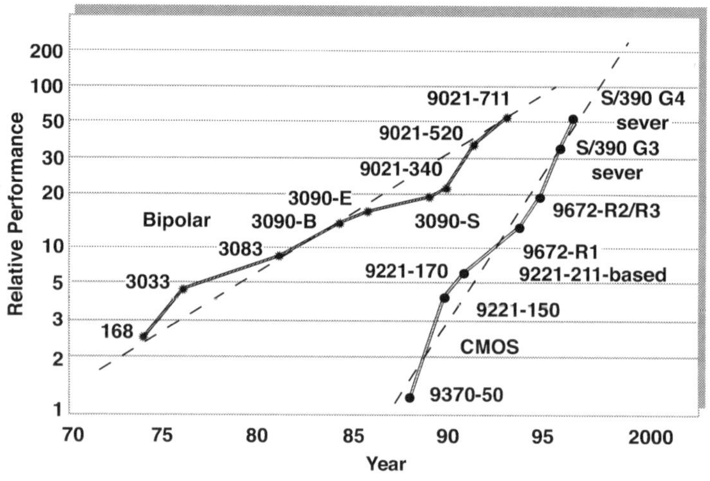

Source: IBM 24780

Figure 6-9. Transition from ECL to CMOS in high end mainframe computers.

HIGH PERFORMANCE MCM USED IN FIGHTER RADAR SYSTEMS

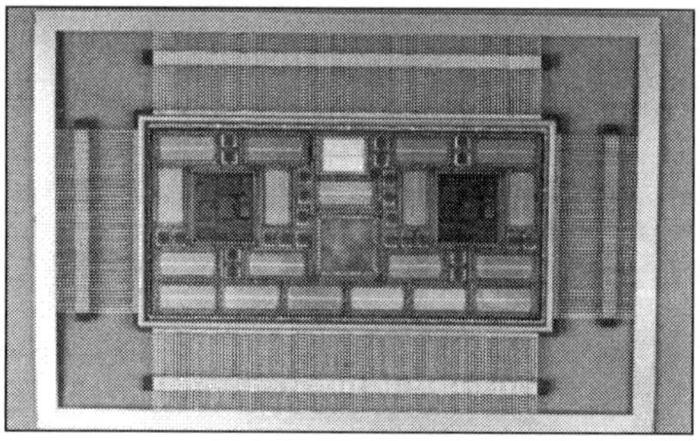

Source: Hughes 24781

Figure 6-10. High performance thin film MCM from Hughes used in the radar system of fighters.

TechSearch International predicts that the MCP market will continue to see strong growth, while the traditional MCM market will be flat or shrink. These projections are shown in Figure 6-12.

There are four elements to the success of the MCP. First is the form factor that allows the handling of the MCM after assembly to be identical to single chip packages. This means the MCP can leverage the existing board assembly infrastructure.

The second element for success is that the substrate used is chosen to be the lowest cost substrate for the given application. MCPs are market pull driven, rather than technology pushed. Most of the applications will be with laminate substrates and wire bonded chips. With cost as a prime driver, some users have referred to this new generation of MCM as standing for Multi Cheap Modules. MCPs can even be fabricated on just simple lead frames, as illustrated in Figure 6-13.

However, when higher interconnect density is required, even cofired ceramic can be cost effective. An example of a high density cofired ceramic MCP for two large flip chip devices is shown in Figure 6-14.

The third element that has lead to the success of the MCP is leveraging conventional package assembly processes. Virtually all package assembly contractors also assembly MCPs. The issue of Known Good Die (KGD) has become almost a non issue. For example, Prismark Partners estimates that in 1997, there were 4.2 billion dice shipped as bare die for use in multiple bare die applications. Only 275 million bare die were shipped with testing beyond wafer probe, in some form of KGD. This is only about 6%. Because most of the modules are low cost, the extra cost of the KGD cannot be justified. Repair is less common than just tossing defective modules.

For high end modules, using more expensive chips, there is a trend toward more effective on-wafer, at speed testing. For example, a new probing technology from FormFactor Inc allows at speed testing on wafer of even high pin count area array devices. They have incorporated an array of microspring contacts, which can be mounted to a ceramic substrate to make contact to all the pads of a die while still on a wafer. Excellent electrical properties are maintained so that at speed testing can be performed. A close up of the microspring contacts is shown in Figure 6-15.

The forth reason for the success of the MCP is finding the right market niche. The chief value an MCP offers is smaller size and potentially shorter time to market with a specialized function. These needs are both strong in the portable and especially wireless markets where time to market and small size are critical. TechSearch International estimates that this is the largest market segment for MCPs followed by portable computers. Their projection is shown in Figure 6-16.

THREE CHIP MCP WITH BGA FOOTPRINT

Source: Motorola 24782

Figure 6-11. Three chip BGA multi chip package.

MCM AND MCP MARKET PROJECTIONS

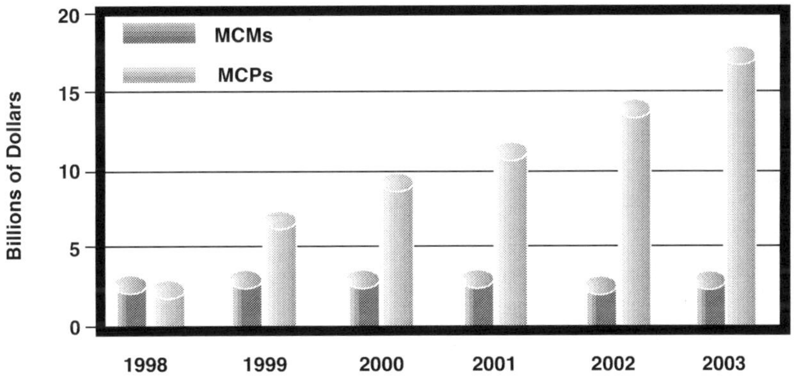

Source: TechSearch International 24783

Figure 6-12. MCP market projections.

LEAD FRAME BASED LOW COST MCPs

Source: Advanced Packaging 24784

Figure 6-13. Lead frame based MCP.

HIGH DENSITY CERAMIC MCP FOR TWO FLIP CHIP DIE

Source: NTK 24785

Figure 6-14. High density ceramic flip chip MCP.

MICROSPRING CONTACTS ON FORMFACTOR PROBE CARD

Source: FormFactor Inc. 24786

Figure 6-15. Close up of microspring contacts of the FormFactor probe technology, which has the potential of revolutionizing at speed wafer test.

In addition to the small size and path for shorter time to market, an MCP can provide a module combining chips that can never be integrated in the future. Typical combinations include:

- Analog and digital ICs
- RF and digital ICs
- Processor and memory- SRAM, Flash, EPROM
- Graphics processor and DRAM frame buffer
- Mixed memory: Flash and SRAM

One example of a mixed technology MCP is the SRAM/Flash module from Fujitsu, NEC and Toshiba. This MCP has two chips on a common laminate substrate, containing a Flash and an SRAM chip. This is shown in Figure 6-17.

Alpine Microsystems

A new MCP technology has been introduced by Alpine Microsystems that has a different approach from all previous MCM products. Rather than the conventional approach of a large area high density substrate to which die are attached and routed, the Alpine approach uses small chip scale pallets with a high density of interconnects, and assembles these onto a large area, low density window frame like substrate.

MARKET SEGMENTS FOR MCPs

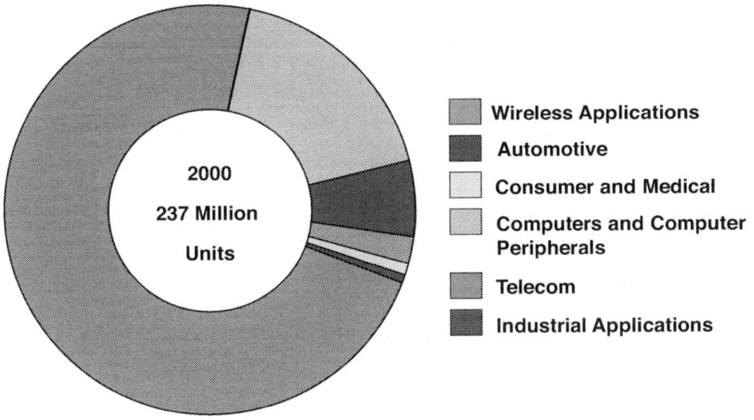

Source: TechSearch International 24787

Figure 6-16. Market segments for MCPs.

TWO CHIP SRAM/FLASH MCP

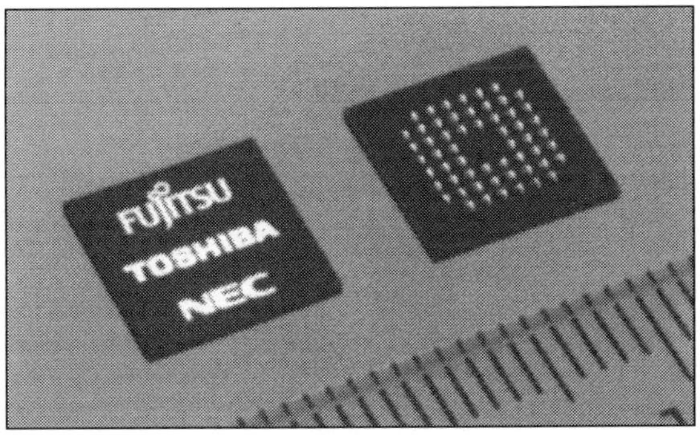

CROSS SECTION OF 2 CHIP MCP

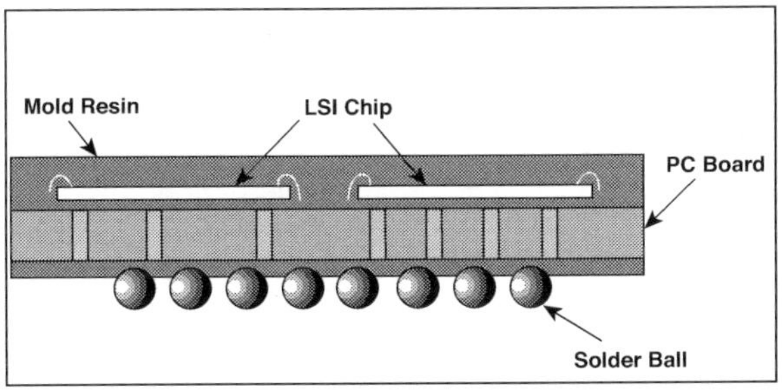

Source: Fujitsu 24788

Figure 6-17. Small memory MCP from Fujitsu, NEC and Toshiba, top view and cross section.

The chip scale carriers, called MicroPallets can be tested, providing a built in KGD capability. The MicroPallets also have traces that provide global routing as pass through connections. The window frame MicroBoard just connects adjacent MicroPallets, with no global wiring. The advantages of this approach for very high density MCPs is KGD, very dense silicon packaging and ability to use off the shelf peripheral bonded chips with very tight bond pad pitch, while still maintaining good electrical performance.

The concept for an Alpine single component solution, termed a Complex IC, is shown in Figure 6-18.

An example of a final complex IC, before and after it is encapsulated, is shown in Figure 6-19.

The Complex IC consists of four parts:

- The bumped chip with peripheral pads
- A custom MicroPallet that the chip is flip chip attached to
- A MicroBoard window frame on which the MicroPallets are flip chip attached
- A single chip package into which the MicroBoard is attached and molded.

A standard chip with peripheral aluminum pads is bumped using the electroless zincate process. Since this is maskless, the cost to bump a wafer can be less than $25 in volume, so the per unit cost can be extremely low. A close up of the gold bumped peripheral pads on a chip is shown in Figure 6-20.

A silicon substrate, termed a MicroPallet, is specially fabricated with up to four layers of thin film copper and BCB dielectric interconnects. Solder pads on the surface match the chip pads that will be bonded to it. The MicroPallet plays two roles. First, it provides a fan out of the chip pads to the periphery of the MicroPallet. Secondly, it provides "pass through" connections that assist in global routing over the module.

SCHEMATIC OF COMPLEX IC CONSTRUCTION

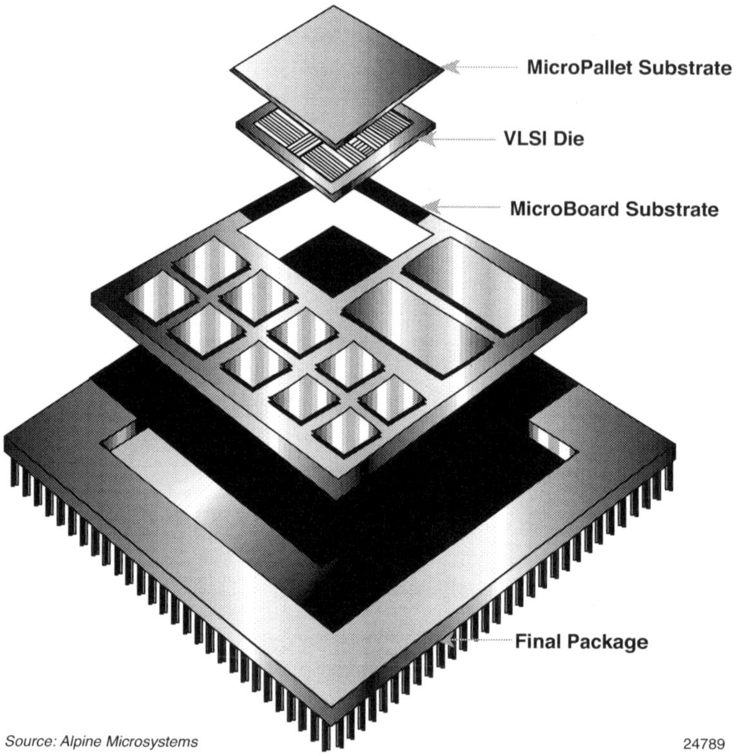

Source: Alpine Microsystems 24789

Figure 6-18. Alpine Complex IC.

COMPLEX IC MCP AFTER ENCAPSULATION

Source: Alpine Microsystems 24790

Figure 6-19. Complex IC assembly before and after encapsulation as a BGA.

Since the MicroPallet is Silicon with a matched TCE to the chip, no underfill is required. The MicroPallet is roughly 20% larger than the size of the chip. With the chip mounted it is almost a CSP carrier. Each die has its own custom MicroPallet. As these are fabricated in a wafer fab process, the chips can be flip chip attached in a wafer process. An example of a wafer of MicroPallets with some chips already attached is shown in Figure 6-21.

The MicroPallets have multiple rows of solder bumps along the perimeter to mount to the window frame MicroBoard. The MicroBoard, shown in Figure 6-22, is a single metal layer silicon substrate that merely connects between adjacent MicroPallets. Figure 6-23 is a close up of the multiple peripheral rows of solder balls on the MicroPallet that would be attached to the matching gold bumped pads on the MicroBoard.

The current applications of the Alpine Complex IC are for graphics controller modules that combine a processor and SRAM frame buffers.

MCP VS SOC SINGLE CHIP INTEGRATION

In addition to providing an integration of multiple die that could never be integrated in one chip due to mixed technologies or feature sizes, an MCP can provide an integrated module with a function that will not be available until a future chip rev. For example, the original HAL Sparc64 CPU was a six chip MCM. In the following generation, most of these functions were integrated into a single chip. The Intel Pentium Pro was a two chip MCM incorporating the processor and L2 cache. In the Pentium II generation Celeron processor, the L2 cache was integrated on chip. In both applications, the higher performance in a small form factor was available in the market before the integrated version was introduced.

There are three factors that can contribute to an MCP implementation providing a quicker path to market or lower cost than a single chip solution:

- If the intended volume is low, the NRE of an MCP is much less ($10k-$50k) compared to the NRE for an integrated ASIC ($100k-$500k)

- If the chips already exist, an MCP can be designed, built and ramped in volume faster than the functionality can be integrated into an ASIC

- If the Intellectual Property (IP) or design data base for all the functions of the single chip are not owned and verified by the ASIC provider, an MCP implementation of the individual die from different vendors may have lower risk and faster time to market.

Under these conditions, an MCP is a low risk, intermediate step to an ASIC implementation. Many view the new trend of System On a Chip (SOC) as the next wave to revolutionize ASICs. With chips capable of 20-50 million transistors, there is the capacity to integrate virtually all the functions of a motherboard or card into one chip. This would certainly produce the smallest and lightest product. On a silicon cost basis, it would also be potentially the lowest cost.

SILICON WAFER OF MICROPALLET CHIP CARRIERS, SOME WITH CHIPS MOUNTED

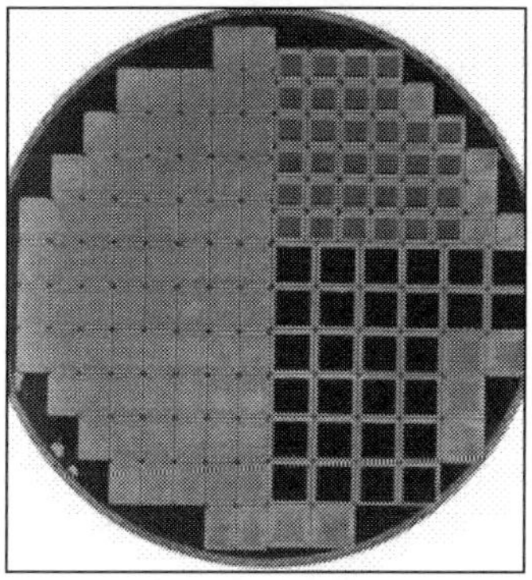

Source: Alpine Microsystems/ICE 24792

Figure 6-21. Wafer of MicroPallets with some chips already flip chip attached.

CLOSE-UP SEM OF GOLD BUMPED CHIP PRIOR TO FLIP CHIP ASSEMBLY TO MICROPALLET

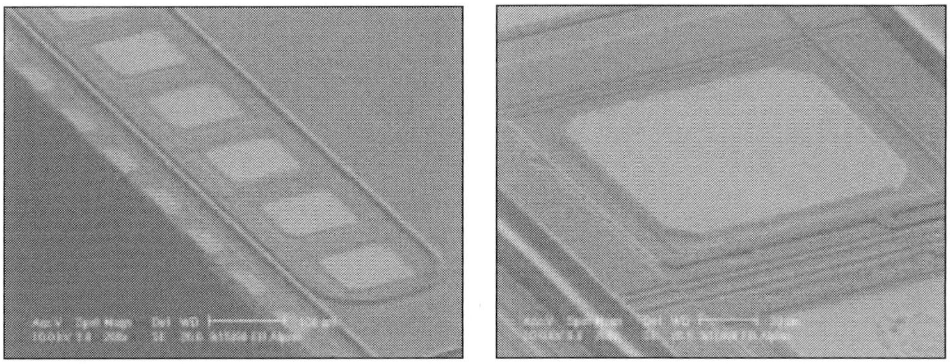

Source: Alpine Microsystems/ICE 24791

Figure 6-20. Bumped peripheral pads of a chip before it is flip chip attached to the solder balls on the MicroPallet.

MICROBOARD SILICON SUBSTRATE WITH ONE LAYER OF INTERCONNECT

Source: Alpine Microsystems/ICE 24793

Figure 6-22. Close up of a silicon MicroBoard that interconnects the MicroPallets. The MicroBoard is then bonded to a package such as a BGA or QFP.

SOLDER BUMPED MICROPALLET I/O CONNECTIONS

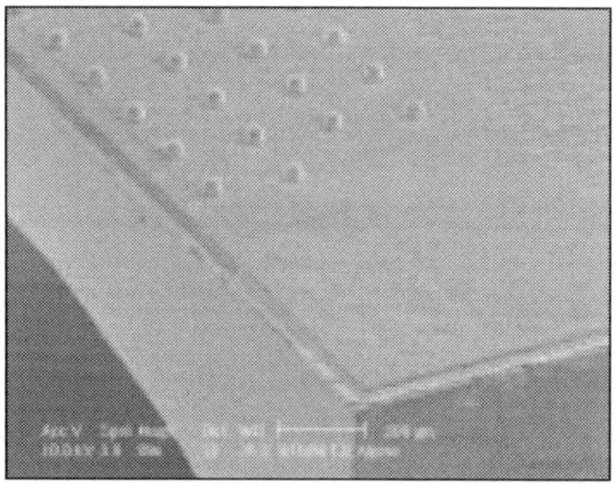

Source: Alpine Microsystems/ICE 24794

Figure 6-23. Solder balls on the MicroPallet to match the pads on the MicroBoard.

However, many barriers exist to the successful implementation of a robust SOC infrastructure. For example, the IP corresponding to each of the functions that are to be integrated must be in a compatible database, at the same feature size and process technology. They must all be available to the ASIC integrating vendor and be tested. Once a final design is identified, it may be many months before all the IP is ready to be converted into mask information. An intermediate step can be to implement the design as an MCP and use the same form factor as the integrated chip. It may be that the key element to the future success of SOC technology will be the multi chip package.

7 Microvia Technology

Conventional Printed Circuit Board Technology

Conventional Printed Circuit Board (PCB) technology is based on mechanically drilling through holes in stacks of laminated inner layers. Each inner layer has double sided copper that has been patterned and subtractively etched. After drilling, the holes are electroless and electroplated with copper making contact to the traces cutting into the sidewalls. The 50 largest merchant bare board vendors produced about $16B worth of "conventional" product in 1998. The top five vendors in 1998 were:

Company	Country	1998 revenue, $millions
CMK	Japan	$1,085
Viasystems	USA	$980
Ibiden	Japan	$727
Hadco	USA	$665
Nippon Mektron	Japan	$660

Of course, "conventional" is a moving target. There are three metrics that define "conventional" boards:

- Hole size
- Line width/space
- Number of layers

One way of establishing a limit to conventional technology is to look at the production volumes. Figure 7-1 shows the transition in line width and space as a percentage of total production, between 1997 and 1998. Though the fall off is at about 6 mil, there is a steady trend toward more boards produced with finer features. This is driven by the need for higher interconnect density.

PCB PRODUCTION OF DIFFERENT LINE WIDTHS IN 1997-1998

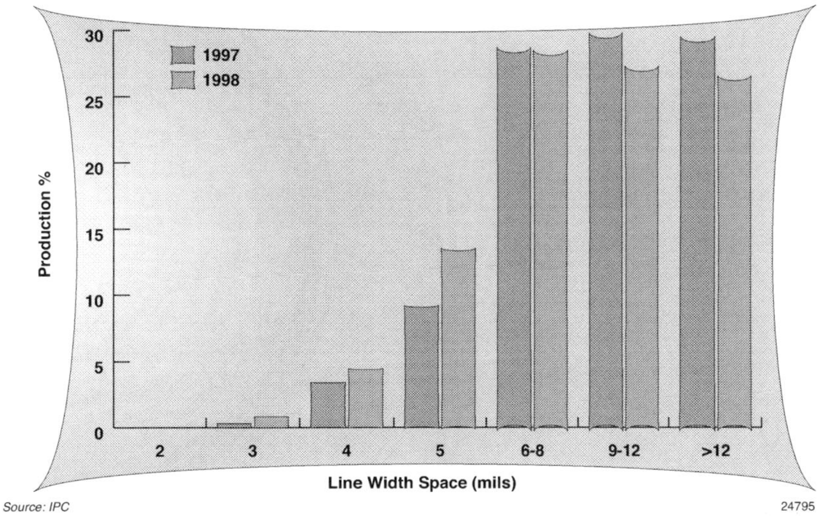

Figure 7-1. Trend in line widths in production from 1997 to 1998. Conventional is defined as 6mil line and space or larger.

In conventional PCB technology, the through holes are individually mechanically drilled with high speed drills and very small drill bits. As the hole size decreases, the cost per hole increases dramatically due to the higher unit cost of drill bits and more rapid wear out. Figure 7-2 shows the estimated cost per hole for various hole sizes.

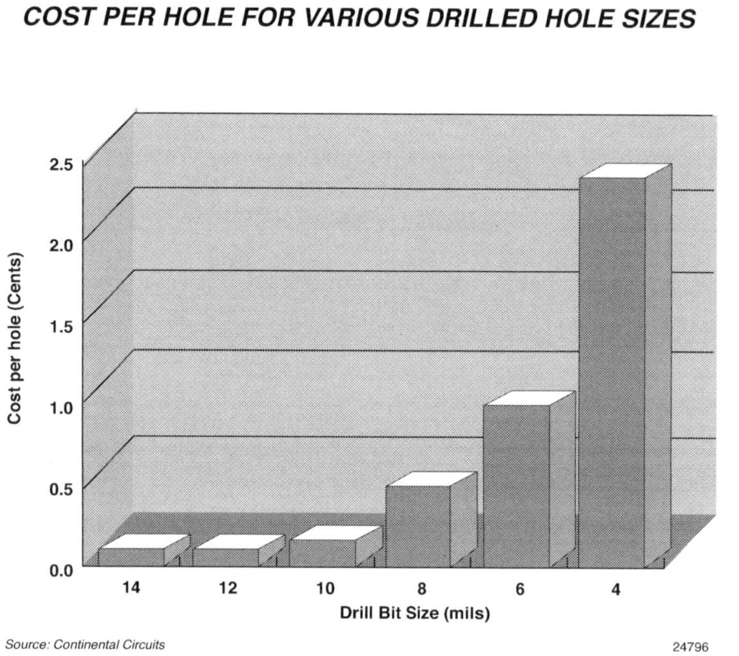

Figure 7-2. Cost per drilled hole for different hole sizes. From a 12mil diameter hole to a 6mil diameter hole is more than a factor of 10 increase in cost!

These two features, trace line and spacing and the hole diameter, contribute to how effectively the PCB can interconnect components placed on the top surface.

The recent product emphasis on smaller form factor and higher functionality has been driving new package technologies with smaller size but the same I/O count. This means a higher pad density on the surface of the board that must be routed by the PCB interconnects. This is illustrated in Figure 7-3. These higher pad densities cannot be interconnected by the gradual improvement of conventional technologies. Figure 7-4 lists some of the new product form factors and the surface pad densities required to interconnect them.

The Microvia Industry

In the last five years, a revolutionary new generation of board technology has been introduced with dramatically higher interconnect density provided by much smaller vias and finer lines. This technology has variously been called:

- BUM Build Up Multilayer
- SBU Sequential Build Up
- HDI High Density Interconnect
- HDIS High Density Interconnect Substrate
- Microvia Technology

These terms all refer to the revolution-via hole generation by non mechanical means, to get much higher hole density, along with finer lines and the ability to interconnect more surface pads per square inch. This new path for enabling higher surface pad density is shown in Figure 7-5.

HDI technology is growing rapidly in production volume, currently dominated by Japan. It is ironic that many of the fundamental processes were developed in the US, but were then commercialized in Japan. This is predominately because the types of products that first required HDI substrates were consumer products. As these were mostly manufactured in Japan, the driving force for immediate HDI applications was in Japan.

The volume of HDI boards in 1998 is estimated to be $1B, with Fujitsu, NEC, Toshiba, Sony, Hitachi, IBM-Yasu and Matsushita as the major suppliers. Over $145M of ALIVH (Any Layer Inner Via Holes) based HDI boards were manufactured for cell phone products by Matsushita alone. In the next three years, the total HDI market is expected to grow to over $4B. This is illustrated in Figure 7-6.

SHRINKING PACKAGING SIZE WITH FIXED PIN COUNT

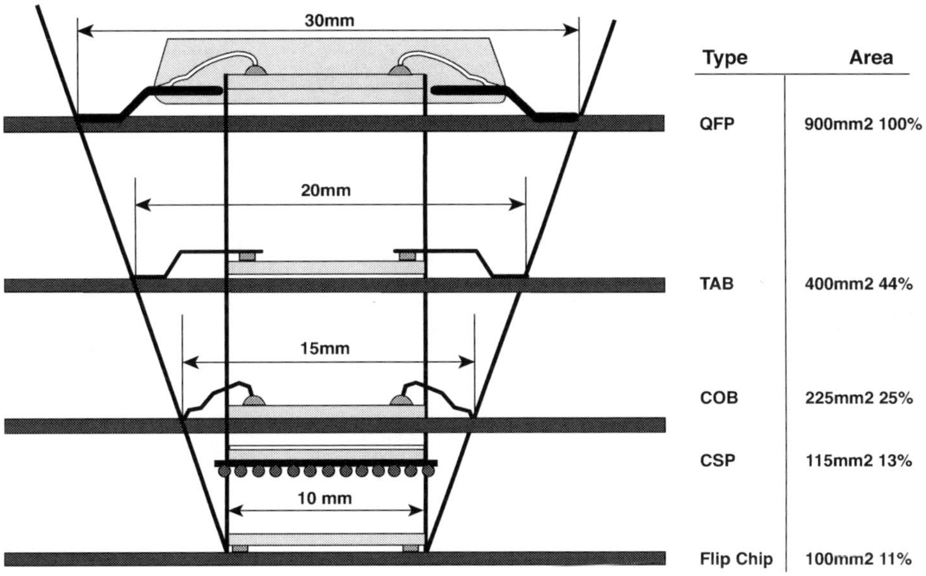

Source: Solution Fitts Inc. 24797

Figure 7-3. Shrinking package size, but same chip size and same I/O count means higher pad density on the surface that must be interconnect by the circuit board.

PAD DENSITY REQUIREMENTS FOR DIFFERENT PRODUCTS

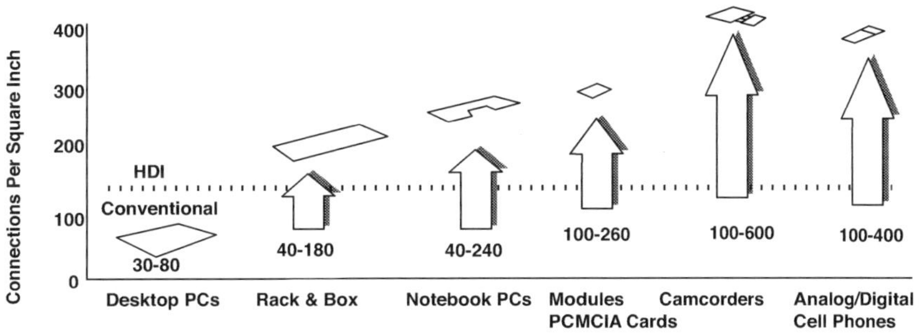

Source: TechLead International 24798

Figure 7-4. Pad density requirements for different products and the limitation of conventional board technology.

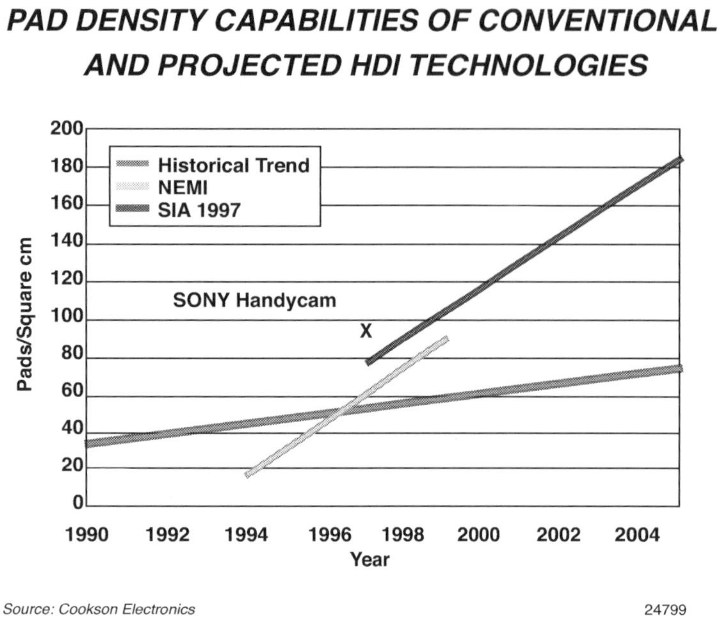

Figure 7-5. The ability to connect higher pad density with Microvia Technology vs. conventional technology.

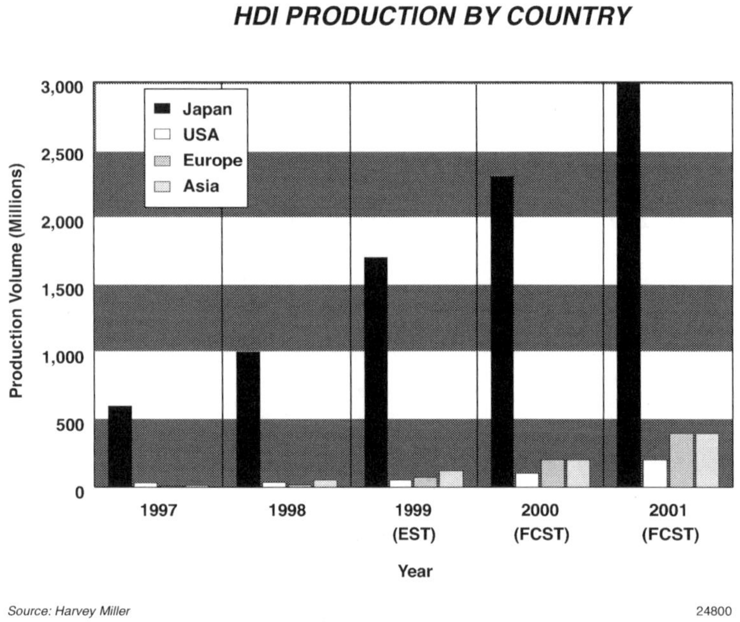

Figure 7-6. Market growth forecast for HDI substrates by country. Japan clearly dominates this industry and will continue to unless radical changes are made in the US.

Microvia Technology

There are three dominant methods of fabricating HDI substrates, based on the via hole generation technology and the metallization process:

- Laser drilled holes
- Plasma etching holes
- Photoimageable dielectric

There are two methods of metallizing the holes: additive, such as electroless copper, and screen printing of a conductive ink, forming "filled" vias.

In the ICE companion publication, **Roadmaps of Packaging Technology**, many of these microvia technologies are described in detail. Some of the larger volume vendors are summarized in Figure 7-7.

The following sections present updates on three promising technologies: laser drilling, ALIVH, and imprint patterning.

Laser Drilling

There are basically two types of laser systems: ultra violet (UV) and infra red (IR). UV lasers are able to drill through dielectric as well as metal, while the IR lasers typically drill through just the dielectric. For the two wavelength ranges, there are two material systems: Nd based, either doped with YLF or YAG and CO_2, either lower pressure RF excited or atmospheric pressure TEA (transverse excited atmospheric).

RF excited CO_2 lasers tend to drill fastest followed by the UV lasers. However, in practice, the actual production rate will depend on the pattern and thickness of dielectric. Figure 7-8 summarizes the relative drill speeds of the various laser types.

HDI TECHNOLOGIES AND VENDORS

PROCESS	COMPANY	MATERIAL	LINES/SPACES	VIA LAND	VIA PROCESS DIAMETER
DV-Multi	NEC	Epoxy Film	80-50/80-50μm	100/250μm	Photo
IBSS	Ibiden	Epoxy Film	Epoxy Film	150-100/250-150μm	Photo
ALIVH	Matsushita	Aramid Epoxy	60/90μm	150/300μm	Laser
PERL (Plasma Etched Redistribution Layers)	Hewlett Packard HADCO Worldwiser	Epoxy Film PI/Aramid	75/50μm and 75/50μm	125-90/250-196μm	Plasma Plasma/ Laser
Build-Up Substrate	Fujitsu	Epoxy	40/40μm	90/140μm	Photo
VB-2	Victor	Epoxy	10-95/100-75μm	200-100μm	Photo
B^2IT	Toshiba	BT Laminate	90/90μm	200/300μm	Paste/Bump
Multi-Layer Build-Up	Shinko	Multiple	40/40μm	50/110μm	Laser/Photo
SLC (Surface Laminar Circuit)	IBM Yasu	Epoxy Liquid	75/50μm anD	125-90/250-165μm	Photo
Hitavia	Hitachi		100/100	200/500	
Viathin	Sheldahl	PI	50/37.5μm	60-25/140-75μm & 85/50/200-165μm	Laser
ViaPly	CTS	PL/Aramid	75/75μm	125/125μm	Photo
TLPS	Ormet	P/I	50/50μm	25/200μm	Photo
DYCOstrate	Dyconex	PI	100/125μm	75/300μm	Plasma

Source: Techlead International

24801

Figure 7-7. *Summary of vendors for HDI substrates and their production processes.*

DRILLING RATES FOR VARIOUS MATERIALS AND LASER TYPES

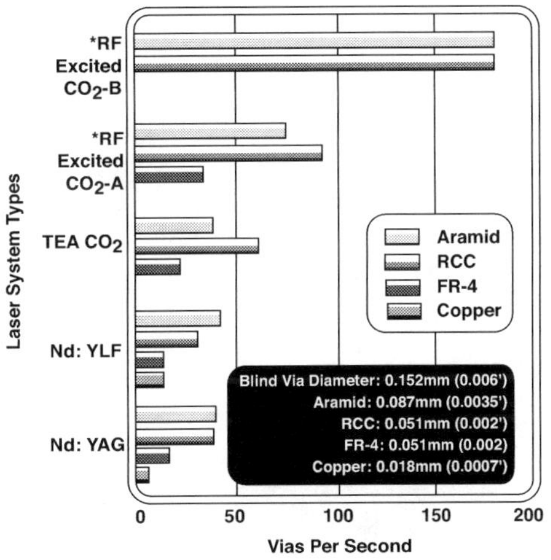

Source: MicroPak Labs

24802

Figure 7-8. *Drilling rates for IR and UV lasers through various materials.*

The laser is used to drill individual holes by precision positioning the beam over the various target locations on the board. The high drill rate is achieved by using light weight Galvanic mirrors for the fine positioning and sliding the table board in X-Y for the gross coverage of the whole board. The optics to do this is shown in Figure 7-9.

In 1998, there were over 400 lasers installed for laser drilling of holes. Of these, almost 300 were installed in Japan. Two of the largest vendors are Lumonics for CO_2 lasers and Electro Scientific Industries for UV lasers. Examples of these lasers are shown in Figure 7-10.

In building a multilayer substrate, more than one HDI layer can be built on each surface of the conventional core. Via connections between the two layers can be either by a pair of staggered vias or by stacked vias. Stacked vias allow a few less processing steps and smaller footprint. A schematic of staggered and stacked vias is shown in Figure 7-11.

Examples of laser drilled microvias are shown in Figure 7-12.

After the microvia holes are drilled, conventional additive electroless copper processes can be used for the metallization.

FINE POSITIONING OPTICS FOR A LASER DRILL

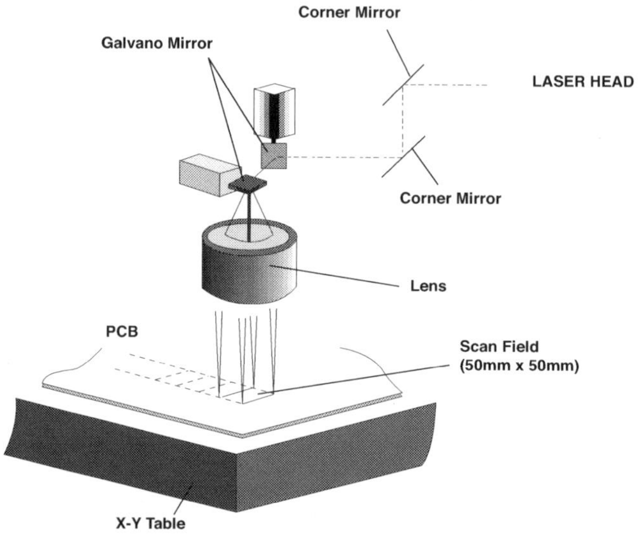

Source: Hitachi 24803

Figure 7-9. Optics to provide fine, rapid positioning and the coarse motion for complete board coverage.

LASERS FOR PCB MICROVIA DRILLING

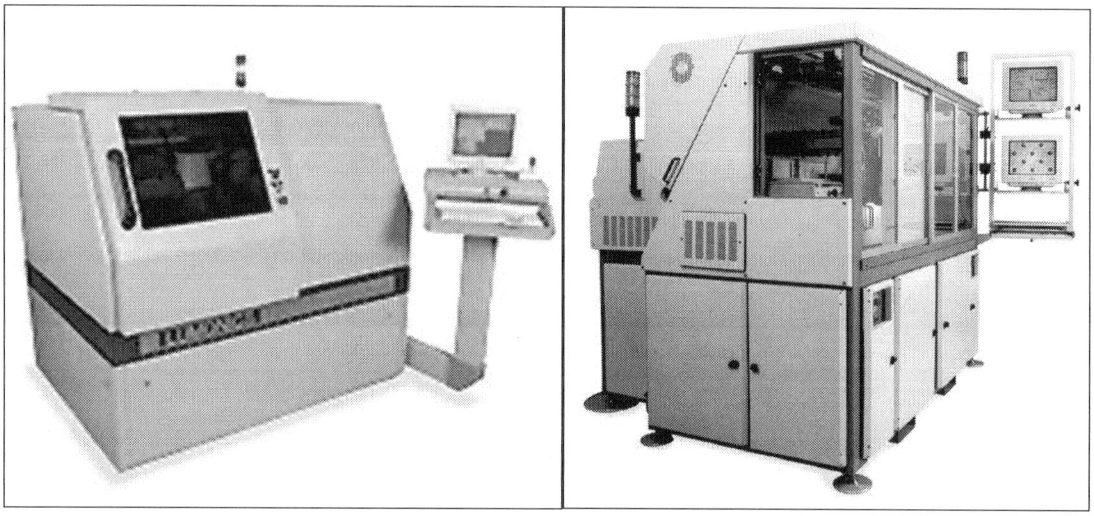

Source: Lumonics Source: Electro Scientific Industries 24804

Figure 7-10. Left: CO_2 TEA laser drill for PCB substrates from Lumonics. Right: UV YAG laser from Electro Scientific Industries.

CONFIGURATION OF STAGGERED AND STACKED VIAS

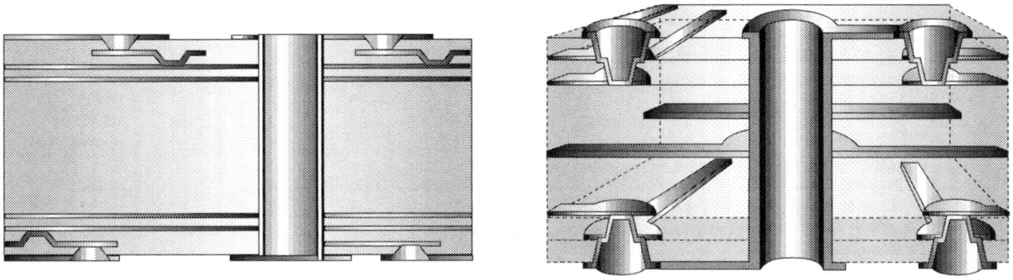

Source: MicroPak Labs

24805

Figure 7-11. Staggered and stacked vias.

25 MICRON DIAMETER LASER DRILLED HOLES IN MICROLAM SUBSTRATES

LAER DRILLED HOLES IN ONE LAYER AND IN TWO

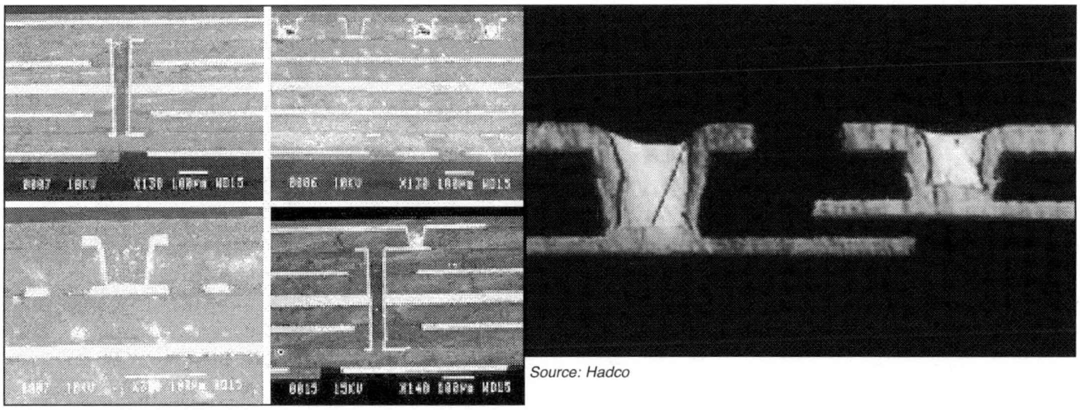

Source: Hadco

Source: W. L. Gore

24806

Figure 7-12. Laser drilled holes. Left: holes in a multilayer Microlam® substrate from W. L. Gore. Right: Holes in an RCC (resin clad copper) layer from Hadco.

Filled Via Technology

In conventional PCB technology, through holes are electrolessly coated with copper and built up by electroplating. The end result is a hole with a thin layer of copper in the walls. This is also the general process for metallizing laser drilled holes. The result is a small, hollow blind via cup. There is an alternative process for metallizing HDI microvias that involves filling the via holes with conductive ink, typically silver filled epoxy. This has been used by Matsushita for filling laser drilled holes, by ProLinx Labs for filling photoimaged holes and by Ormet to produce conductor traces and vias with photoimaged patterns. These approached are described in this section.

Matsushita has incorporated laser drilling with conductive epoxy filled vias to create a low cost, light weight, very high density substrate, termed ALIVH (Any Layer Inner Via Hole). The material for each layer is a sheet of random aramid fiber reinforced epoxy. Holes are laser drilled and screen print filled with silver filled epoxy. Copper foil is laminated on each side of the dielectric sheet and conventionally patterned. Additional layers can be co laminated as required. This manufacturing process is illustrated in Figure 7-13.

MANUFACTURING OF ALIVH LAYERS

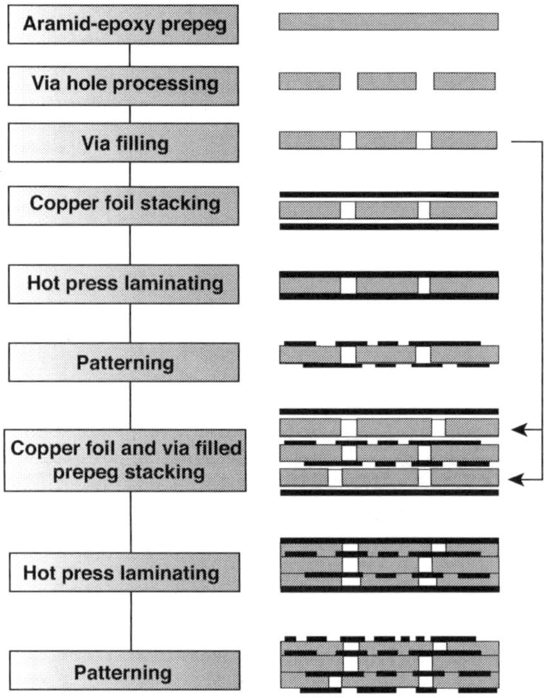

Source: Matsushita 24807

Figure 7-13. Manufacturing process for the ALIVH microvia HDI substrates.

This technology has been applied to chip scale packages, BGA packages, multichip modules and motherboards. Figure 7-14 is a schematic of an MCM mounted to a motherboard, both fabricated with this technology. Figure 7-15 is an example of an MCM substrate fabricated with ALIVH, currently shipping in notebook computers. Matsushita has incorporated a low cost version of flip chip, termed SBB (stud bump bonding) to flip chip attach chips to the top surface.

SCHEMATIC OF MCM AND MOTHERBOARD FABRICATED WITH ALIVH LAYERS

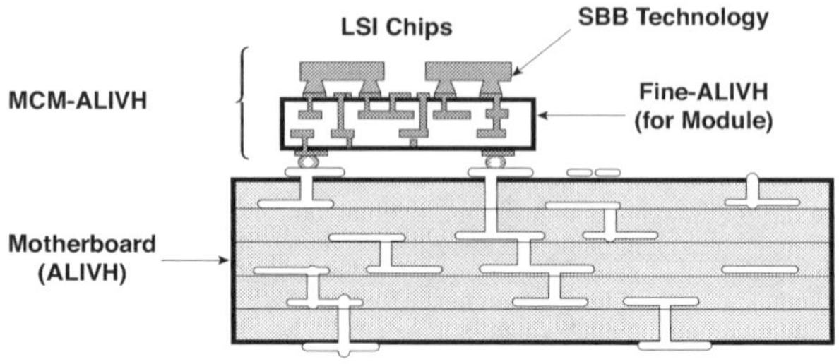

Source: Matsushita 24808

Figure 7-14. Schematic of an MCM and motherboard, fabricated with the ALIVH HDI technology.

NOTEBOOK MCM FABRICATED WITH ALIVH AND SBB

Source: Matsushita 24809

Figure 7-15. Example of a small MCM used in notebook applications. The substrate is fabricated with ALIVH layers and the chips are attached with the SBB process.

In a similar implementation of filled via technology, ProLinx Labs fabricates BGA packages. On top of a solid copper core with large insulated feedthroughs, multiple HDI layers are built up. The dielectric is a photoimageable epoxy. Into the imaged holes, silver filled epoxy is screen printed. Copper foil is then laminated on top and print and etched using conventional technology. This process is illustrated in Figure 7-16.

A cross section of two filled vias is shown in Figure 7-17.

PROCESS FLOW FOR HDI LAYERS IN BGA SUBSTRATE

1. Form isolation vias on solid copper core.
2. Apply photoimageable dielectric, image and develop, fill micro-via with siver paste.
3. Laminate copper foil, print, etch circuitry.
4. Repeat sequential buildup for additional circuit layers.
5. Ni/Au plate, pattern etch and score to singulate.

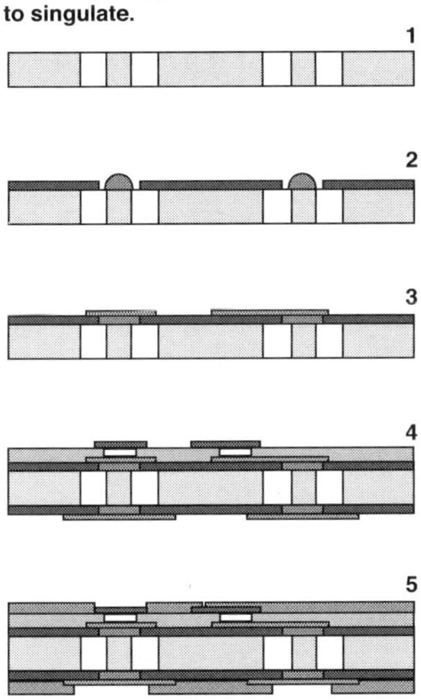

Source: Prolinx Labs 24810

Figure 7-16. Fabrication process for ProLinx Labs copper core BGA (C^2BGA) substrates.

Ormet, a supplier of transient liquid phase sintering (TLPS) polymers, has demonstrated the fabrication of interconnect and vias using photo imageable polymers and a screen printed conductive filler. In their approach, conductor patterns are imaged in the dielectric as trenches. Into these, the conductive polymer is screen printed and filled in. A second layer of photopolymer is then laminated and via holes opened up. Another layer of conductive filler is added. In this way a multilayer HDI substrate can be built up. This process sequence is shown in Figure 7-18. This process has the limitation of a lower conductivity conductor system. The metal system in the Ormet paste has a final conductivity about 10 x lower than copper, which is comparable to tungsten used in cofired ceramic substrates.

CROSS SECTION OF STACKED VIA IN PROLINX HDI SUBSTRATES

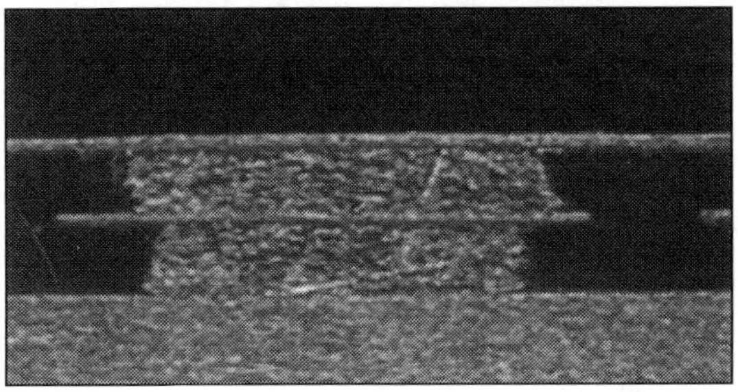

Source: Prolinx Labs 24811

Figure 7-17. Cross section of filled vias in ProLinx Labs HDI substrates used to fabricate BGA packages.

Imprint Patterning

There is a technology, currently used for very high volume production, capable of producing micron size holes over a field of more than 10 inches at a cost of pennies per square inch. Though it sounds a lot like via formation in HDI boards, it is applied to a completely different technology- the fabrication of compact disks. The technology: embossing. A master is used to imprint its mirror image pattern into a soft resin surface and is able to replicate millions of copies. Though this concept is old, its application to the packaging and interconnect world is new.

This basic approach of near perfect pattern replication has been experimentally applied to the production of fine line interconnects and microvias by Dimensional Circuits. There are two short term applications Dimensional Circuits is pursuing, patterning of surface features to enhance SMT assembly and low cost and fine features for HDI substrates. Figure 7-19 is an example of small features embossed in a polymer coating on the surface of a conventional PCB. The guide holes were imprinted to increase yield by self locating the components and prevent solder bridging.

PROCESS FLOW FOR HDI LAYERS IN ORMET SUBSTRATES

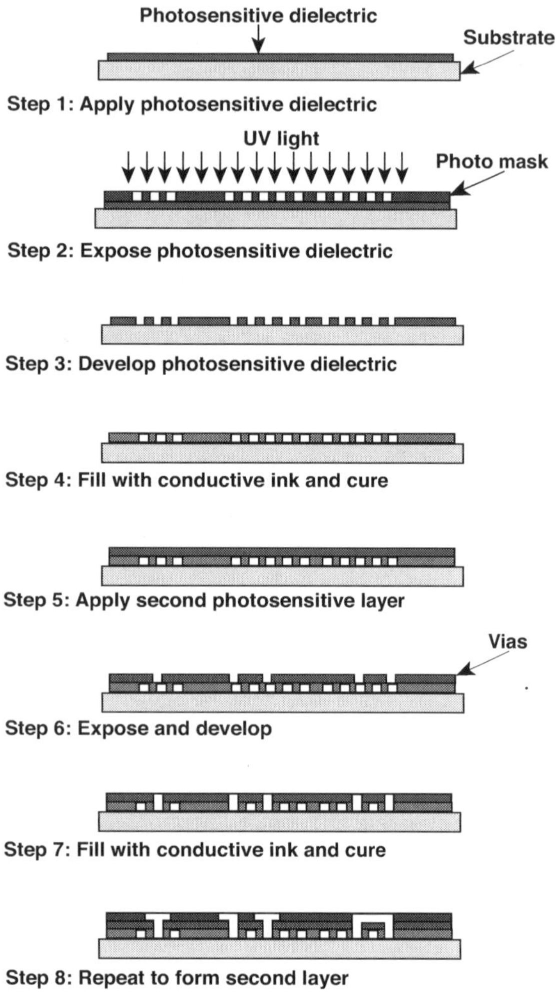

Source: Ormet 24812

Figure 7-18. Process sequence for Ormet HDI layers.

The basic approach to imprint patterning is to emboss a pattern in a specially formulated, heavily filled epoxy based thermoset material that is laminated to the surface of a conventional PCB. The embossed pattern can be the via hole connections to underlying metal, and at the same time, trenches for the conductors on that layer. The embossing master tool is not restricted in punching only one depth of impression. A long post can imprint a via connection while a low ridge can imprint a conductor line. When a via is to make contact to an underlying layer, the bottom of the embossed hole still needs to be cleaned out with a plasma cleaning process. Figure 7-20 shows a via cross section before and after plasma cleaning.

IMPRINT PATTERNED ALIGNMENT GROOVES

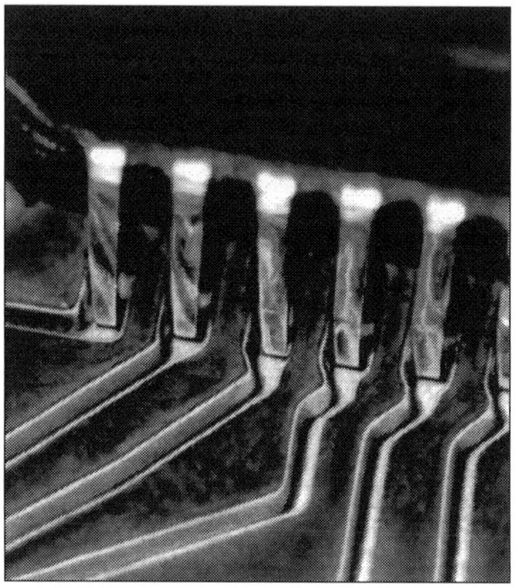

Source: Dimensional Circuits 24813

Figure 7-19. Channels in the surface of a conventional board created by imprint patterning of a surface coating.

One way of metallizing this pattern is to squeegee a conductive ink, such as silver filled epoxy, into the holes and grooves. This would pattern and metallize all in one step, similar to the Ormet process.

An alternative method of creating a patterned metallization is to blanket coat the entire surface with electroless and then electroplated copper. The top surface of the copper will be the replicated embossed surface. On top of this patterned surface, etch resist material can be squeegee deposited so that it fills the holes and grooves. This is illustrated in Figure 7-21.

VIA HOLE BEFORE PLASMA CLEANING — VIA HOLE AFTER PLASMA CLEANING

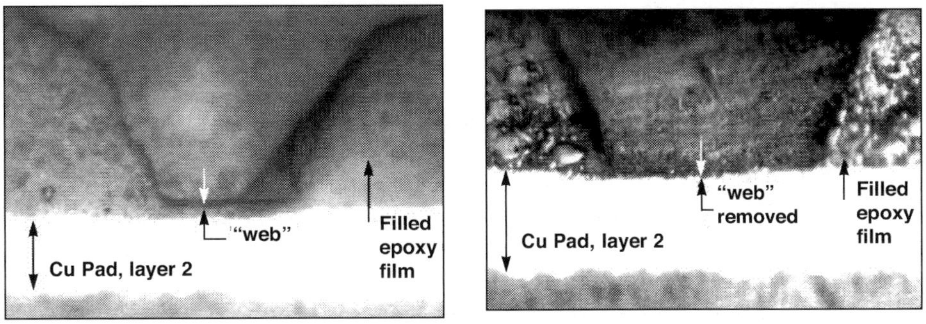

Source: Dimensional Circuits 24814

Figure 7-20. Cross section of via hole created by embossing a hole into the filled thermoset material, before and after plasma cleaning.

SQUEEGEE PROCESS FOR FILLING COPPER VALLEYS WITH ETCH RESIST

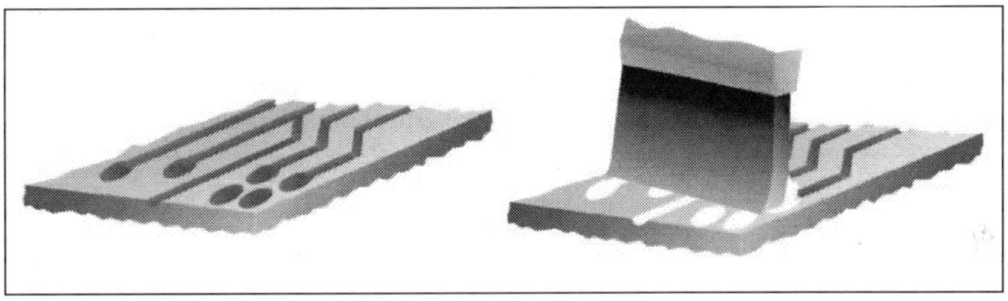

Source: Dimensional Circuits 24815

Figure 7-21. Squeegee printing of the etch resist into the copper plated holes and grooves.

At this point, the copper making up the via connections and surface traces is protected by the etch resist. The exposed copper can be etched off. Then the resist stripped. The resulting board is now a patterned HDI layer. An additional feature of this process is etching the edge of the copper to below the surface of the board. Figure 7-22 illustrates this step.

The copper traces on the surface form a recessed cup in the surface. The dielectric between adjacent traces can act as a natural solder dam without the need for any solder mask. An example of this feature is shown in Figure 7-23.

A new layer of thermoset polymer can be laminated to this surface and the process repeated. This entire process is illustrated in Figure 7-24.

Multi layers of imprint patterned HDI layers can be fabricated sequentially by staggering the vias. A two layer build up is illustrated in Figure 7-25.

This technology has the potential of being extremely low cost. The only imaging step is in creating the master tool, using conventional electroform technology, currently used for micron sized CDs and laser discs. When silver filled epoxy is filled in the holes and trenches, there is no wet chemical processing that is required. Features on the order of 25 microns can be embossed and filled. The limitation is in the registration from layer to layer.

This technology has the potential of moving HDI substrates into mainstream, high volume, low cost applications.

ETCHING OFF THE COPPER FORMING RECESSED CUPS

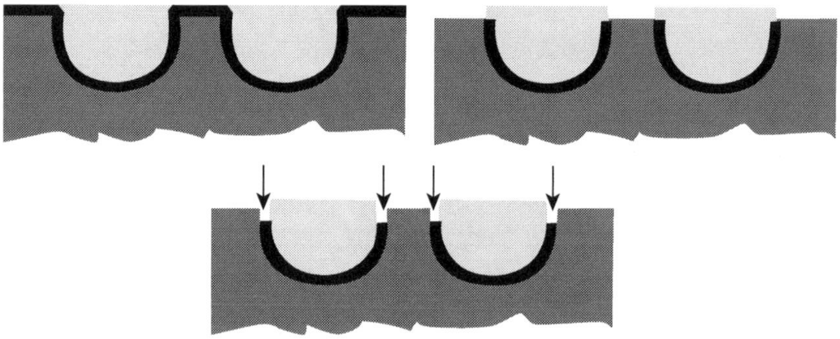

Source: Dimensional Circuits 24816

Figure 7-22. Process steps of etching off the removed copper and forming a recessed cup in the copper trench.

NATURAL SOLDER DAMS FORMED BY COPPER CUPS ON SURFACE LAYERS

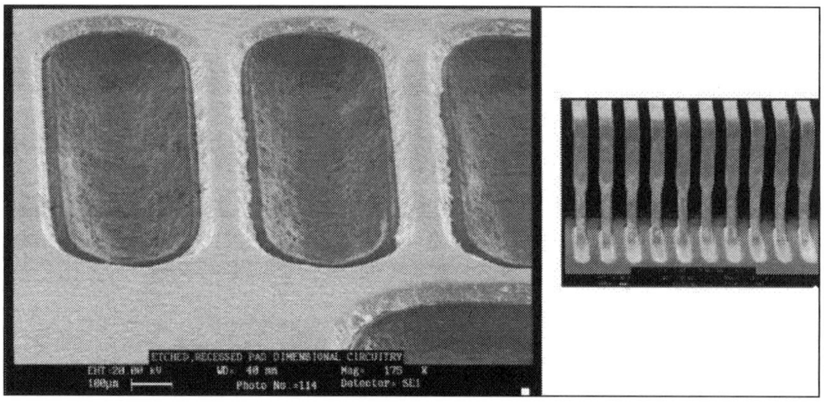

Source: Dimensional Circuits 24817

Figure 7-23. Example of the natural solder dam capabilities of the etched copper cup.

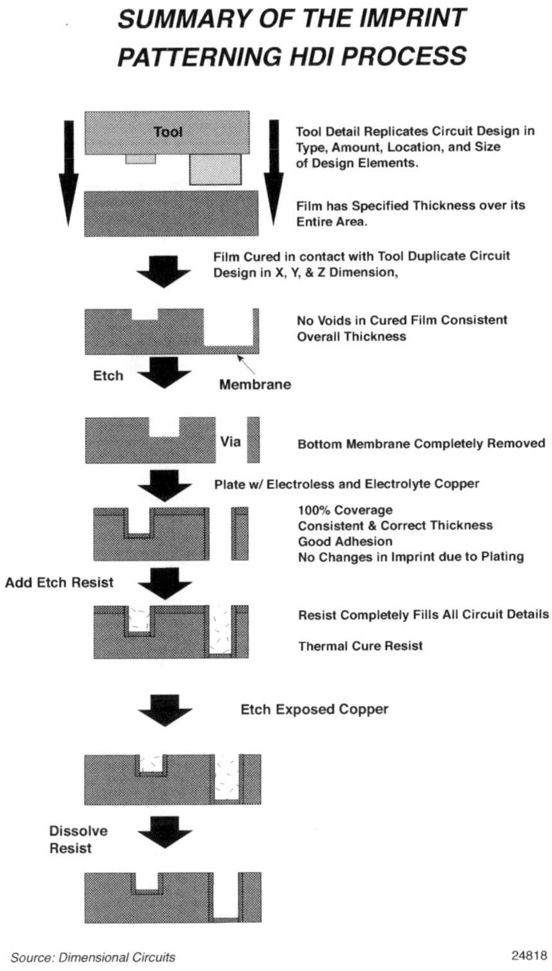

Figure 7-24. Imprint patterning process.

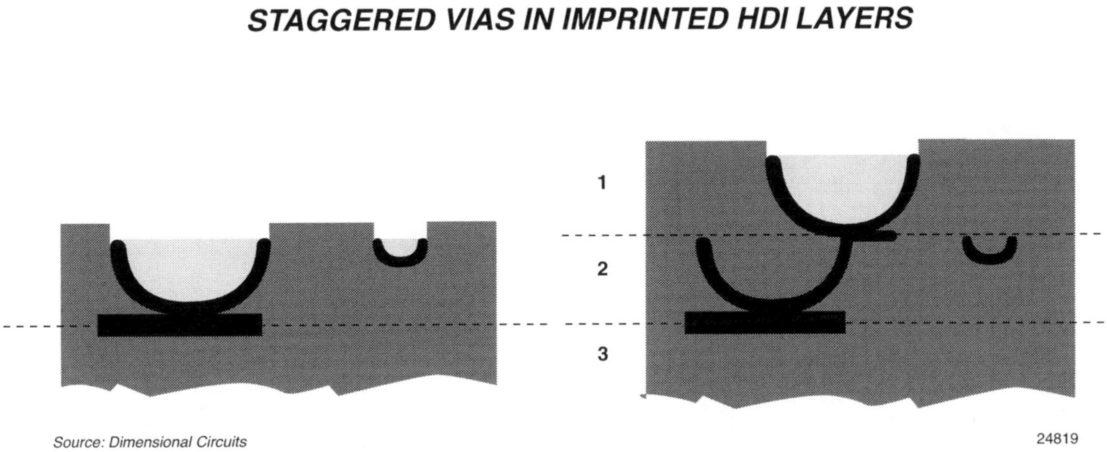

Figure 7-25. Staggered vias in an imprint patterned HDI substrate.

8 Integrated Passive Devices (IPDs)

CONVENTIONAL PASSIVE COMPONENTS

Passive elements include resistors, capacitors, inductors and diodes. They play the critical roles of:

- Terminating unwanted reflections on transmission lines
- Establishing voltage thresholds
- Decoupling noise in the power and ground distribution
- Filtering noise out of signal lines
- Protecting circuits from ESD
- Reducing EMI
- Signal processing by filtering high or low frequencies
- Establishing a resonant frequency as a reference

In a typical high speed digital system, there are as many as 20x more discrete passive components than active semiconductor devices. This is evident in the close up of a motherboard for an AMD K6-2 processor, shown in Figure 8-1. The number of passives used in various generations of Intel processor motherboards is shown in Figure 8-2.

The situation is often worse on RF devices that use more passive components especially for filtering. An example of a Nortel dual band phone showing the large number of discrete passives is shown in Figure 8-3.

AMD MOTHERBOARD CLOSE UP

Source: Bogatin Enterprises

24860

Figure 8-1. Close up region of an AMD motherboard showing the large number of resistor and capacitor passives.

GROWTH IN PASSIVES ON PC MOTHERBOARDS

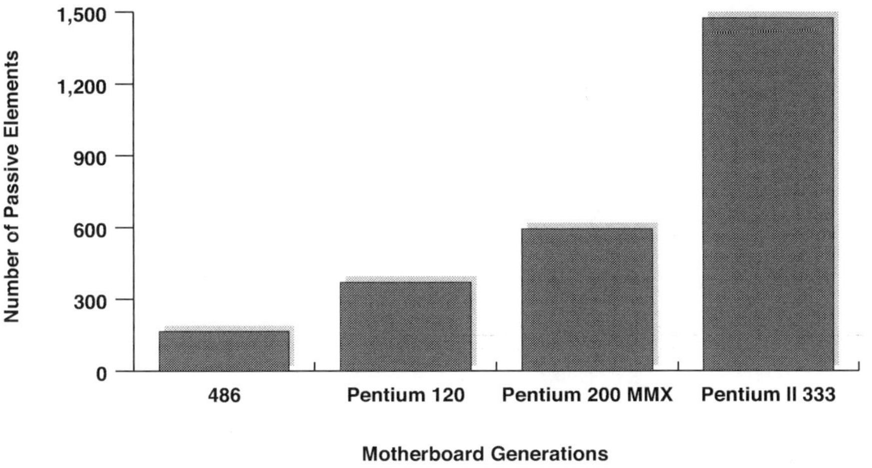

Source: AVX 24861

Figure 8-2. Growth in the number of passive elements needed by PC motherboards.

NORTEL UAL BAND PHONE WITH MANY DISCRETE PASSIVES

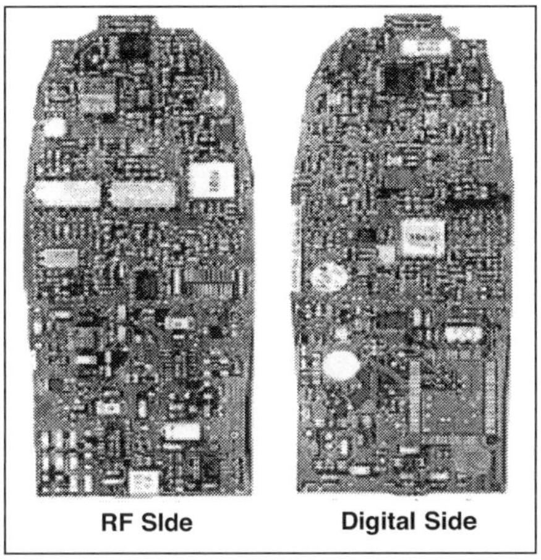

Source: DuPont 24873

Figure 8-3. Nortel dual band cell phone loaded with passives.

The driving forces on all products: smaller, faster cheaper, NOW!, have been driving passives as well. The transition from through hole to surface mount device (SMD) allowed a large reduction in the size for a passive element. Figure 8-4 shows the difference between a typical through hole resistor and its surface mount counterpart.

The SMD resistor is often termed a "chip resistor" because it looks like a small integrated circuit chip. The package designation of chip components: resistors, capacitors and inductors, are defined by their outer dimensions. The descriptor is two pairs of numbers. The first is the dimension between solder terminals, in 10 mil increments. The second number is the width of the SMD element. For example, the SMD resistor above is in a 1206 package, since the length between end terminals is 120 mils and the width is 60 mils. This is one of the largest package sizes for chip SMD devices. Other standard package sizes are 0805, 0603, 0402 and 0201. It should be noted that a grain of salt is about 20 mils on a side. The 0201 size is actually smaller than a grain a salt. These relative sizes are shown in Figure 8-5.

RELATIVE SIZES OF SMD RESISTORS

Source: SMT Magazine 24862

Figure 8-4. Comparison of through hole and surface mount resistor elements.

RELATIVE SIZES OF SMD CHIP COMPONENTS

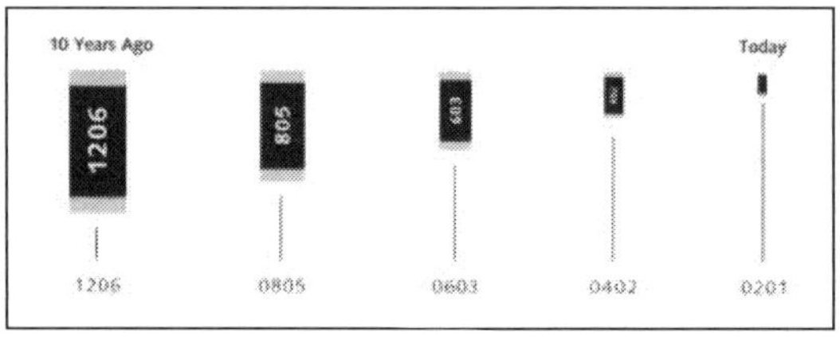

Source: SMT Magazine 24863

Figure 8-5. Relative sizes of standard SMD chip components.

The drive for smaller components has motivated the use of smaller and smaller SMD discrete passives. The 0630 is the most popular size in use, with 0402 starting to gain volume. Figure 8-6 illustrates this transition.

MARKET SHARE OF PASSIVE COMPONENTS BY SIZE

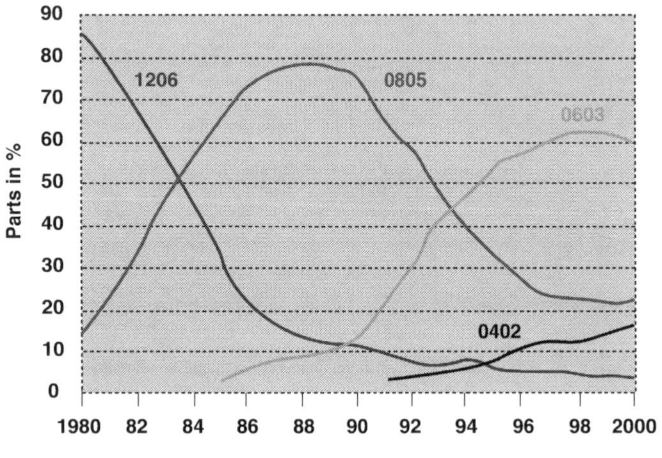

Source: Circuits Assembly Magazine 24864

Figure 8-6. Market share for the different size SMD chip components.

Assembling thousands of SMD chip components that are the size of a grain a salt on every board cannot be a long term, cost effective path. The industry is just starting to transition to an alternative approach that integrates the passive components before assembly on the board. The motivation is similar to what drove the introduction of the integrated circuit: smaller size, higher performance and lower cost. These new devices have been termed integrated passive devices (IPDs).

INTEGRATED PASSIVE DEVICES

In its simplest form, an IPD is nothing more than a substrate that carries multiple, independent passive discretes, each with independent terminals. In many applications, one end of the passives might be connected to the same terminal, so the busing can be done on the substrate, in this way reducing the number of terminals needed almost in half. A simple integrated resistor array is shown in Figure 8-7.

The revolutionary introduction of IPDs have the potential of matching the capabilities of the revolutions in packaging and substrate interconnections in achieving the faster, smaller and cheaper goals by:

- reducing the board area used for passives (smaller)
- improving performance by reducing the parasitic impedance of the leads and enabling new functions for high speed applications (faster)
- reducing the total cost of ownership by reducing assembly related costs (cheaper)

There are three general classes of integrated passive device:

- Arrays
- RCLD combinations, often using thin film on silicon (TFOS)
- Integral passives

The bright future projections for the market volume of these various forms of IPDs are shown in Figure 8-8.

GENERAL VIEW OF A DIPPED SIL R PACK

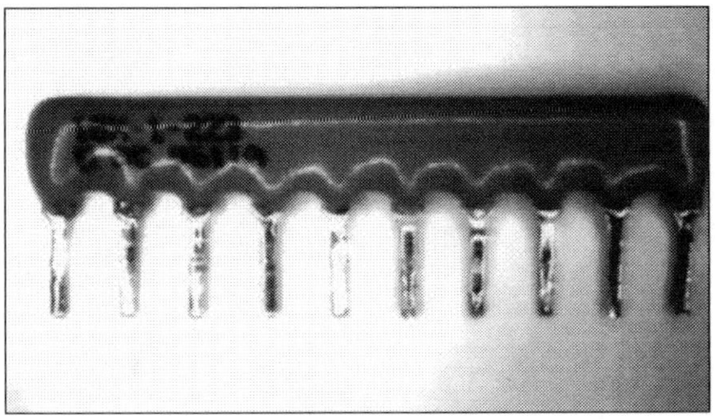

Source: ICE 21905

VIEW AFTER DECAPSULATION SHOWING RESISTIVE AND CONDUCTIVE LAYERS WITH PROTECTIVE GLASS

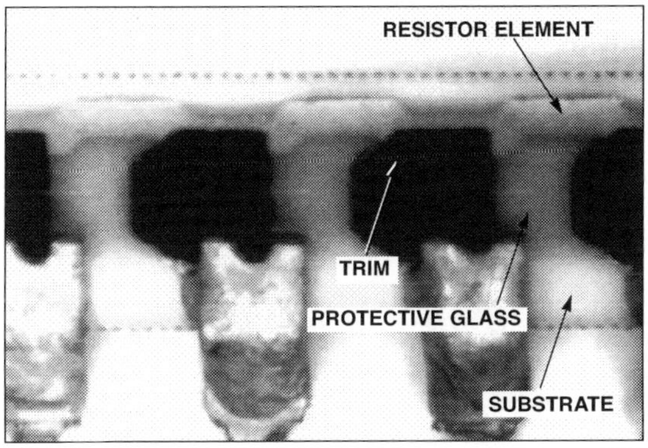

Source: ICE 21906

Figure 8-7. Integrated resistor array consisting of a ceramic substrate with thin film resistor material sputtered down and terminals to one side. The second end of the resistor array is common. Top: SIP (Single In-line Package) of the resistor array. Bottom; close up of the resistor elements that make up each integrated resistor.

INTEGRATED PASSIVE DEVICE ARRAYS

As their name implies, IPD arrays are collections of the same passive type, on a common substrate. The most common arrays are resistor and capacitor arrays. All the top vendors for resistors and capacitors offer these components in array formats. These include:

- Bourns
- AVX
- California Micro Devices
- Kemet
- KOA Speer Electronics
- Murata Electronics
- Philips Integrated Passive Components
- Vishay
- CTS
- IRC
- Intarsia
- Hadco
- Ohmega Technologies

Resistor arrays can be fabricated with a thick film paste screen printed and fired onto a ceramic substrate. They can also be fabricated with thin film, typically tantalum nitride, sputtered onto either ceramic, silicon or glass substrates. Though most IPDs use peripheral I/O with a lead pitch typically of 20mil (0.5mm), there is a growing trend to implement an area array form factor. An example of a nine element resistor array with a BGA foot print on 0.5mm pitch is shown in Figure 8-9. As pointed out in a previous chapter, this footprint is a standard CSP footprint.

Discrete ceramic chip caps are typically fabricated by laminating multiple layers of a high dielectric constant ceramic, such as barium titanate and conductive layers such as silver palladium. After firing, the sheets are cut and the edges metallized. This is illustrated in Figure 8-10.

Capacitor arrays can be fabricated in the same way, with the electrodes separated on the edge. An example of capacitor arrays is shown in Figure 8-11.

INTEGRATED RCLD DEVICES

In many applications, multiple passive elements are combined together in a circuit for a special function. This usually involves filtering or wave forming of some kind. Integrated passive components are ideally suited to provide a single component with these filter operations.

The most common type of circuit is a simple RC. When applied to the end of a transmission line, the RC can minimize the reflections, yet keep DC power consumption to a minimum. Figure 8-12 shows the schematic of how an RC circuit would

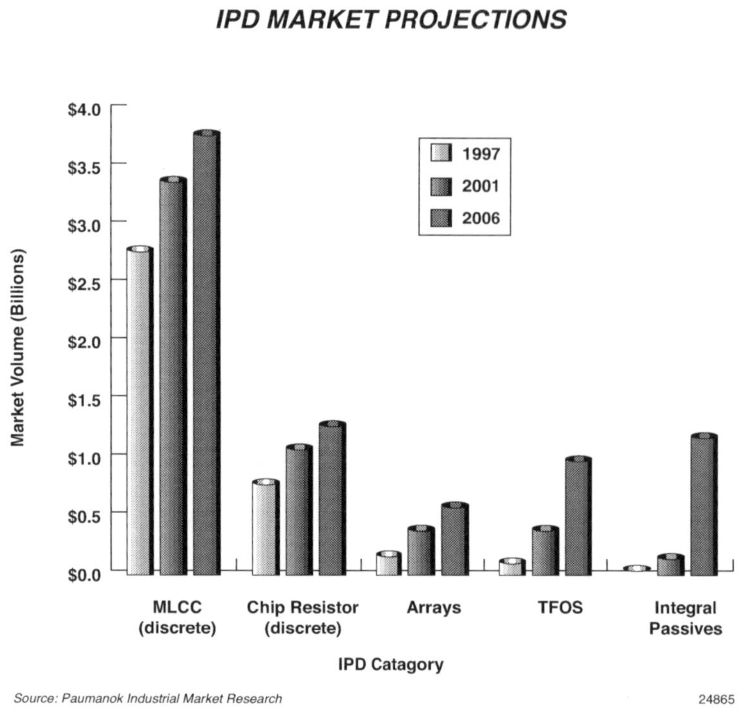

Figure 8-8. Future market projections for IPDs.

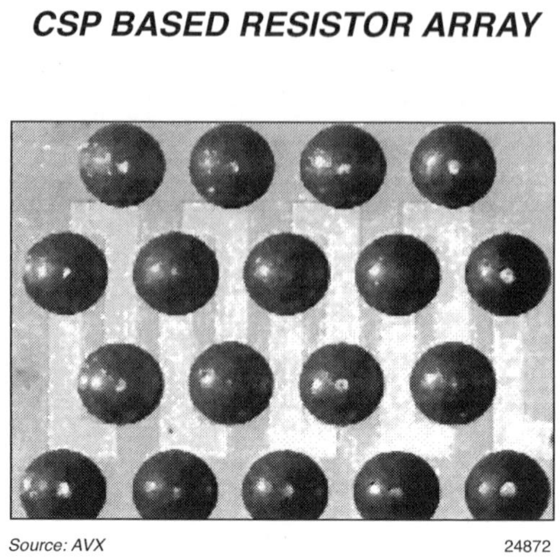

Figure 8-9. Nine element resistor array with BGA footprint on 0.5mm centers. This is often termed a chip scale package.

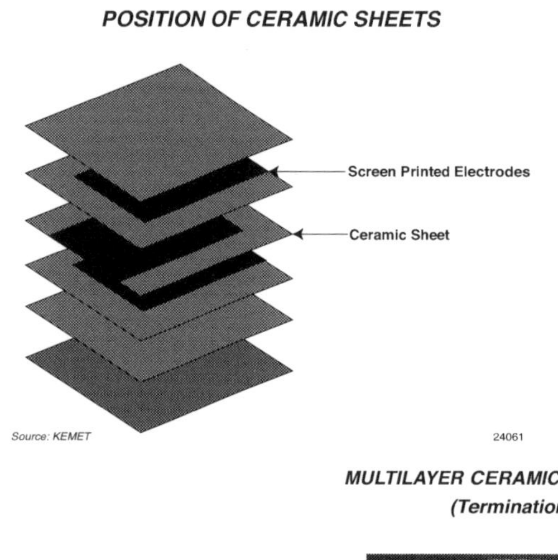

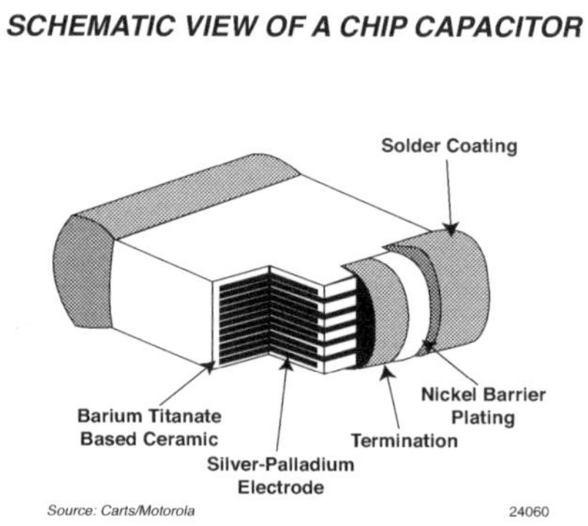

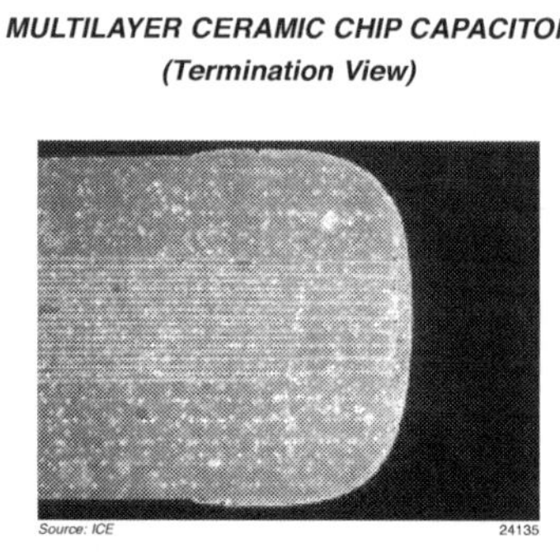

Figure 8-10. Fabrication of discrete ceramic chip caps. Left: lamination process. Right: metallization of the edge. Bottom: Cross section showing the thin ceramic layers and edge termination.

terminate a transmission line and the resulting improvement in signal integrity over no termination. An example of an integrated RC terminator array is shown in Figure 8-12.

RC arrays are typically formed by adding a thick film resistive material to the conventional multilayer ceramic capacitor. AVX has introduced a new resistive electrode material laminated inside the multilayer capacitor. This is called a Z Chip device. These approaches are illustrated in Figure 8-13.

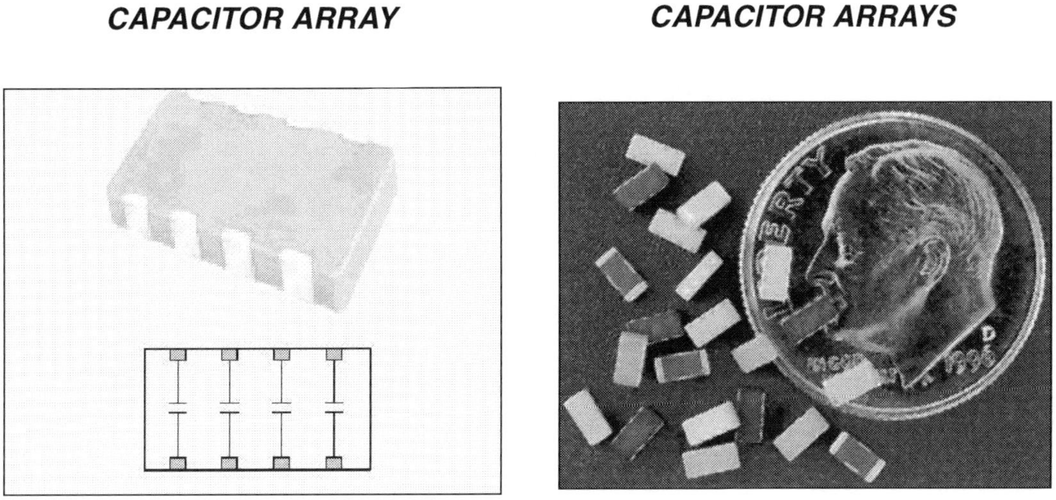

Source: AVX

24867

Figure 8-11. Ceramic capacitor arrays in small SMD packages.

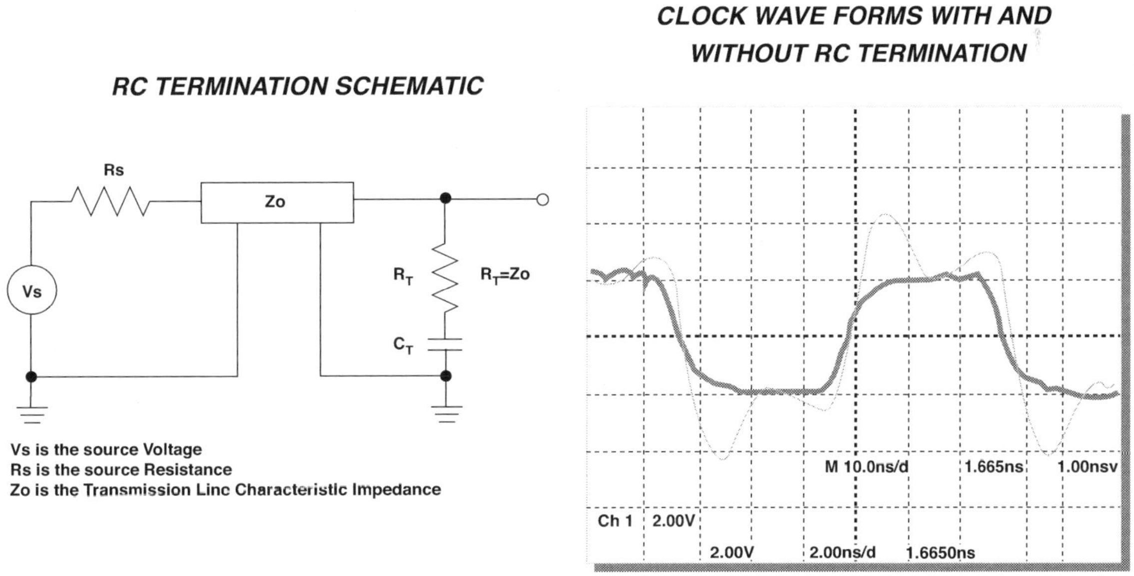

Source: AVX

24869

Figure 8-12. Top: RC termination schematic. Bottom: 80MHz clock waveform measured at far end with and without the RC termination.

INTEGRATED RC DEVICES

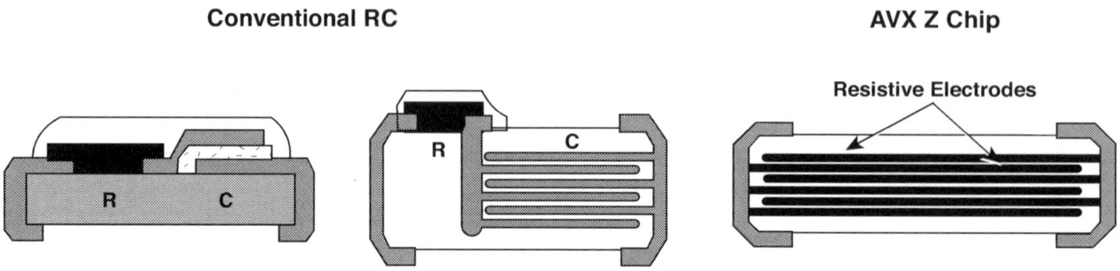

Figure 8-13. Conventional approach to constructing an integrated RC device and the new AVX Z Chip that uses resistive electrode materials.

In addition to RC circuits, diodes and inductors can be added as needed. One application for diodes is ESD protection, common in protecting I/O lines from possible static charge contributed by contact from ungrounded operators. When many passive devices are added to a single component, the value can be high, while the cost to manufacture is low. An example of a highly integrated passive device from California Micro Devices which provides filtering and ESD protection for two USB ports on a PC is shown in Figure 8-14.

INTEGRAL AND EMBEDDED PASSIVES

The various IPDs described above are themselves discrete components which are surface mount assembled onto circuit boards. They are much faster to assemble, take up less room and because they have fewer solder joints, are more reliable than discrete passives. A new class of passive devices is built right into the circuit board or interconnect substrate. In this sense they are integral to the board and have been termed "Integral Passives" or "Embedded Passives". The two most common substrates to incorporate integral passives are low temperature cofired ceramic (LTCC) and printed circuit board (PCB) substrates.

LTCC substrates are most commonly used for RF and microwave devices where the passive components are resistor, capacitor and inductor elements used in the filtering of RF signals. Inductors are fabricated as flat spirals of conductor material. Resistors are screen printed traces and capacitors are overlapping layers. An example of an integrated LC filter for cell phone applications is shown in Figure 8-15.

Passives have also been embedded into printed circuit bards. The two most common applications have been for termination resistors and decoupling capacitors. These are the most common application of passives for high speed digital products.

Omega Technologies offers a thin film material coated on copper foil. Once laminated to the resin, the resistive material, trade named Ohmega-Ply, can be patterned independently of the copper metallization. The typical sheet resistance is 25Ohms/square. For a 50Ohm resistor, for example, two squares of the resistive material in series is all that is needed. The cross section of a laminate layer is shown in Figure 8-16.

These embedded resistors can be applied to motherboards as well as single chip packages that are made from PCB substrates. An example of series termination resistors designed into a BGA is illustrated in Figure 8-17.

IPD FILTER FOR DUAL USB PORTS

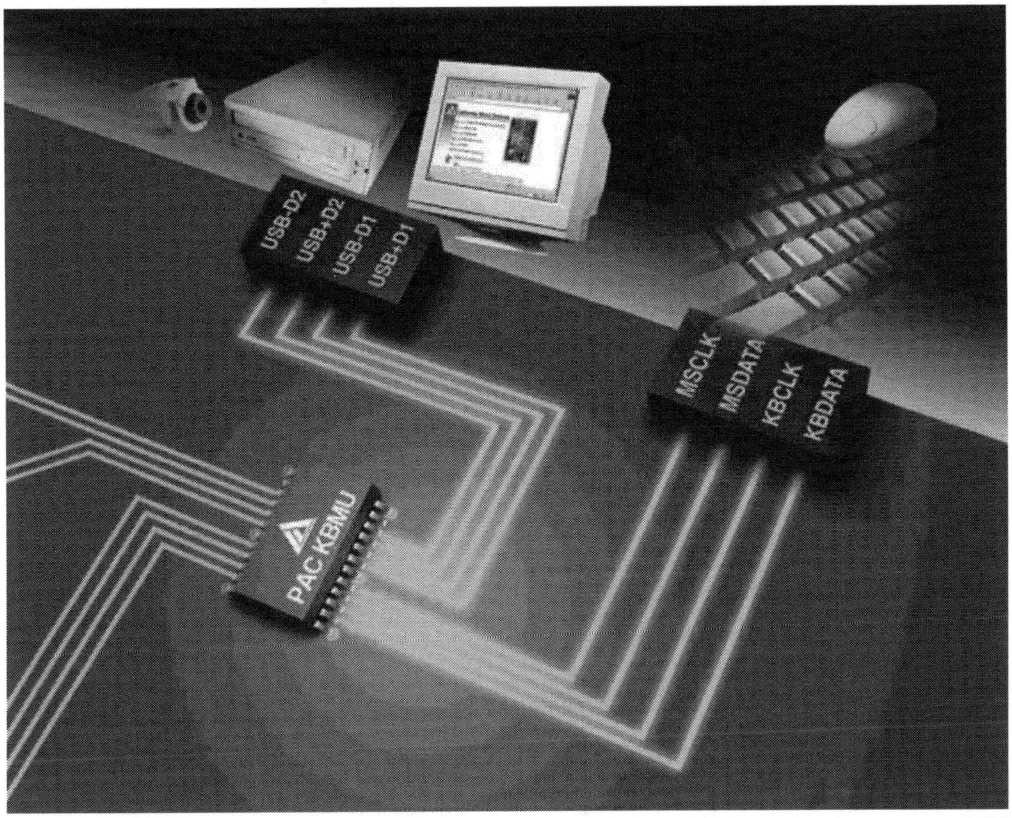

Source: Calif Micro Devices 24859

Figure 8-14. IPD performing complex filtering on two independent USB ports.

The second element that is sometimes embedded in PCB substrates is capacitor layers. Any two adjacent layers in a PCB provide capacitance. The capacitance is proportional to the overlap surface area of the conductor layers, the dielectric constant of the material between the conductors and inversely to the spacing, h, between the layers. For h in mils, the capacitance per square inch is:

$$C_{area} = \varepsilon_r \times \frac{0.225}{h} \frac{pF}{sq.\ in.}$$

For example, in standard FR4, with $\varepsilon_r = 4.5$ and h = 10mils, the capacitance per area is about 0.12nF. In a typical board that is 12 inches on a side, this is a total capacitance of about 18nF. When the layers are the power and ground planes, capacitance is very important. It can have a significant effect in decreasing the switching noise and EMI. Discrete ceramic chip capacitors, with typical values of about 1nF to 100nF are often placed on the board to provide this high speed decoupling. A typical value of decoupling required for a low power IC is about 1000nF, typically supplied by 10-20 discrete capacitors. If nothing special is done in the board, its power and ground plane intrinsic capacitance of 0.1nF in the vicinity of an IC, is not enough to provide adequate decoupling.

Hadco offers a technology for increasing this integral power and ground plane decoupling capacitance, they term EmCap. It is a laminate of FR4 epoxy filled with a Barium Titanate ceramic power having a thickness of 4mils and dielectric constant of 50. When this is used as the layer between power and ground planes, it can provide an intrinsic capacitance of 2.75nF/sq inch. With his level of decoupling, it may not be necessary to add any discrete capacitors to the top surface of the board with values less than 100nF. An example of the cross section of a PCB with an EmCap layer between the power and ground planes is shown in Figure 8-18.

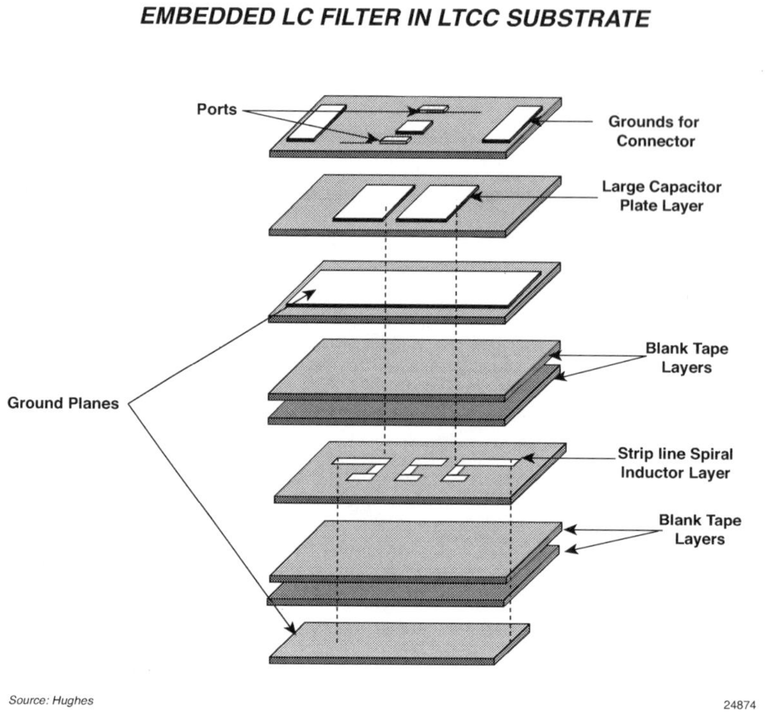

Figure 8-15. Integrated LC module for wireless applications built with LTCC.

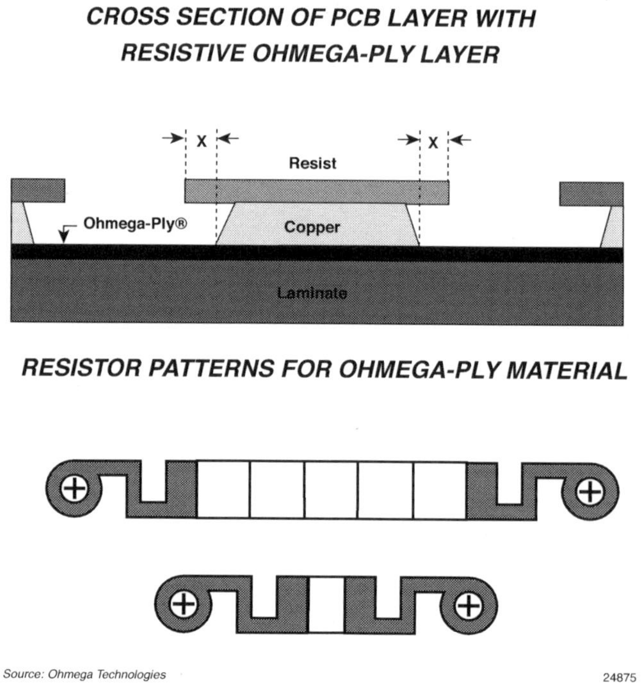

Figure 8-16. Cross section of the laminated Ohmega-Ply layer against the resin surface and top view of possible buried resistor patterns.

PBGA WITH EMBEDDED TERMINATION RESISTORS

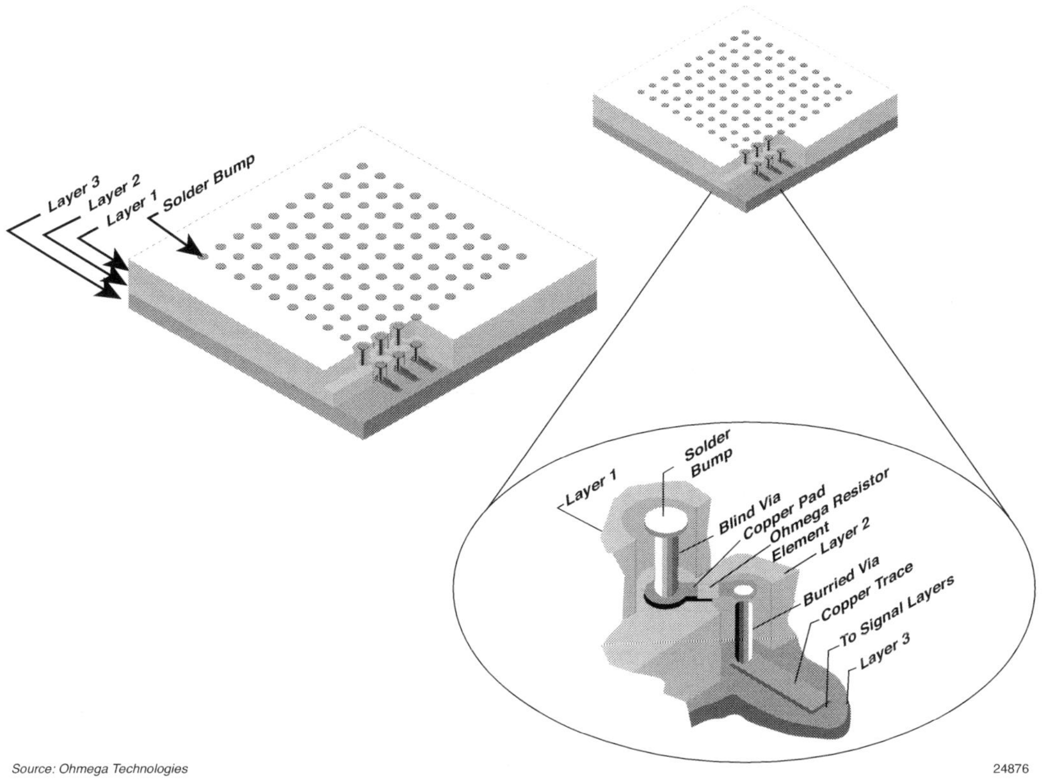

Source: Ohmega Technologies 24876

Figure 8-17. PBGA with embedded resistors.

INTEGRATION OF EMCAP LAYERS IN PCB

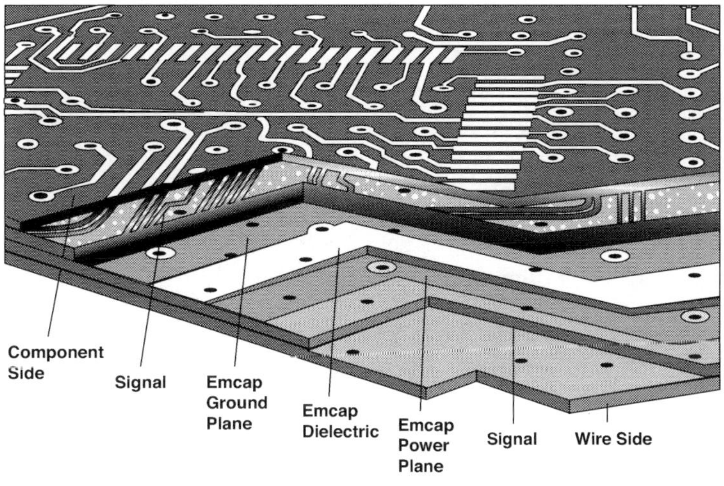

Source: Hadco 24879

Figure 8-18. EmCap layers in a PCB.

9 Contract Manufacturing Services (CMS)

Every new product is a custom design. To reduce time to market and cost, one strategy is to use as many standard, off the shelf components as possible. While to add specialized functionality and differentiation, some subsystems are customized, such as:

- Special function ICs and their packaging
- Software
- Circuit board
- Enclosure

In the 70s and 80s, a vertically integrated company, such as IBM, AT&T, HP or Sony, would have the internal resources devoted to designing, fabricating, assembling and testing all the subsystem elements and their integration into a final product.

With pressures on reducing cost, reducing time to market and being able to rapidly adjust to changing product needs, the manufacturing infrastructure required to be effective for all these elements is large. Every dollar spent on manufacturing process development means not spending it on shrinking the product introduction cycle time. Increasingly, it is not the manufacturing technologies that differentiate products, but the product design, software and market presence.

In the last five years, there has been an increasingly rapid migration away from the vertically integrated organization to a specialized organization where non core competencies are outsourced to independent service providers. The combination of many independent providers all contributing to part of the value added chain of a product has been termed a "virtual" corporation.

There are four merchant industries growing in market size to support this trend of outsourcing the custom design, manufacturing and assembly operations of subsystem components: silicon foundries, package assembly, printed circuit board fabrication, board level assembly and box integration.

SILICON FOUNDRIES

These companies manufacture silicon wafers under contract by customers who provide the design information. In 1999, about 10% of ICs produced were fabricated in foundries. This is expected to grow to 35-50% over the next 15 years.

In this business model, companies that use foundries exclusively and do not manufacture their own chips are called "fabless" semiconductor companies. Companies that design and fabricate their own chips are termed Integrated Device Manufacturers (IDMs). Many IDMs also use foundries to add capacity as needed, rather than paying for the overhead of supporting unused captive lines.

Typically, the fabless customer is responsible for the IC design, sometimes down to the actual mask set. In other cases, the fabless customer will provide block level or functional design and leave the actual implementation of the design to the design services bureau of the foundry. As SOC (System On a Chip) becomes more prevalent, the design libraries that foundries have access to will become an important value add. Even a large IDM may not have the intellectual property (IP) assets that a foundry might have. A foundry with a strong IP library may displace the current role of the ASIC vendor in the near future.

The three largest foundries are:

- Chartered Semiconductor (Singapore),
- TSMC (Taiwan Semiconductor Manufacturing Co.)
- United Microelectronics Corp (UMC)

PACKAGE ASSEMBLY

Package assembly is sometimes called back end assembly or test assembly and packaging (TAP). This involves wafer level test, package design, selection and fabrication and assembly of the chip into the package. According to Dataquest, the total market for this market segment was $17B in 1996. It will be $43B in 2001. Outsourced contract assembly was 28% of the market in 1996 but will grow to 35% of the market in 2001. This is shown in Figure 9-1.

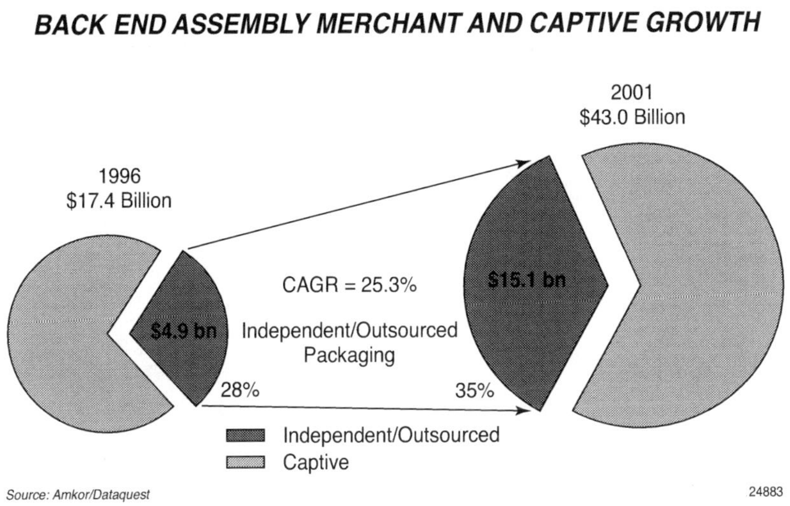

Figure 9-1. Market segment for captive and merchant package assembly.

Outsourced package assembly is used by both captive IC fabs and merchant foundries. A typical modern assembly line is shown in Figure 9-2. It used to be the labor content in assembly operations was as much as 25%. In an automated facility, such as Abpac, the labor content of the finished parts is less than 2%. Most of the cost is in the materials.

As the distinction between the package and chip becomes blurred, there will be a growing integration between foundries and package assemblers. For example, in 1998, Amkor purchased a fab line from Anam Semiconductor, which has been qualified for a 0.25 micron 5 metal layer process. Amkor can offer a complete turnkey solution from the chip design, library database, chip fab and package assembly. This type of full service capability under one subcontractor will become more common in the future, as the chip and package design becomes more integrated.

PWB (PRINTED WIRING BOARD) FABRICATION

A bare board, without any components assembled is usually called a printed wiring board. After the components are added, the assembled board is called a printed circuit board. According to Frost and Sullivan, the total PWB market for the US was $8.7B in 1997. This is expected to grow at the rate of about 9% CAGR. The US holds about 30% of the world market. Advest estimates the worldwide PWB market was about $30B in 1997 and $33B in 1998.

The transition from captive to merchant PWB market is nearly complete in the US, where only about 5% of the PWB market is still captive. While in Europe it is about 20% still captive and in Asia it is about 25% captive. This landscape is also migrating to more outsourced operations.

The largest merchant bare board vendors are

Company	Country	1998 revenue, $millions
CMK	Japan	$1,085
Viasystems	USA	$980
Ibiden	Japan	$727
Hadco	USA	$665
Nippon Mektron	Japan	$660

FINAL ASSEMBLY OPERATIONS IN A MODERN PACKAGE ASSEMBLY PLANT

Source: Abpac 24882

Figure 9-2. Modern chip package assembly line, at Abpac in Phoenix, Az, designed for BGA assembly.

BOARD LEVEL ASSEMBLY AND SYSTEM INTEGRATION

The key element of all electronics products is the printed circuit board that contains all the ICs and interconnects them to each other and the outside world. The process of assembling the components onto the circuit boards is generally referred to as assembly operations, not to be confused with chip into package assembly.

Dataquest estimates that about 14% of the world wide assembly market is performed by outsourced, contract manufacturers. In 2001, this market share will grow to 23%, for a total value of $178B. With such a huge market potential, this industry has been receiving a lot of attention recently. This market growth is shown in Figure 9-3.

This attention has lead to the creation of many terms to describe the same operations. Some of these terms to describe the service providers for board and box level assembly are:

- CM: Contract Manufactures
- CMS: Contract Manufacturing services
- CEM: Contract Electronics Manufacture
- CEMS: Contract Electronics Manufacturing Services
- EMS: Electronics Manufacturing Services
- EMSI: Electronics Manufacturing Services Industry
- EMPS: Electronics Manufacturing Products and Services
- ES: Electronics Services

The four top EMS providers are:

Company	Headquarters	1998 Sales
SCI Systems	Alabama	$6.8B
Solectron	California	$5.3B
Celestica	Ontario, CN	$3.3B
Jabil Circuits	Florida	$1.3B

According to a survey conducted by the IPC, it is the largest companies which will be growing the fastest, and will continue growing. They estimate the 1997 to 1998 growth rate is 25% for the highest volume vendors and only 17% for the smallest. This is shown in Figure 9-4. The conclusion is that in this market, it really is the economies of scale that will help to keep costs low and profits high.

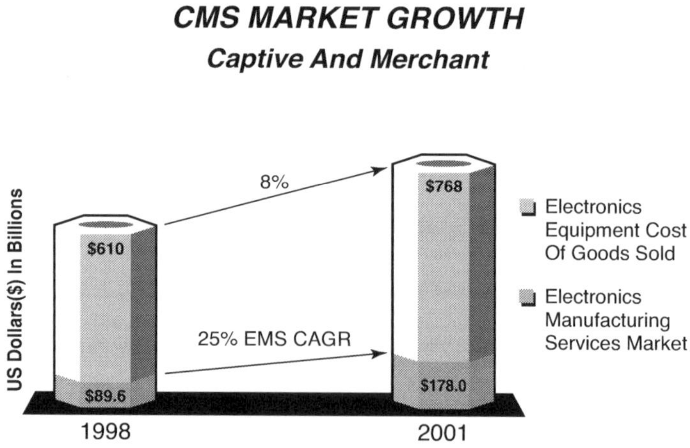

Source: Solectron 24880

Figure 9-3. Market growth of the assembly operations both total and merchant market.

EMS GROWTH BY COMPANY SIZE

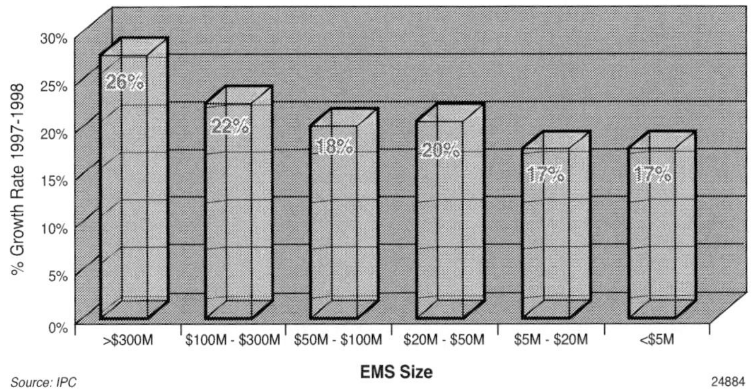

Figure 9-4. Growth in the EMS industry by company size.

In the 1970's and 80's, the contract manufacturer's role was to merely build specific products using materials consigned for the build. In the 1990s and into the next century, the role of the CEM is to take on more of the supply chain management and provide a turnkey solution from design to ship to the final customer. This evolution in the role of the CEM is show in Figure 9-5.

EVOLUTION IN THE ROLE OF THE EMS

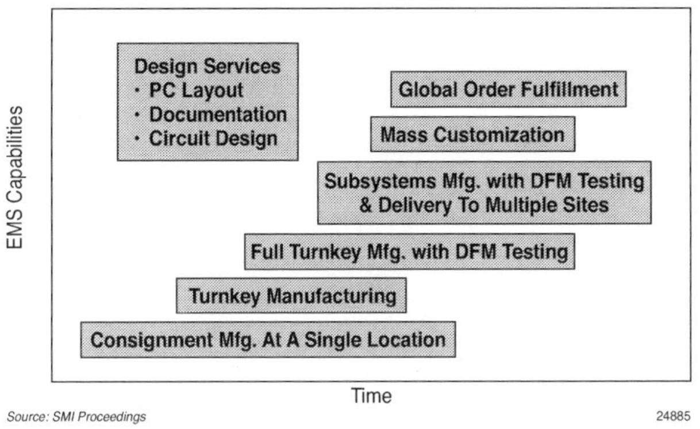

Figure 9-5. Evolution of the role of the CEM, in taking more responsibility and value add.

FUTURE BUSINESS MODELS

As OEMs focus more on product design, software and marketing, the outsourced vendor base will grow. The relationship between the contract manufacturer and the OEM will need to be much tighter, with more intellectual property and proprietary information passing between them.

The growth path for the CEM is in three directions: Larger market share of the existing business, expanding to global operations and migrating up and down the value add chain. All the top tier CEMs have been purchasing the captive lines of many of the previously vertically integrated OEMs, who are shifting to outsourcing, such as HP, IBM, DEC and NCR. With a global market place for the OEM, having final assembly and ship in the country of final sale means lower tariffs and faster time to market. Figure 9-6 illustrates the value add for CEMs in taking on more design responsibility and supply chain management.

This new business model for manufacturing leadership will have an impact on new packaging and interconnect technology. The vertically integrated companies that have insight into their future product form factors and requirements will still be in the driver seat for new technologies.

Only the largest contract manufacturers will become technology innovators. They will be able to support the R&D staff needed to develop and implement new technologies. They will also have the broad customer base to provide insight into future product needs. Those CEMs that have close relationships across the spectrum of foundry, package assembly, board assembly and box assembly will be positioned to develop optimized system level packaging.

Any market can be divided up into four segments, based on the metrics of margin and volume. Companies in a high margin, high volume market are generally monopolies. Companies that are in a high margin, low volume are niches. Companies that are in a low margin, high volume market are commodities. And companies that are in a low margin, low volume business are typically unstable, unprofitable and on their way to collapse. These four market segments are illustrated in Figure 9-7.

CHANGING ROLE OF THE CONTRACT MANUFACTURER

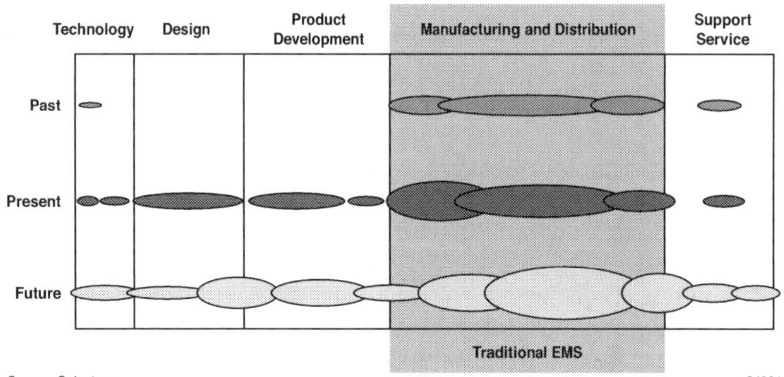

Source: Solectron 24881

Figure 9-6. Changing role of the CEM.

The largest contract manufacturers are typically in the commodity business. The differentiators for them will be how much of a one stop shop and complete turnkey operation they offer, how quickly they can ramp product to volume and how much infrastructure they have in place to manage the information flow required for product design, supply chain management and multiple product line work in progress (WIP). The smaller, successful contract manufacturers, will have clearly defined niches. A key effort for them will be to identify the elements of their niche, and how to grow value within it.

FOUR MARKET SEGMENTS OF ANY INDUSTRY

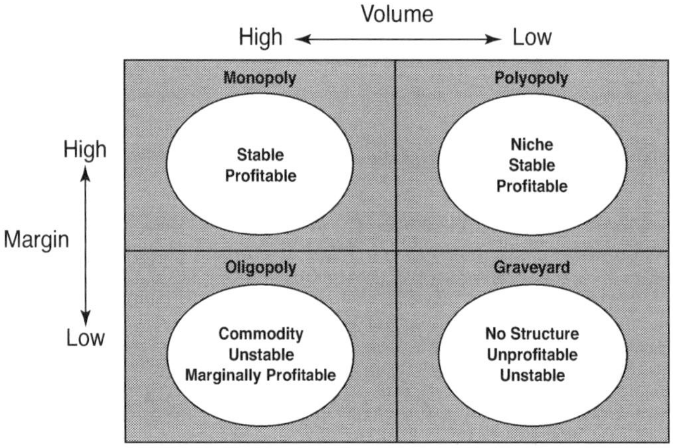

Source: Ray Alderman/Electronic Design 24886

Figure 9-7. Four market segments for any industry.

10 Designing for High Speed

PHYSICAL DESIGN OF THE INTERCONNECTS AFFECTS PERFORMANCE

The last few years have catapulted us into a new design regime for high speed digital products, where clock frequencies on-chip, on-board and in serial links are routinely over 100MHz. In these systems, rise times are typical less than 1 nsec. Figure 10-1 shows the future predictions from the SIA (Semiconductor Industry Association) roadmap for on-chip and off-chip clock frequency trends. The growth in the number of installed high speed local area network (LAN) ports for ATM, running at 622MHz and of Fibre Channel running at 2.4GHz, has a CAGR (Compound Annual Growth Rate) of almost 100%. This trend is shown in Figure 10-2.

PREDICTIONS FOR GROWTH RATE OF HIGH SPEED LAN PORTS

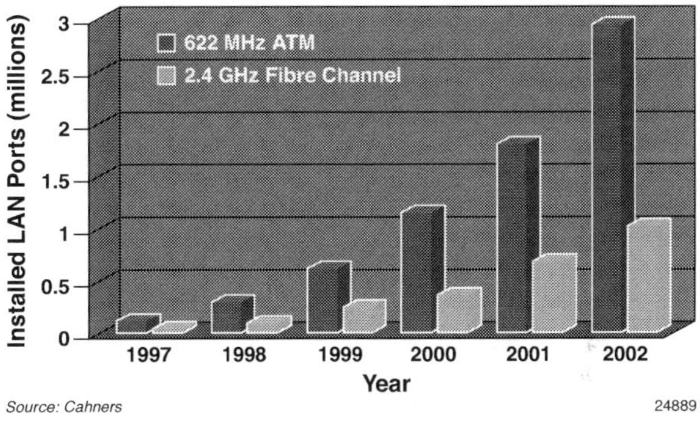

Figure 10-2. The growth in high speed LANs.

To first order, the maximum clock frequency is determined by the intrinsic gate delay of the integrated circuits and how they are connected. This is the prime factor that determines the "speed" of the system. As pointed out in the ICE companion publication, **Roadmaps of Packaging Technology**, the packaging, boards and other interconnects can never increase the clock frequency above what the chips are capable of. They will only degrade the system performance. The goal of the designer is to minimize this detrimental impact. If special consideration is not taken in the design and the selection of packaging technologies, invariably, there will be problems with high speed operation.

PREDICTIONS FOR ON-CHIP AND OFF-CHIP CLOCK FREQUENCIES

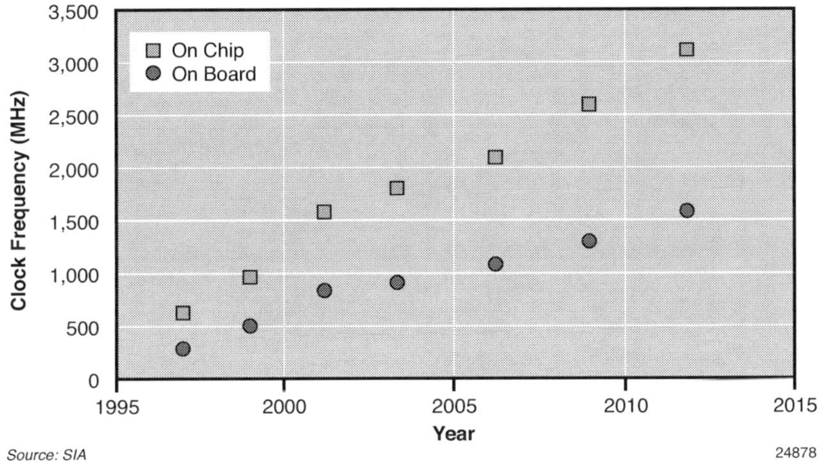

Figure 10-1. Clock frequency increases.

The packaging and interconnect will degrade system performance in two ways: by adding timing delays and by adding noise. The noise effects are typically grouped under the general heading of signal integrity. This broad term includes four distinct noise sources arising from the interactions of the signals from the chips and the physical structures of the packaging and interconnects. These four noise sources, summarized in Figure 10-3, are:

Signal quality- impedance changes in the signal path and its return cause reflections and distortions

Cross talk- voltage and current noise is transferred between nearby traces due to stray electric and magnetic fields

Switching noise- finite impedance in the power and ground planes will cause voltage noise when current switches

ElectroMagnetic Interference (EMI)- the high frequency components of the various currents will radiate and interfere with adjacent equipment or fail an FCC certification test

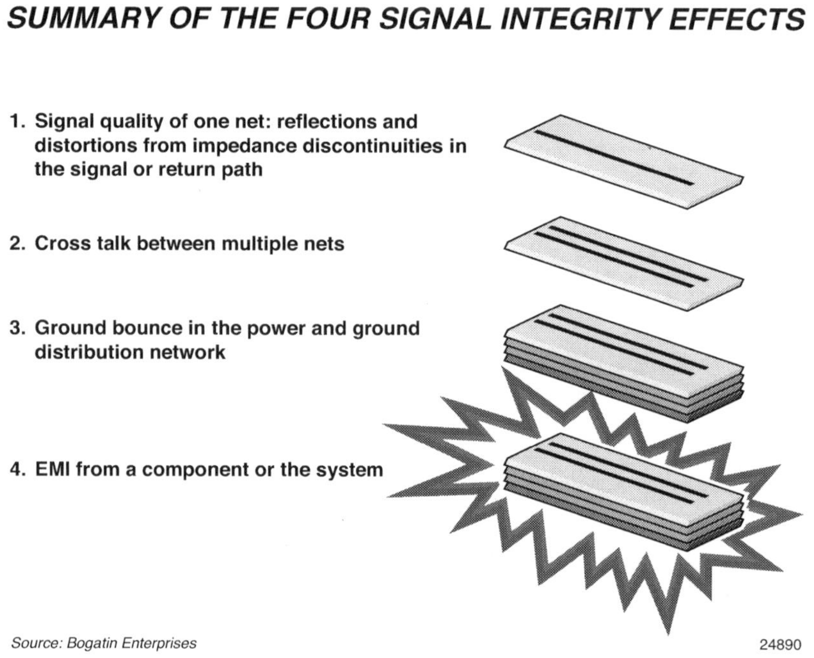

Figure 10-3. Summary of the four signal integrity related noise sources.

When clock frequencies are greater than about 50MHz, some or all of these problems will occur unless specifically designed out. Correct high speed operation doesn't happen by luck or chance. These problems can be minimized by correct design and by leveraging new technologies. In the following sections some of the design principles and new technologies to optimize the packaging and interconnects for high speed operation are described.

TIMING DELAYS

The first hurdle in designing high speed digital systems is meeting the timing spec. This means fitting all the gate delays, set up times, hold times, wiring delays and skews within the shorter and shorter cycle time budget. When the cycle time is only 5nsec, the interconnect related delays can be as much as 50% of the total delays. Figure 10-4 illustrates the increasing contribution of the interconnect to timing delays.

The most important quality of the interconnects that affects the timing delay is the time of flight of signals down the various paths. The time delay, TD, depends on the length of the interconnect, L, and the speed at which the signal propagates down the trace, v:

$$TD = \frac{L}{v} = \frac{L\sqrt{\varepsilon_r}}{12\,in/n\,sec}$$

There are two ways of minimizing interconnect related timing delays: decrease interconnect lengths and decrease the dielectric constant of the interconnect dielectrics. The driving force in the industry to increase the interconnect density is also moving in the right direction to decrease timing delays.

CONTRIBUTIONS TO THE TIMING BUDGET

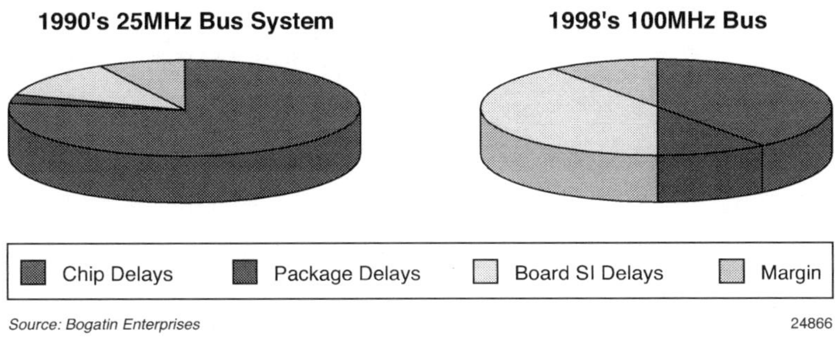

Figure 10-4. Fraction of the timing delays contributed by the interconnect for different clock frequencies.

The introduction of new materials with lower dielectric constant is also helping to reduce timing delays. One of the features of HDI (High Density Interconnect) microvia technology is the lack of a glass fiber reinforcing web. The glass has a dielectric constant of 6.5, compared to the epoxy resin of 3.5. Without the glass, the dielectric constants used in HDI layers are lower than conventional FR4. Figure 10-5 lists the dielectric constants of some of the new HDI substrate materials.

DIELECTRIC CONSTANTS OF COMMON HDI DIELECTRICS

Material	Dielectric Constant
Photoimageable Dielectric (PID) Epoxy	3.8
Epoxy Acrylate	3.8
Epoxy (RCC)	3.5
Epoxy Aramid	3.5
Polyimide Film	3.4
Microlam® ePTFE	3.3
FR4 (Glass Weave)	4.1-5.2
Driclad (IBM)(Glass Weave)	4.1
Cyanate Ester (E-Glass)	3.8
Bismaleimide Triazine (BT) (Glass Weave)	4.1

Source: Bogatin Enterprises 24888

Figure 10-5. Dielectric constants of HDI materials.

Even with heroic efforts to eliminate the last picosecond of delay from the devices, the packages, the boards and the connectors, meeting the timing spec does not guarantee the system will work.

SIGNAL INTEGRITY

The second hurdle in high speed digital design is fitting all the signal integrity noise sources within the noise budget. The fundamental problem with ever higher clock frequencies is that the noise sources all increase with shorter rise times of the signals. Design techniques used in the last design may not work in the next design with rise times decreased and noise magnitudes increased by 20%-30%.

It will always be more profitable to pay extra, if necessary, to design a product right the first time than to try to fix it later in the product development cycle. In the product life cycle, often, the first six months in the market are the most profitable. If a product is late, a significant share of the life cycle profits may be lost. Time really is money.

All four of the signal integrity effects mentioned above can be minimized by following specific design principles and with the use of new technologies recently introduced, which are reviewed in the following sections.

SIGNAL QUALITY ON A SINGLE NET

Signal quality on a single net depends as much on the features of the signal trace as in its return path. Any change in the impedance a signal sees propagating down the net will cause a reflection and distortion. These discontinuities can arise from the topology or routing, the terminations at both ends and from added components. When a trace branches into two, the impedance changes and some signal will reflect back to the source and some will continue down the branches in reduced and distorted form.

The first step to minimize reflection problems is to design the circuit boards with controlled impedance traces. In such boards, the cross section of interconnects is chosen to achieve a target characteristic impedance, such as 50Ohms, or 65Ohms. This cross section is kept uniform throughout the entire board. Many different cross sections are suitable for controlled impedance. Some of these possibilities are shown in Figure 10-6.

The second step in controlling reflections is to terminate traces that are long. If the interconnect has a time delay (TD) that is shorter than about 20% the rise time, the reflections may not be so large as to cause problems. However, if the length increases beyond this limit, the reflections at the ends will cause "ringing" noise and false triggering. Figure 10-7 illustrates the waveforms at the far end as the interconnect length increases beyond 20% the rise time. If lines this long are not terminated, the product will not function. In order to minimize the need for terminations, interconnect traces should be kept as short as possible. This is achieved with closely spaced CSP packages, mounted on HDI substrates, for example.

Termination can be done in a variety of ways, illustrated in Figure 10-8.

SIMULATED REFLECTION NOISE FOR DIFFERENT LENGTH UNTERMINATED TRANSMISSION LINES

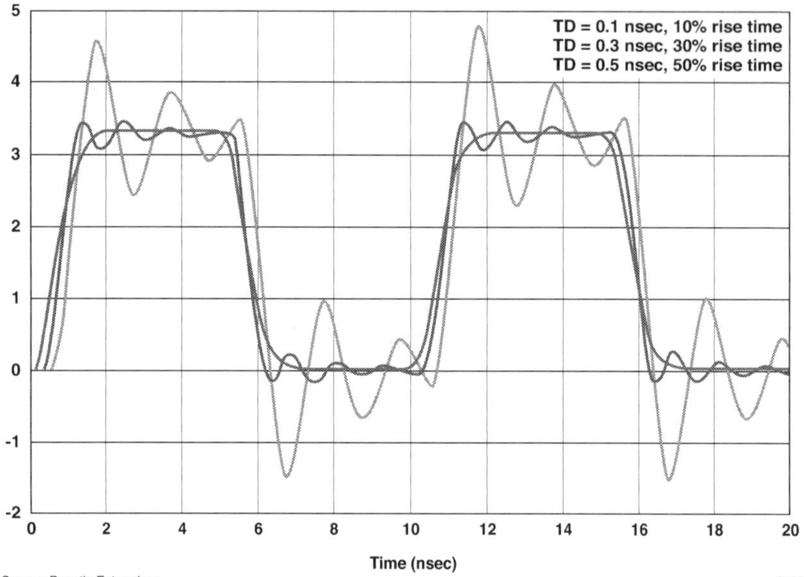

Source: Bogatin Enterprises 24893

Figure 10-7. Reflection noise will increase beyond acceptable levels when the TD is greater than 20% of the rise time, unless the ends are terminated.

Many of these components can be added by using arrays of resistors, or integrated RC circuits as integrated passive devices (IPDs), described in a previous chapter. Figure 10-9 shows an example of IPD arrays from Intarsia and the resulting cleaned waveform using an RC termination.

Even a uniform trace will show attenuation from resistive losses and dielectric losses. This will degrade the rise time, increasing the timing delay.

CROSS SECTIONS USED IN CONTROLLED IMPEDANCE INTERCONNECTS

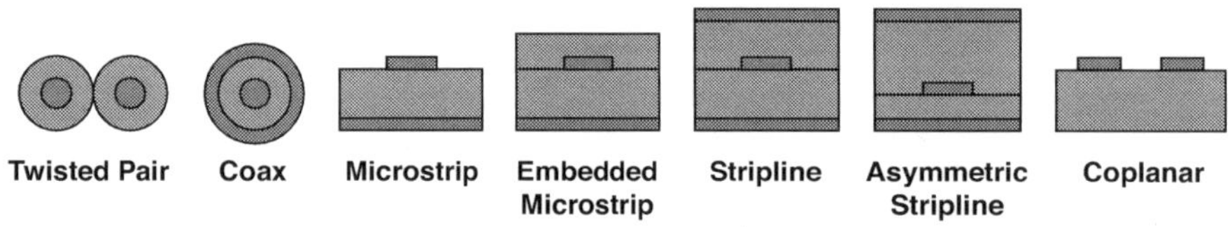

Source: Bogatin Enterprises 24891

Figure 10-6. Different cross sections can be used as controlled impedance interconnects, as long as the cross section is uniform down the length.

TERMINATION STRATEGIES FOR TRANSMISSION LINES

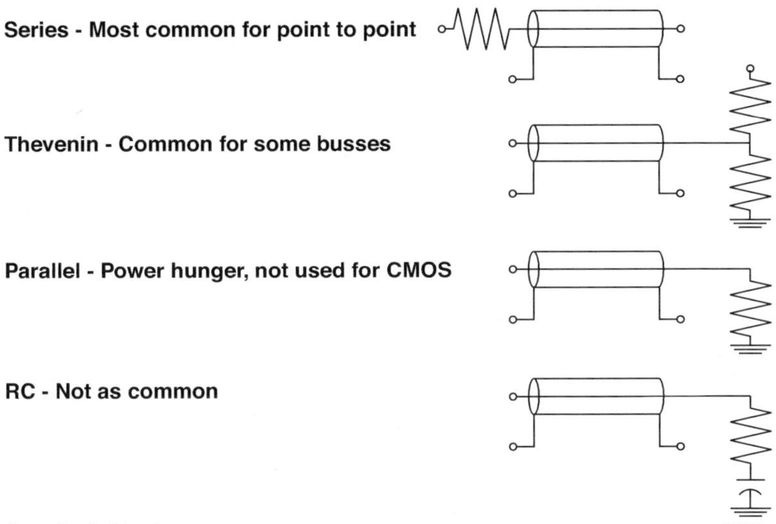

Source: Bogatin Enterprises 24892

Figure 10-8. Various termination strategies for transmission lines.

With high speed serial links, excessive attenuation may result in a collapse in the eye diagram and bits dropped. The dielectric loss, or dissipation factor, of the substrate dielectric, will set a fundamental limit on how long an interconnect can be and still have enough signal at the far end to be received. The lower the dissipation factor, the less loss and the longer the acceptable interconnect length.

Figure 10-10 identifies the maximum allowable value of the dissipation factor for a given length for GHz clock signals and 10mil wide traces. It can be seen that FR4, the most common board material, with a dissipation factor of 0.02, is the worst material, limiting the maximum interconnect length to about 20 inches at 1GHz. For longer lines, common in backplanes, lower dissipation factor materials must be used. And, the maximum usable interconnect length is getting shorter with higher clock frequencies. This is driving the introduction of new low loss materials such SpeedBoard from W.L. Gore.

INTEGRATED PASSIVE DEVICES

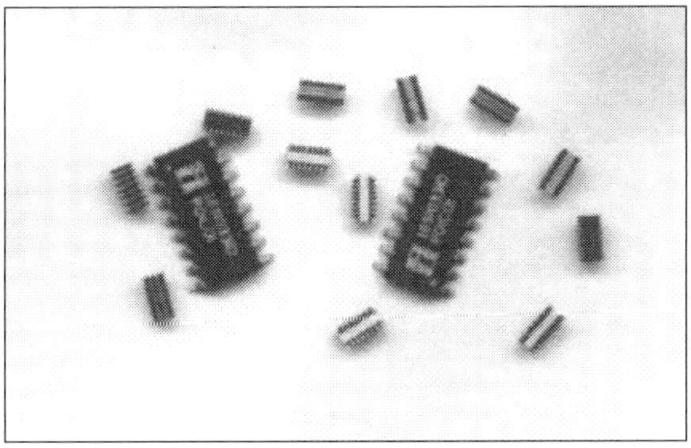

Source: Intarsia 24868

SIMULATION OF RC TERMINATED TRANSMISSION LINES USING IPD RC ARRAYS

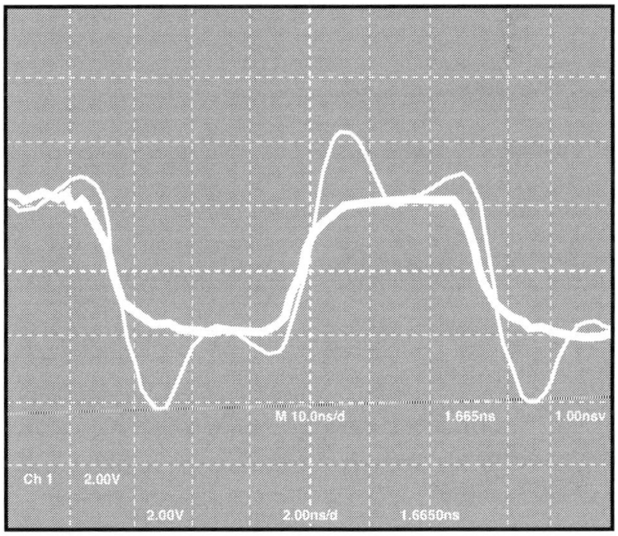

Source: AVX 24870

Figure 10-9. IPDs from Intarsia and the waveform at the end of a trace with and without an RC termination.

MAXIMUM USEABLE LENGTH FOR GHz CLOCKS WITH DIFFERENT DISSIPATION FACTORS

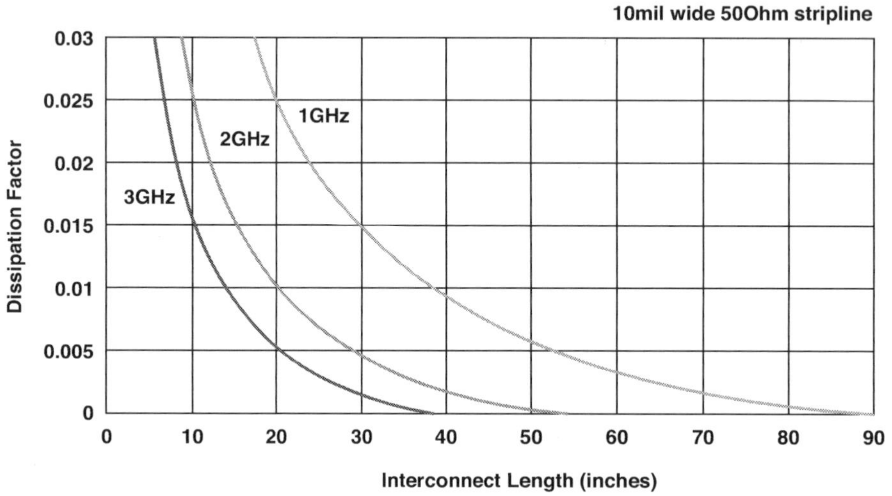

Source: Bogatin Enterprises 24894

Figure 10-10. Maximum usable interconnect length with an acceptable signal with a 1, 2 and 3GHz clock for a given dissipation factor.

CROSS TALK

Noise can couple between two or more adjacent nets by capacitive coupling or inductive coupling. These combine in different ways to produce two flavors of noise in transmission lines: near end and far end. An example of the near end and far end cross talk noise induced in an adjacent microstrip trace is shown in Figure 10-11.

Far end coupling, prevalent whenever the dielectric is inhomogeneous, such as microstrips in PCB traces and most connectors, increases in magnitude with the coupling length between the traces and with decreasing rise times. Shorter rise times, with higher clocks, will give rise to higher far end cross talk for the same board design rules. For example, in two surface microstrip traces, the far end voltage noise might be about 100mV for a 10 inch parallel run with 1nsec rise times. This might be within the noise budget. But with a rise time reduced by 1/5 to 200psec rise times, the noise will be increased 5x larger, to 0.5v, far outside the noise budget. The most effective way of reducing far end noise is to use a stripline stack up. This structure does not show any far end noise.

The near end noise voltage reaches a maximum value, called the saturation value, when the time delay of the coupled length is equal to the rise time. Near end noise can always be reduced by keeping the co-parallel run length shorter than the saturation length. In FR4, a 4nsec rise time has a saturation length of 24 inches. It's possible to layout busses with co parallel lengths less than 12 inches. But, with a 0.5nsec rise time, the saturation length is 3 inches. This almost guarantees that buss lines will have the maximum near end noise, which can be as high as 100mV. The saturation length for various materials and signal rise times is shown on Figure 10-12.

When bus widths are 128 bits, it may be required to route dozens of data lines adjacent to each other over most of the board. The most effective way of reducing cross talk to an acceptable level is to establish a separation design rule that keeps the saturated near end noise to an acceptable level. Figure 10-13 is a simulation from the Ansoft Maxwell 2D Extractor field solver, of the near end cross talk coefficient for 50Ohm adjacent traces. A microstrip and stripline stack up are compared, each with 5mil wide traces.

NEAR AND FAR END CROSS TALK

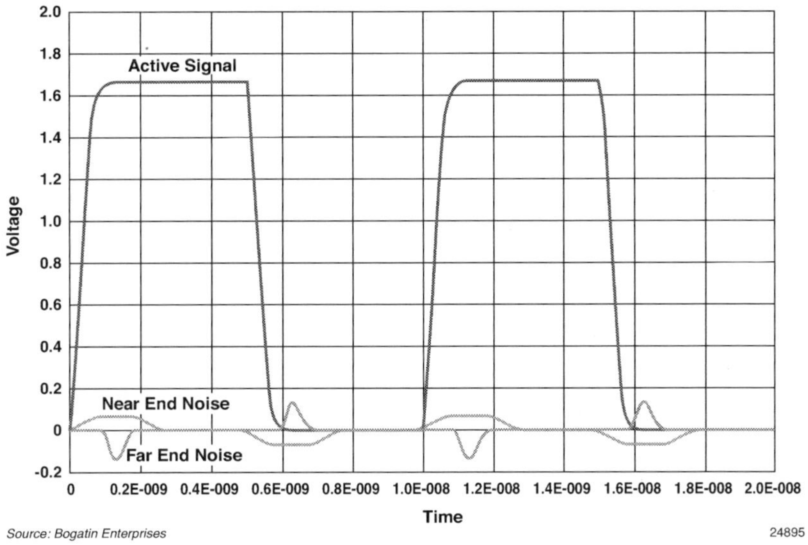

Figure 10-11. Simulation of near and far end cross talk in an adjacent microstrip trace.

SATURATION LENGTH OF NEAR END CROSS TALK

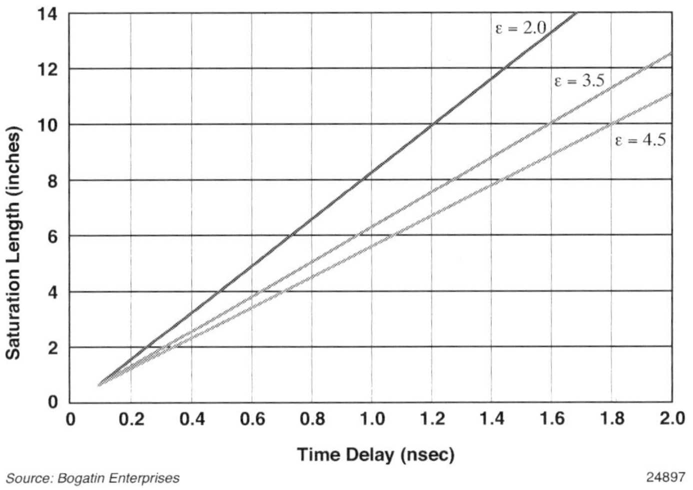

Figure 10-12. Saturation length of near end cross talk in coupled transmission lines.

From this plot, it can be seen that for cross talk on the order of 2%, typical of many specs, both stack ups require a comparable spacing. There is no real advantage using one or the other. However, in mixed signal applications, where high isolation between traces is important, a stripline structure clearly offers superior isolation over a microstrip. Of course, the added advantage of a stripline structure is the absence of far end cross talk.

There is another important way to decrease cross talk: use a lower dielectric constant laminate. In order to achieve a 50Ohm stripline line with a 5mil wide trace in FR4, with a dielectric constant of 4.5, requires a dielectric thickness of 12mils. But, if the dielectric constant is reduced to 2.9, as for example, using a liquid crystal polymer (LCP) dielectric with a dielectric constant of 2.9, the required dielectric thickness to achieve 50Ohms is only 9mils. The closer spacing of the reference planes will decrease the cross talk between adjacent traces. An example of the comparison is shown in Figure 10-14.

At a spacing of 10 mils, for example, a lower dielectric constant material can provide a 10dB greater isolation for the same size lines, over FR4. Likewise, if the pitch is cross talk limited, the traces can be brought closer together, and the product form factor decreased, by using a lower dielectric constant material. Products that need to shrink can leverage lower dielectric constant materials such as liquid crystal polymer and SpeedBoard® from W. L. Gore.

POWER AND GROUND DISTRIBUTION NOISE

Virtually all high speed digital products are based on a synchronous clock. All gates in the system switch based on the timing information from a master clock. This means that many gates will be switching simultaneously. When they switch, they draw current from the power and ground distribution. The current surge through the power and ground leads and planes will cause voltage drops due to the finite impedance of the power and ground. This noise is often called:

- Simultaneous switching noise (SSN)
- Simultaneous switching outputs (SSO)
- Ground bounce
- Switching noise
- Power and ground collapse
- Rail collapse
- Delta I noise

The magnitude will increase with shorter rise times and increase with more bits switching simultaneously. Both trends are happening: rise times are decreasing, and buss widths are increasing. This means switching noise is getting harder to prevent. There are two main ways of decreasing switching noise: decreasing the series inductance in the power and ground path and increasing the parallel capacitance across the power and ground distribution.

To first order, the inductance of a lead depends on its length. The most important way of decreasing the series inductance of a connection is making it shorter. A flip chip connection with a 5mil long solder ball may have only 0.1nH of self inductance, while a 50mil long wire bond might have a self inductance of 1.3nH, a factor of 10 larger.

The lead in a CSP, only 50mils long, will have 1.3nH self inductance, while the lead in a SOP, 250 mils long, for example, might have a self inductance of 6nH. The introduction of CSPs for glue logic is a very important step. An example of the small size advantage of a CSP over a TSOP is shown in Figure 10-15.

When connections are not short, planes should be used to transport the power and ground distribution. The loop inductance associated with two adjacent planes, separated with a spacing, h, for a width, w and length, len, is:

$$L_{loop} = \mu_0 h \frac{len}{w} = hx\frac{len}{w}33\frac{nH}{inch}$$

NEAR END CROSS TALK IN IDENTICLE MICROSTRIP AND STRIPLINE

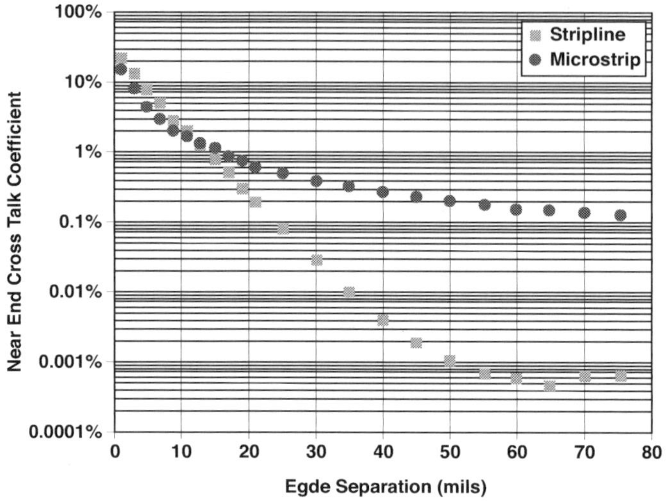

Source: Bogatin Enterprises 24896

Figure 10-13. Near end cross talk for microstrip and stripline, 50Ohm traces, each 5mils wide, in FR4.

NEAR END CROSS TALK IN IDENTICLE STRIPLINE TRACES, WITH DIFFERENT DIELECTRIC CONSTANTS

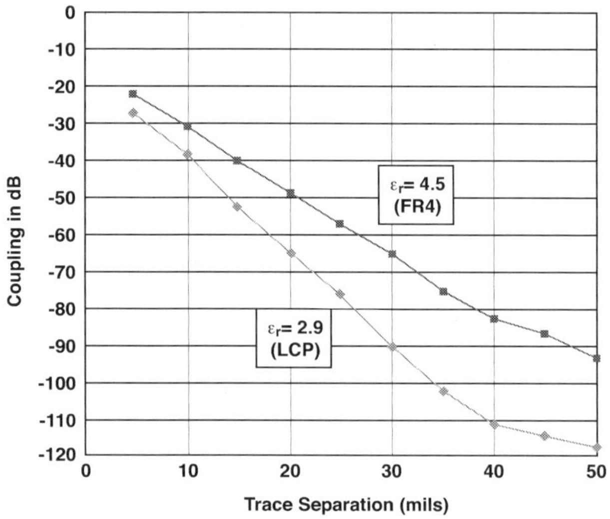

Source: Bogatin Enterprises 24898

Figure 10-14. Compares the cross talk between two pairs of 50Ohm traces, each 5mils wide, but with different dielectric constants.

BODY SIZE SHRINK IN MIGRATION TO CSP

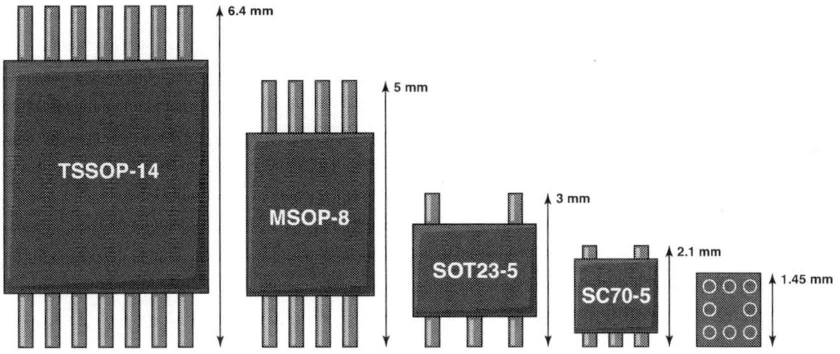

Source: National Semiconductors 24877

Figure 10-15. Use of CSP will offer much shorter leads and lower inductance leads than a TSOP.

This is illustrated in Figure 10-16.

LOOP INDUCTANCE OF POWER AND GROUND PLANES

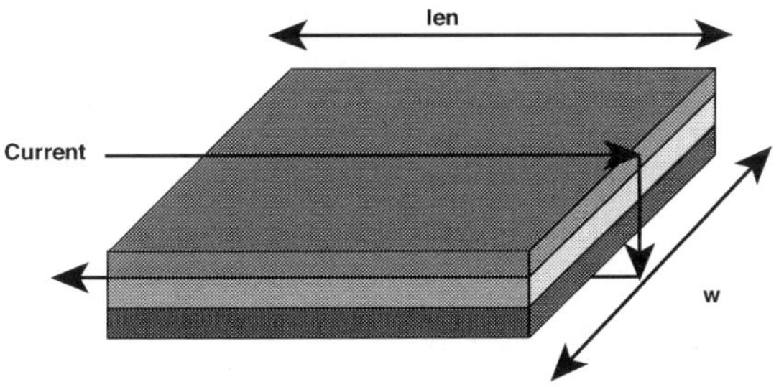

$$L_{loop} = \mu_0 h \frac{len}{w} = h x \frac{len}{w} 33 \frac{nH}{inch}$$

Source: Bogatin Enterprises 24899

Figure 10-16. Loop inductance for two planes.

In order to minimize the loop inductance of power and ground planes, the thickness of the planes should be kept to a minimum. This can be achieved by using ultra thin laminates, such as used in HDI microvia substrates. This is an advantage of high performance BGA packages fabricated with HDI technology: the power and ground planes can be made very thin, and hence, low inductance.

The second way of decreasing the switching noise is adding low inductance decoupling capacitors. The key is low inductance. When the chip looks into the power and ground network, it is important for it to see low impedance up to the switching frequencies. The intrinsic inductance of a capacitor, related to its geometry, will increase its impedance at higher frequencies.

The useful high frequency limit for a capacitor will be set by its impedance. One way of increasing the useful range of a capacitor is to mount it along the short axis. Figure 10-17 illustrates the typical impedance curve of two 0.1microFarad capacitors, one mounted in the traditional fashion of 1206 and the other in the low inductance manner of an 0612. Just by changing the orientation, the useful frequency range of a capacitor can be increase by a factor of two.

An even lower inductance capacitor can be provided by careful internal design and arrangement of current flow in adjacent planes. An example of the Low Inductance Capacitor Array (LICA) capacitor from AVX is shown in Figure 10-18.

IMPROVED HIGH SPEED PERFORMANCE OF 0612 CAPACITOR STYLE

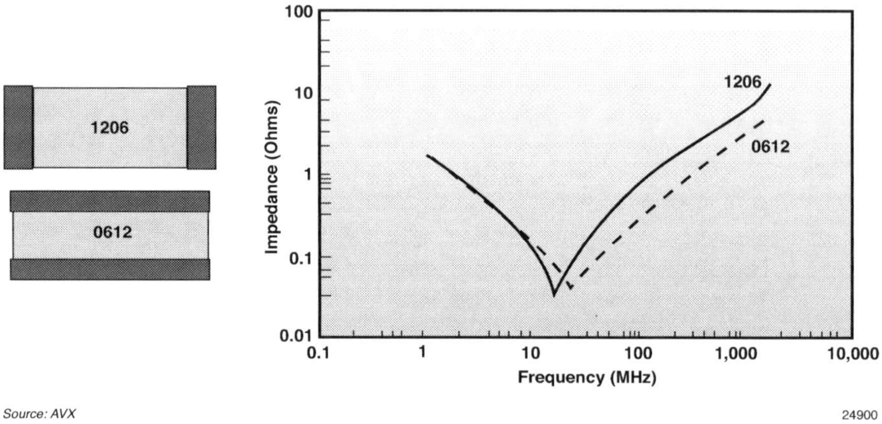

Figure 10-17. Impedance of decoupling capacitors mounted as 1206 and 0612.

LICA CAPACITOR

LICA CAPACITOR INTERNAL STRUCTURE

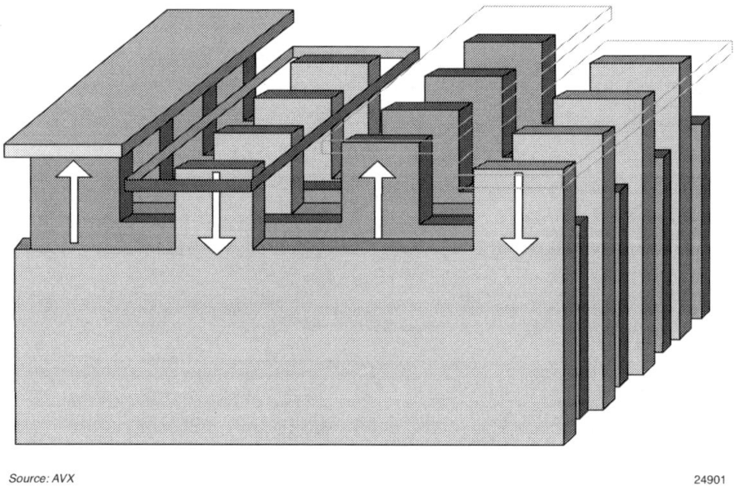

Figure 10-18. LICA capacitor from AVX with less than 100pH of internal self capacitance.

EMI

With clock frequencies in the 100-300MHz range, the first few harmonics are within the common communications bands of TV, FM radio, cell phone and PCS. This means there is the very real possibility of interfering with communications unless emissions are kept in control. Unfortunately, without special design considerations, EMI will get worse at higher frequency. The radiated far field strength from common mode currents will increase linearly with frequency and from differential mode currents will increase with the square of the frequency. This has prompted many signal integrity engineers to say, "...there are two kinds of designers, those that have EMI problems and those that will." Figure 10-19 displays the maximum radiated field intensity allowed by the FCC, to pass a CLASS B test, suitable for home or office environment.

FCC CLASS B 3M EMISSIONS LIMIT

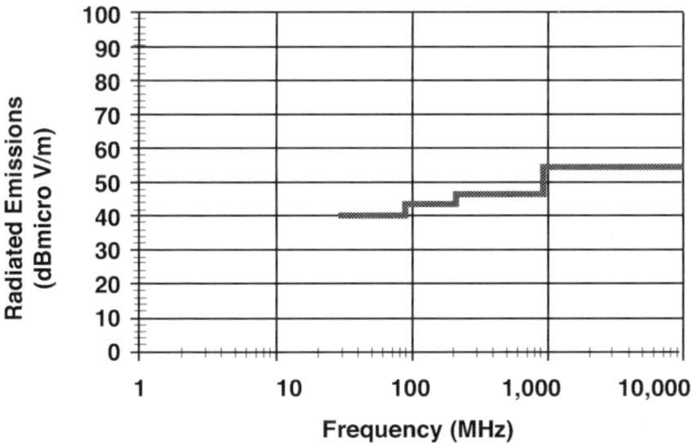

Freq (MHz)	µV/m	dB µV/m
30-88	100	40
88-216	150	43.5
216-960	200	46
>960	500	54

Source: Bogatin Enterprises 24903

Figure 10-19. FCC CLASS B conditions for acceptable radiated emissions at 3m.

It takes three things to have an EMI problem: a source of noise, a pathway to a radiator and an antenna. Every source of signal integrity problem mentioned above will be a source of EMI. What makes EMI even more insidious is that even if the noise is low enough to meet the signal integrity noise budget, it may still be large enough to cause serious radiated emissions.

Managing EMI is a three tiered defense. First is managing the bandwidth of the clocks and signals. Everything possible should be done to keep the bandwidth as low as possible, tough to do as rise times decrease. Where possible, sharp rise time signals should be filtered. Many connectors offer the option of having integrated filters so that I/O lines will have a reduced bandwidth. The reduced bandwidth means less energy at the high frequencies available to radiate. Figure 10-20 is an example of connectors with integrated filters, and the resulting attenuation possible.

Another popular method of decreasing the bandwidth of signals is to modulate the clock frequency a small amount, typically a few megahertz. This spreads the narrow band of radiation from the clocks into a broader bandwidth and drops the average radiated intensity. Figure 10-21 shows the reduced emissions from a Spread Spectrum Clock Generator (SSCG). Reductions of 5-10dB are routinely possible.

The second step to reduce EMI is to minimize the generation of noise, especially common mode noise on the ground distribution, which might have the potential of exiting the product. To keep the ground noise low, power and ground planes should be used, and kept as close together as possible. An example of the reduction in emissions possible with 2mil spaced power and ground layers available from Hadco, termed ZBC layers, is shown in Figure 10-22. By converting two pairs of layers from conventional to ZBC layers, emissions were reduced by over 10dB at some frequencies.

Next, everything possible should be done to control the return path of the signal lines. Just as much care should be taken in routing the RF return path as in the signal paths. If a trace passes over a gap in the return plane, signal integrity may not be noticeably affected, but the RF current flow in the plane will change and can dramatically increase the common mode noise.

FERRITE BASED FILTER PIN

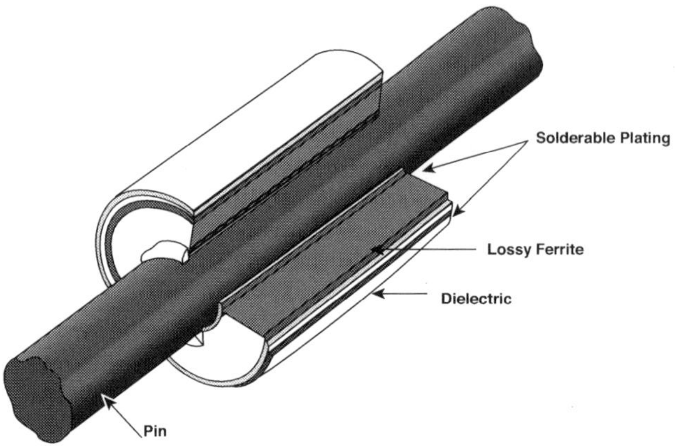

Source: AMP

24904

ENHANCED ATTENUATION OF FERRITE FILTER PIN CONNECTORS

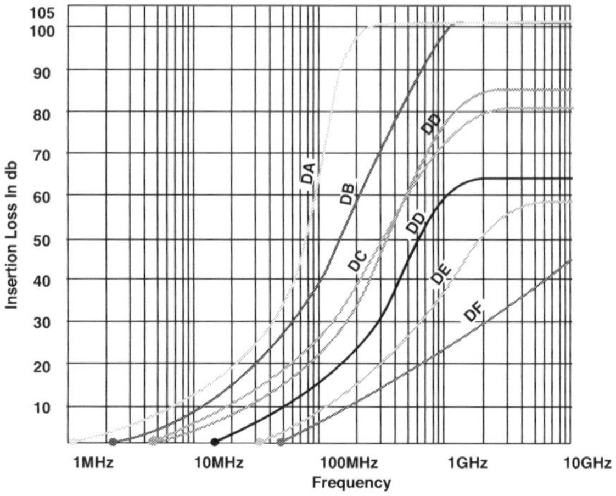

Source: AMP

24906

STANDARD CONNECTOR FORM FACTORS WITH INTEGRATED FILTER PINS

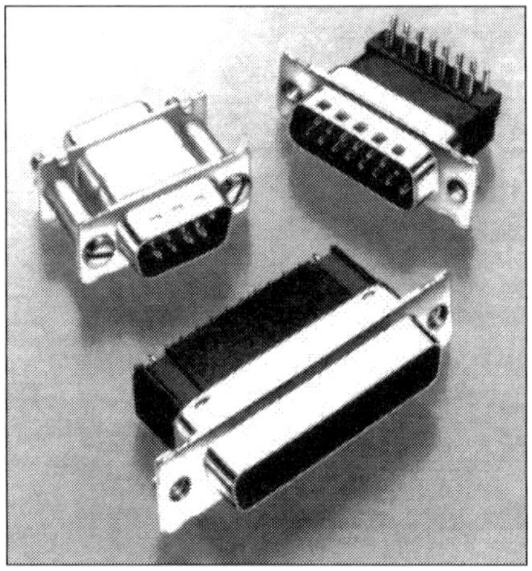

Source: AMP

24905

Figure 10-20. Integrated ferrite filters in conventional connectors. Top left: example of the ferrite core providing the filtering. Top right: response curve of the attenuation from a variety of filter designs. Bottom: examples of standard style connectors with integrated filters for reduced emissions.

Sometimes the gaps under signal traces are unintentional. If clearance holes through the planes are relaxed and large, they can overlap in a field of vias, such as a connector or BGA site. This will create regions of the board where the ground plane is not continuous. Merely reducing the clearance hole size may decrease the common mode currents and reduce emissions. Figure 10-23 illustrates the problems that can arise with a signal passing over a via field if the clearance holes in the ground plane are too large. The problem can be eliminated if the clearance holes are reduced in size and the gaps prevented.

REDUCED EMISSIONS AMPLITUDE FROM SSCG CLOCK CHIP

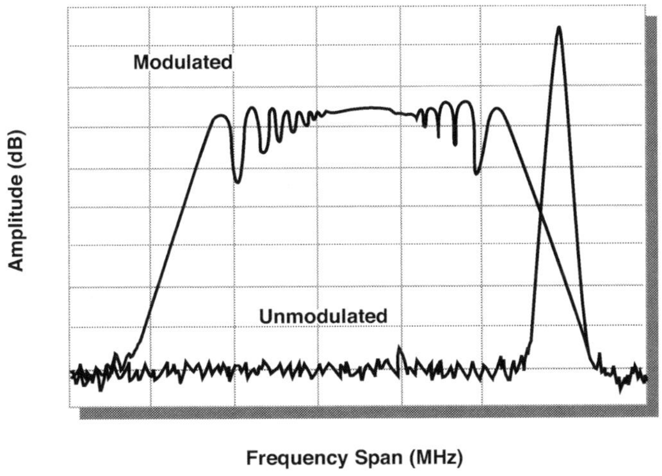

Source: IC Works 24907

Figure 10-21. SSCG can spread the narrow clock spectrum into a broader band, dropping the average emission level. The vertical scale is 10dBmV/div.

The third line of defense against EMI is shielding. Many of the ills of poor board design can be fixed with a good shield. This shield can be added locally to the surface of a board, after the fact, by screen printing a conductive ink. An example of a post fab EMI shield is shown in Figure 10-24.

In many mixed signal products, such as portable wireless, noisy digital devices are a fraction of an inch away from very sensitive analog front end receivers. Over 120dB of isolation is often required. This is accomplished by using guard traces around signal lines in a stripline stack up and by enclosing any surface components in miniature Faraday cages which can be surface mounted to the boards. Figure 10-25 shows the increased isolation possible in a shielded stripline compared with the same stripline pair, but with no guard trace.

EMISSIONS WITH AND WITHOUT THE THINNER ZBC LAYERS

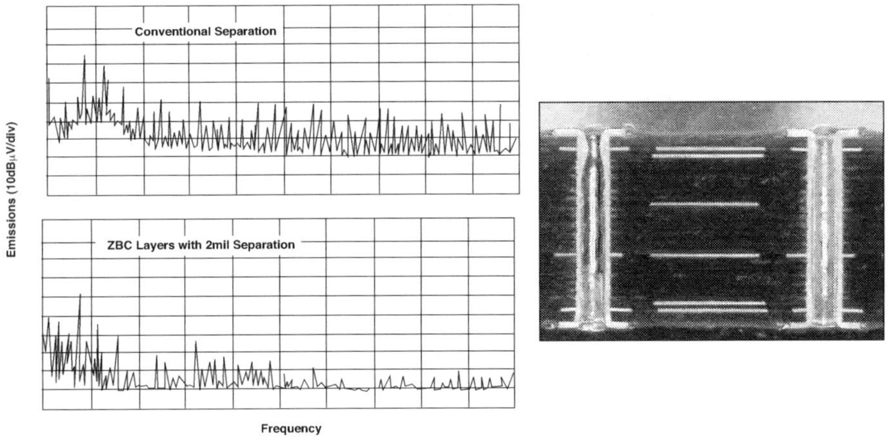

Source: Hadco 24908

Figure 10-22. Emission reductions by thinner dielectric in the power and ground distribution using the ZBC layers from Hadco. Also shown is a cross section of the board with two pairs of ZBC layers.

CLEARANCE HOLES IN RETURN PATH PLANE

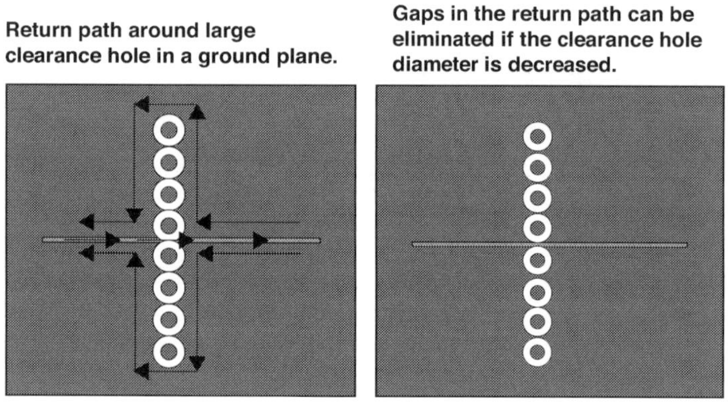

Source: Bogatin Enterprises 24909

Figure 10-23. How clearance holes in the ground plane can cause inadvertent gaps under signal paths.

SCREEN PRINTED LAYERS PROVIDING EMI SHIELD

Source: DuPont 24913

Figure 10-24. EMI shield screen printed by conductive ink available from DuPont.

For additional isolation, a mechanical shield can be provided locally inside the enclosure, as with a small formed metal housing. An example of a custom internal EMI shield is shown in Figure 10-26.

A product with a great shield will still need to have connecting cables to the outside world, for communications, for peripherals or for interfacing. Perhaps the biggest source of noise in cables is common mode noise from the ground connections getting on the outside of the cable shield. This can be reduced by adding a common mode ferrite choke around the outside of the cable. An example of a ferrite on a printer cable is shown in Figure 10-27.

As clock frequencies increase, and rise times decrease, it becomes increasingly difficult to meet the timing and signal integrity requirements. It is by detailed analysis and design with the incorporation of new technologies specially developed to solve signal integrity problems, that the next generation of high speed products will be made possible.

SHIELDING EFFECTIVENESS OF GUARD TRACES

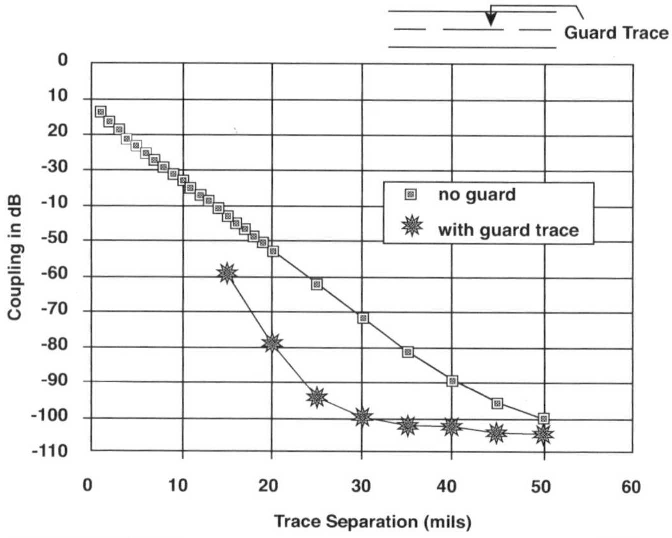

Source: Bogatin Enterprises 24911

Figure 10-25. Comparing isolation advantage with and without a guard trace between two 50Ohm stripline lines in FR4. Over 30dB isolation can be gained with a guard trace.

INTERNAL SMT EMI SHIELD

Source: Holdt 24910

Figure 10 26. Custom internal EMI shield.

FERRITE ON OUTSIDE OF PRINTER CABLE FOR REDUCED COMMON MODE CURRENTS

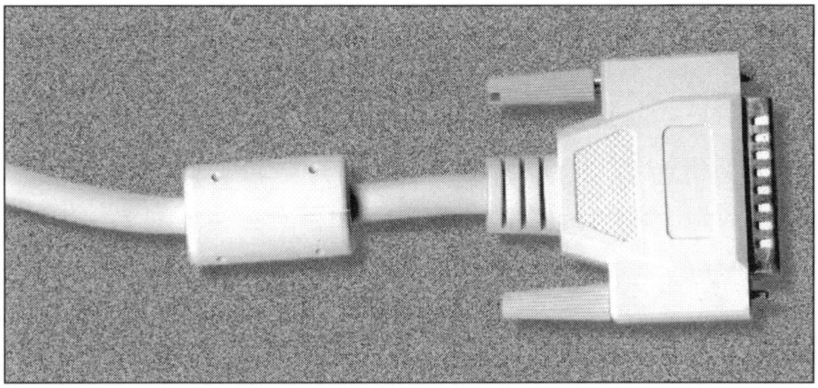

Source: Bogatin Enterprises 24912

Figure 10-27. Example of a ferrite on the outside of a printer cable to minimize common mode currents.

11 CAE Tools

All multilayer packages, MCMs and circuit boards for every new product, are custom. This means a package or substrate design step is involved in all new product development. Even though all 256 ball BGAs, for example, have the identical foot print, the inside bonding shelf or pin to ball assignment and routing may be very different. Some chips may require the lower inductance of a power and ground plane, while others may allow the lower cost of a simple two layer package.

It used to be that the package or MCM design was done on a CAD (Computer Aided Drawing) station and the package designer was a mechanical designer whose sole concern was laying out the traces for the package so as to meet connectivity and manufacturing requirements. This was labor intensive and could take as long as five weeks to complete the drawings for a 250 pin package.

Making a small change to one or two traces, typically in AutoCAD, might mean having to redraw the whole package. The drawings would be reviewed by an experienced engineer and after approval, would be translated into the artwork, either in Gerber or GDSII format.

After the first article was built on a rushed fast track, it would be tested. If it checked out, the rest of the run was committed and production proceeded. If it didn't work, the laborious process of debug would start and the package, MCM or substrate would be redesigned. In the days of 25MHz clocks, this process, often called the "design by correcting" process, illustrated in Figure 11-1, might have worked satisfactorily. To assist in the debug of the design, a breadboard model of the product would often be constructed.

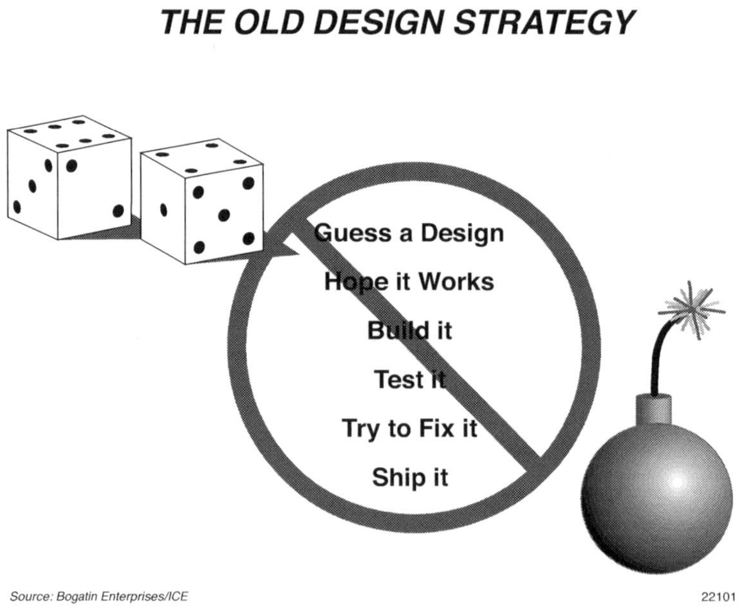

Figure 11-1. The old design method of "design by correcting".

However, with current generation clock frequencies over 100MHz, a breadboard cannot be built. The poor electrical performance of breadboards will cause signal integrity and timing problems. Only production quality units can be realistically tested. And with shorter time to market as a powerful driving force, a new method of creating the physical design of a package, MCM or substrate that will have an excellent chance of functioning correctly the first time, is critical. As pointed out in the previous chapter, and reviewed in the companion ICE publication, **Roadmaps of Packaging Technology**, the physical design of the package and interconnects strongly influences the electrical performance. To meet tighter time to market windows, the physical design process has to speed up and the impact of the physical design on electrical performance has to be incorporated in the design flow.

The new generation of design tools couple automated design with analysis and are grouped under the general heading of CAE (Computer Aided Engineering) tools. CAE tools are grouped under the broader heading of EDA (Electronic Design Automation) tools. Typically EDA tools include the broad class of chip design and analysis tools as well as circuit board layout.

In the new methodology, a candidate prototype design is completed in a design tool leveraging automation features. The design, still as a virtual prototype, is analyzed and its performance is simulated. This process may involve multiple design iterations, but each one can be done rapidly. This is the virtual design and virtual test process. An example of a virtual design of a BGA package is shown in Figure 11-2.

In the next generation design process, the performance simulation is done while the design is in process, rather than at the completion of the physical design. In this way, a new physical feature is not added to the existing design unless it meets a specified performance spec. This process is called "correct by design" or synthesis. The evolution of the design processes from design by correcting, virtual prototyping and synthesis is illustrated in Figure 11-3.

VIRTUAL BGA IN ADVANCED PACKAGE DESIGNER

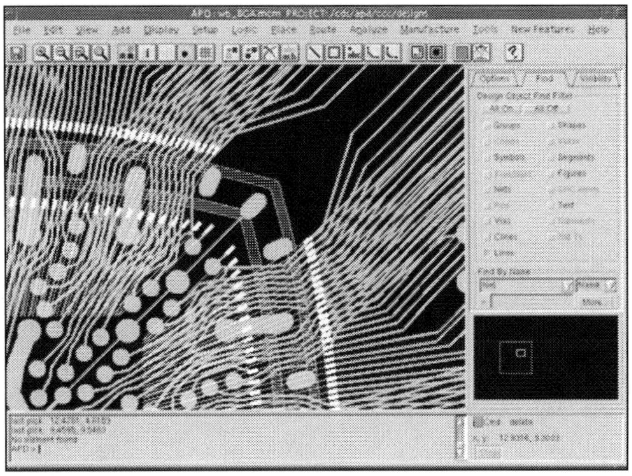

Source: Cadence 24916

Figure 11-2. Example of a virtual prototype BGA package as designed with Cadence Advanced Package Designer.

EVOLUTION OF DESIGN METHODOLOGIES FOR FASTER TIME TO MARKET

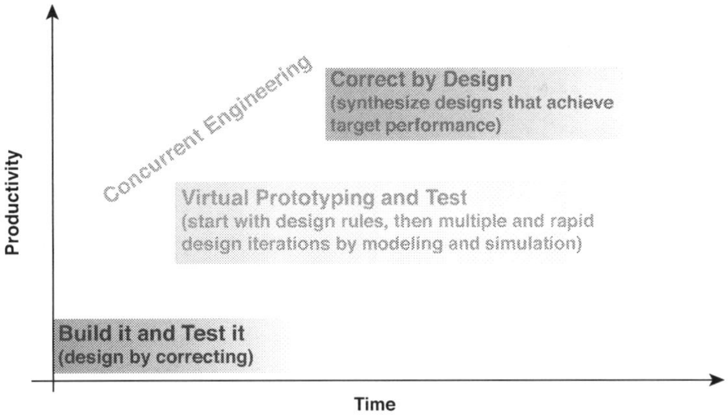

Source: Bogatin Enterprises 24917

Figure 11-3. Evolution of design processes for faster time to market.

It is always the case that finding and fixing high speed or other design problems as early in the design cycle as possible will result in the shortest development cycle time and lowest development cost product. This means extensive test and evaluation at every phase of the design process. The product design process flow for a package, MCM or circuit board is shown in Figure 11-4.

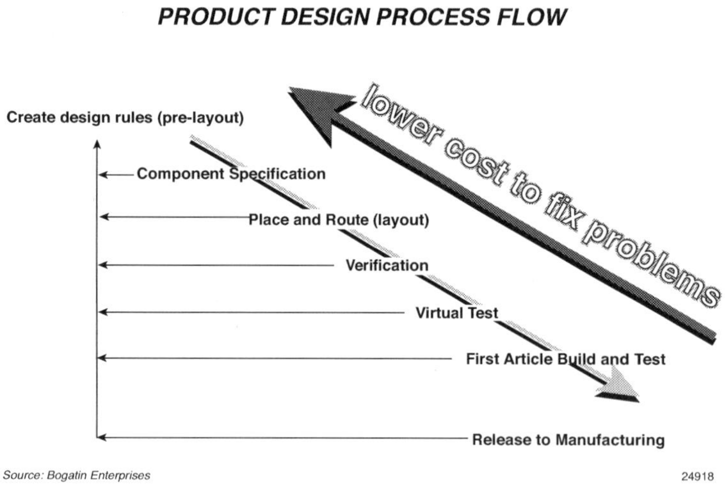

Figure 11-4. Product design process flow and the opportunity for evaluation and design iteration.

In high speed products, where the electrical performance of the packaging and interconnects will affect product operation, there are four steps in the design process:

- Design rule generation
- Layout, Routing and ERC, DRC
- Parasitic Extraction
- Simulation

In order to design a package, it is no longer a CAD engineer, but a system engineer who must be knowledgeable of each of these steps. These four operations are reviewed in the following sections.

DESIGN RULE CREATION

The physical design of a BGA, CSP, MCM, HDI substrate or printed circuit board, will influence the electrical properties, such as characteristic impedance and cross talk. These terms can be controlled by the appropriate choice of stack up geometry, line widths, dielectric thickness and trace spacings. For example, the characteristic impedance of a microstrip stack up, common in a four layer BGA, can be estimated by the following approximation:

$$Z_0 = \frac{87}{\sqrt{\varepsilon_r + 1.41}} \ \ln\left(7.5\frac{h}{w}\right) \text{Ohms}$$

where:
Z_0 = characteristic impedance
h = dielectric thickness below the trace
w = line width

By sweeping the line width for a given dielectric thickness, the design space can be mapped out. In this way, the design rule that specifies a specific line width and dielectric thickness can be established that will result in a target characteristic impedance.

For more accurate estimates of the design rules, a 2D field solver should be used to predict specific design rules. Fundamentally, a field solver will solve Maxwell's equations for a given geometry and selection of material properties. The first parameters calculated are the electric and magnetic fields. An example of the electric fields calculated by the field solver from Hyperlynx is shown in Figure 11-5.

From the fields, the various capacitance and inductance matrix elements are calculated. From these quantities, all electric properties such as characteristic impedance, time delay and cross talk can be calculated. The most commonly used field solver vendors are:

- Ansoft (www.ansoft.com)
- ApSim (www.apsimtech.com)
- InCASES (www.incases.com)
- OptEM Eng (www.optem.com)
- Pacific Numerix (www.pnc.com)
- Polar Instruments (www.polar.co.uk)
- Quantic Labs (www.quantic-emc.com)
- Viewlogic (www.viewlogic.com)
- HyperLynx (www.hyperlynx.com)

ELECTRIC FIELDS SIMULATED WITH 2D FIELD SOLVER

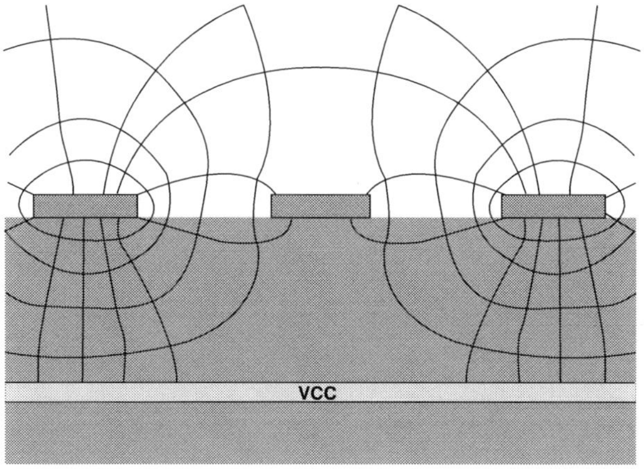

Source: HyperLynx 24919

Figure 11-5. Electric field calculation from the Hyperlynx tool.

The approximation above is compared to the results from the Ansoft Maxwell 2D field solver, in Figure 11-6. It is seen that for FR4 type materials, it can be accurate to 5% for characteristic impedances greater than about 50Ohms. For low impedances, however, it can be off by as much as 50%. This is further motivation to always use a field solver for final design rule verification, rather than relying on an approximation.

USING A FIELD SOLVER TO EVALUATE THE ACCURACY OF AN APPROXIMATION

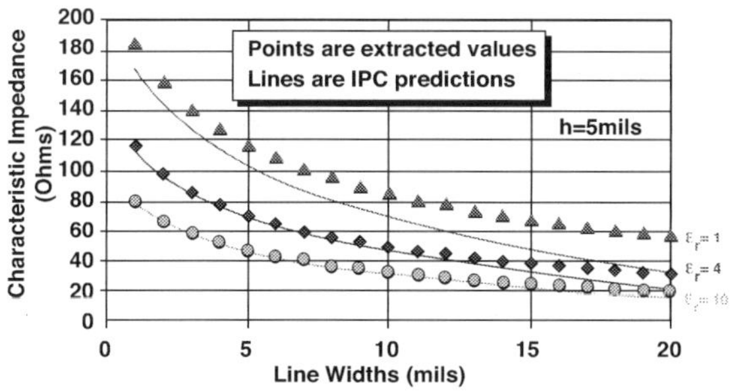

Source: Bogatin Enterprises 24920

Figure 11-6. Comparison of a popular approximation and the predictions of a 2D field solver.

The real value of a field solver is being able to cre-

ate accurate design rules that include second order effects so that before hardware is actually built, there is high confidence that the fabricated parts will meet the target performance spec. For example, with a 2D field solver, it is possible to predict the impact from a solder mask covering, common to all BGA packages and many circuit boards. In Figure 11-7, the decrease in characteristic impedance is calculated as the solder mask thickness is increased. It can be seen that for a typical thickness of 2mils, the characteristic impedance can drop by as much as 5Ohms, often exceeding typical tolerance limits.

EFFECT OF SOLDER MASK ON CHARACTERISTIC IMPEDANCE

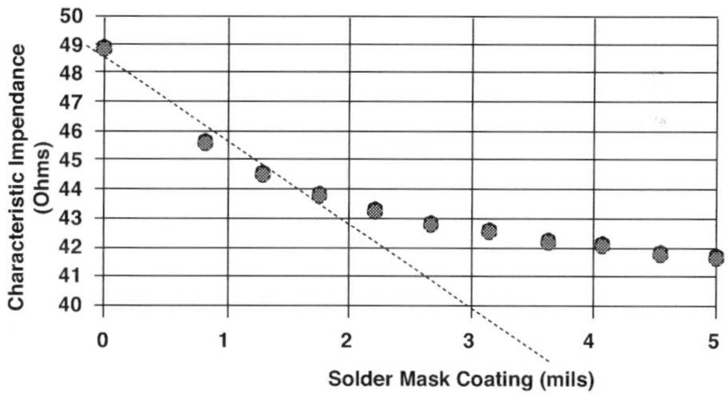

Source: Bogatin Enterprises 24921

Figure 11-7. Predictions from the Ansoft Maxwell 2D field solver for the influence of solder mask coating.

As illustrated in the previous chapter, 2D field solvers can also establish the design rules for cross talk in any stack up geometry. Once the physical design rules are established they can be used as a starting place to layout and route the traces for the package.

AUTOMATED LAYOUT

Though a BGA might look like a small circuit board, the design process, input information and database management requirements are very different. In particular, there must be a tight coupling between the chip design information and the package design information. The relationship between information flow between the IC design, a package design and the concurrent engineering and analysis that must go on for the package analysis is shown in Figure 11-8.

VLSI Technology Inc. has offered a list of seven important criterions for an efficient BGA design tool:

- Ability to start a design without a netlist
- Ability to build a hierarchical library containing components unique to BGAs, such as pads, staircase via stacks, bond fingers, fiducials and array patterns
- Interactive and automatic routers that can achieve very high trace density
- Automatic bond finger generation
- Integrated design and manufacturing rule checking (DRC)
- Integration of analysis software in the design process for detailed analysis and characterization
- Ability to import and export data in commonly used formats such as DXF, GDSII and Gerber.

With these features in a design tool, the process can change from one of intensive manual manipulation to a streamlined flow. Figure 11-9 compares the old design process flow involving the transfer of design information between the IC vendor to the package subcontractor with the new process flow, used by VLSI Technology, after incorporating one of the new BGA design tools from Xynetix.

There are five vendors offering automated design tools with specialized features for BGA and MCM design:

- Xynetix: Encore
- Cadence: Advanced Package Designer
- Pads: Power BGA
- CDS: Electrical Package Designer
- Zuken-Redac: CR-5000

They all incorporate some of the new features listed above. For example, the Xynetix Encore tool is able to create a package design without a netlist, route at any angle and automate the wire bond pad genera-

PROCESS FLOW FOR BGA DESIGN

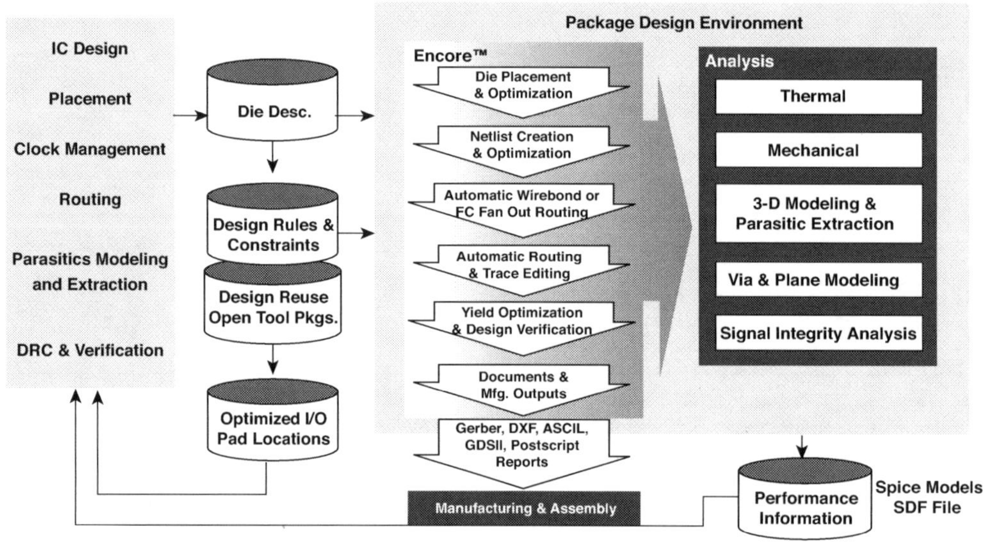

Source: Xynetix

24922

Figure 11-8. Tight integration between chip design and package design and analysis.

tion process. An example of a BGA design with this tool is shown in Figure 11-10. This new generation of automated design tool can reduce the design cycle time from 25 days to less than 5 days.

PARASITIC EXTRACTION

At the completion of the package or substrate layout, an equivalent circuit model of all the interconnect features can be created. This model can be used to compare to a target spec or can be used to add to a circuit simulation that includes the chip device driver models and a virtual test performed. The process of building an equivalent circuit model is often called parasitic extraction. This process is typically performed with a 3D field solver. Of the automated BGA design tools mentioned above, three of them integrate their geometry output to one or more 3D field solver tool:

- Xynetix-Ansoft Maxwell 3D Extractor
- Cadence -Pacific Numeric Turbo Package Analyzer
- Zuken-Redac-Apsim Technology

VIRTUAL BGA DESIGN

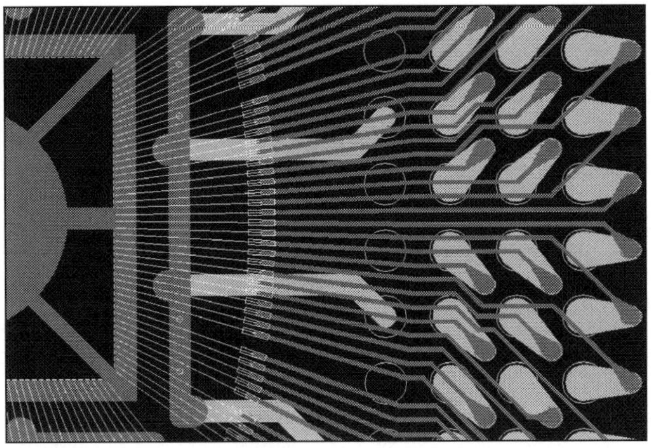

Source: VLSI Technology 24924

Figure 11-10. Example of BGA design with Xynetix Encore BGA.

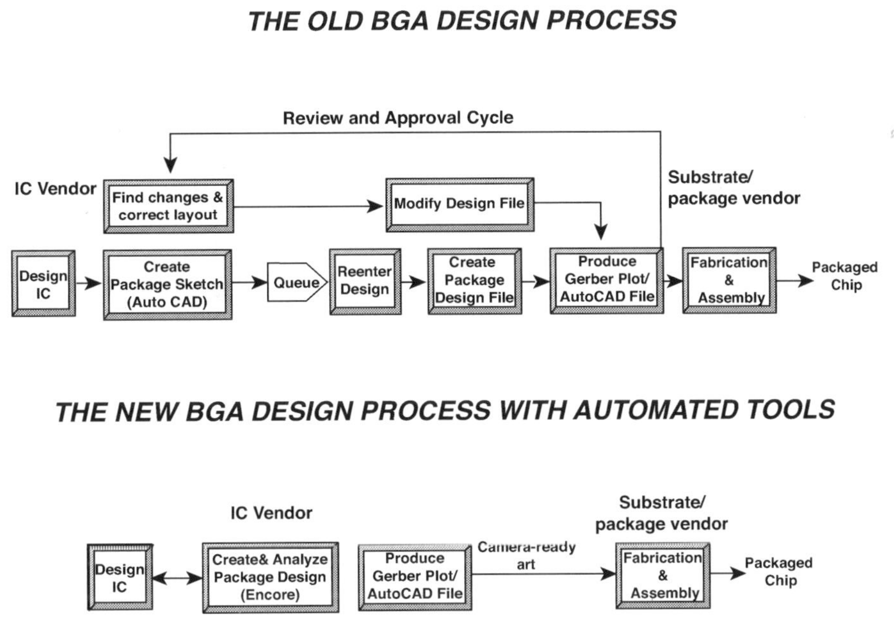

Source: VLSI Technology 24923

Figure 11-9. Old and new BGA design process flow used at VLSI Technology Inc.

For example, Xynetix Encore can export the geometry information of the BGA features to Ansoft Maxwell 3D Extractor. The geometry information can then be used to create a circuit model or calculate current flows. Figure 11-11 illustrates the translation of the BGA layout information into a 3D solid model.

VIRTUAL DESIGN OF A BGA PACKAGE AND ITS TRANSLATION INTO A 3-D SOLID MODEL

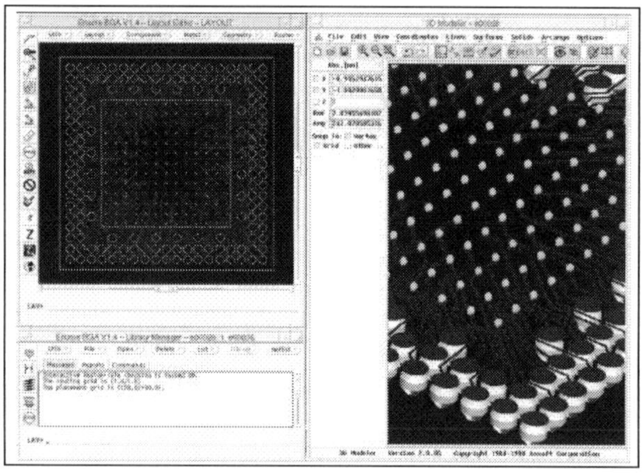

Source: Xynetix 24925

Figure 11-11. Encore BGA design translated into a 3D solid model in Ansoft Maxwell 3D Extractor.

All the geometry information, such as wire bonds, vias and solder balls can be recreated in the 3D solid model. An example of three leads of a BGA and the calculated current distribution in a lead and adjacent ground plane is shown in Figure 11-12.

The electrical circuit model for a collection of leads in a BGA consists of the capacitance matrix values, the inductance matrix values and the resistance values. These three matrices for a collection of leads would then be fed into a SPICE simulator for waveform analysis. Figure 11-13 is an example of the three sets of matrices for eight leads in a BGA.

Routine parasitic extraction of all the leads and planes in a BGA package, CSP or MCM substrate is still an emerging process. The tools need to evolve to be more automated, solve faster and be more user friendly to the increasing number of design engineers who are not electrical experts.

PERFORMANCE SIMULATION

The final step in performing a virtual test is simulating the electrical performance of the package, chip and any other relevant system components. There are two principle types of circuit simulators, those based on SPICE (Simulation Program with Integrated Circuit Emphasis) and those based on IBIS (Input/output Buffer Interface Specification).

SPICE was originated in Berkeley in the early 1970s as a tool to simulate the circuit performance of integrated circuits based on process and fabrication parameters. It has evolved as the workhorse circuit simulator to calculate the voltage and current waveforms for any circuit schematic. To be able to simulate a circuit in SPICE, the interconnect must be described by one or more of the following five elements:

- Resistors
- Capacitors
- Inductors
- Mutual inductors
- Transmission lines

Some versions of SPICE allow additional elements. In particular, HSPICE from Avant! introduces the W element, which can describe distributed, lossy transmission lines.

Once the schematic is created, along with the models for active devices, waveforms can be simulated at any node. An example of a circuit schematic and simulated waveform is shown in Figure 11-14.

SPICE is available from a variety of vendors, such as:

- Avant!
- OrCAD
- Ansoft
- Analogy
- Applied Simulation
- Protel

3-D SOLID MODEL OF THREE LEADS IN A BGA

CURRENT DISTRIBUTION SIMULATED IN ANSOFT MAXWELL 3-D EXTRACTOR

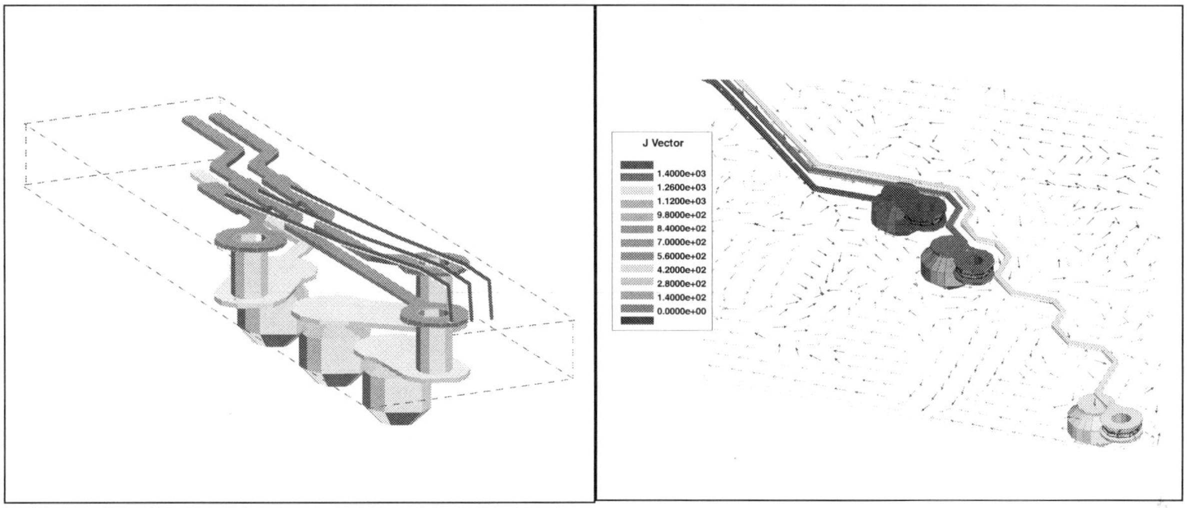

Source: Ansoft 24926

Figure 11-12. Recreation of three leads with wire bonds and solder balls in the Ansoft Maxwell 3D Extractor modeling tool.

EXTRACTED R, L AND C MATRICES THAT FULLY CHARACTERIZE THE CIRCUIT MODEL FOR 8 LEADS IN A BGA PACKAGE

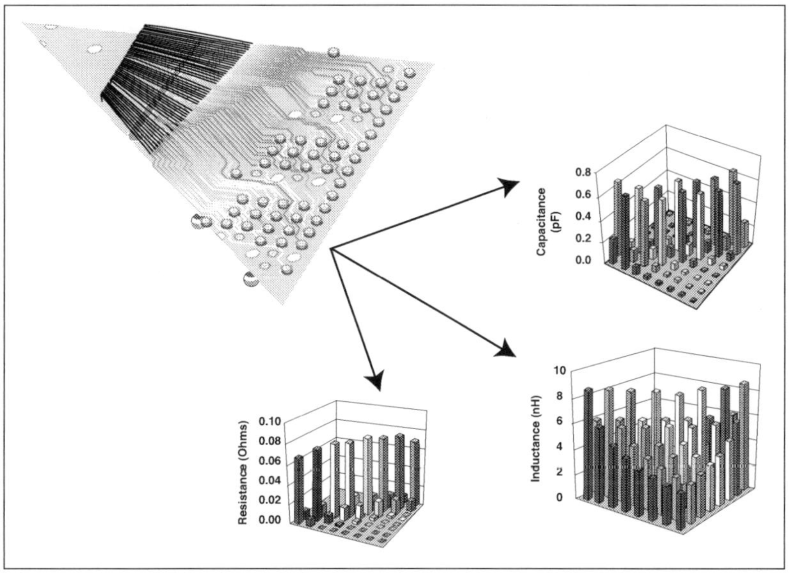

Source: Bogatin Enterprises/VLSI Technology Inc. 24927

Figure 11-13. Circuit model information extracted for eight leads in a BGA package.

EXAMPLE OF SCHEMATIC AND ITS SPICE SIMULATION

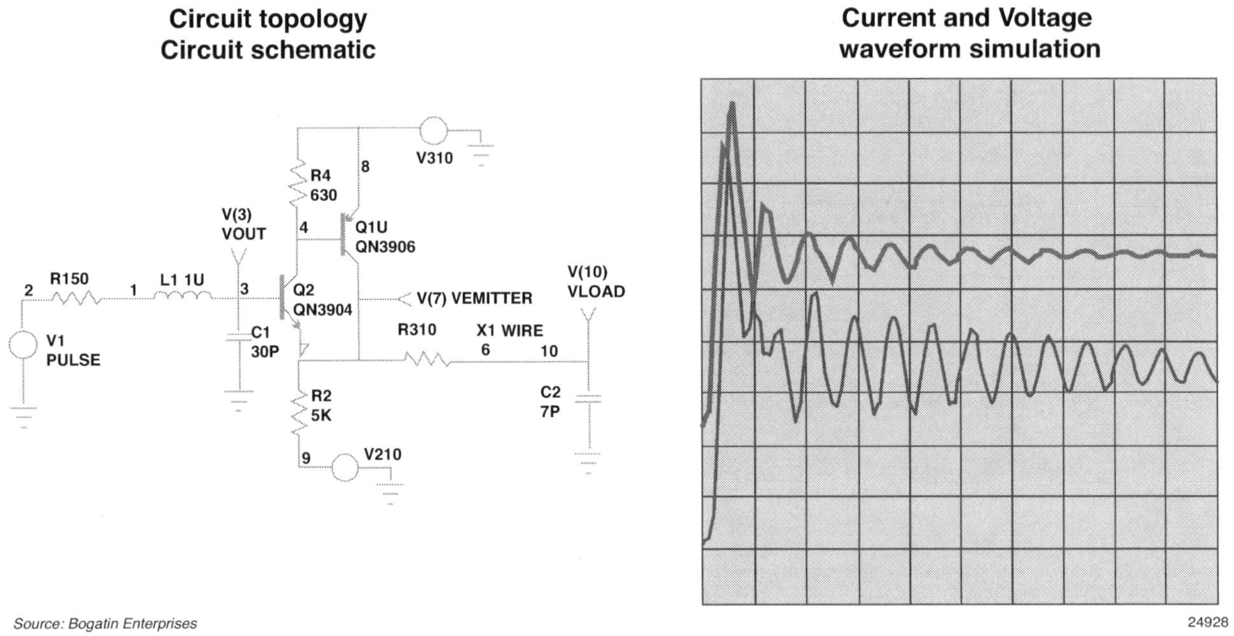

Figure 11-14. SPICE circuit and simulation.

There are two limitations to SPICE. For complex circuits, such as an entire circuit board with devices and packages, the simulation time can be days, if it is even able to converge to a solution. Secondly, accurate circuit models for active devices contain information that can be used to reverse engineer the features, designs and fabrication technology of the integrated circuit chips. This is information that many semiconductor vendors consider proprietary and are reluctant to release to customers. If device models are unavailable, then it is impossible to perform virtual testing before a package or system is built.

To get around these two limitations, a new simulation format, termed IBIS, has been created in the mid 1990s under the leadership of an adhoc industry committee. In this format, devices are described by their I-V output curves- tables of numbers. Interconnects can be described as transmission lines and packages in terms of their RLC matrices. Simulators based on the IBIS format are blazingly fast. An entire board with 1000 nets and 100 active devices can be simulated with all waveforms on all nets available for viewing in just a few hours with some tools.

An IBIS based simulator performs a similar function as SPICE. A circuit model is defined with device models and interconnect elements. Transient waveforms are then calculated of the voltages expected at any node in the system. An example of an IBIS circuit diagram and the resulting simulated waveforms, from Hyperlynx, is shown in Figure 11-15.

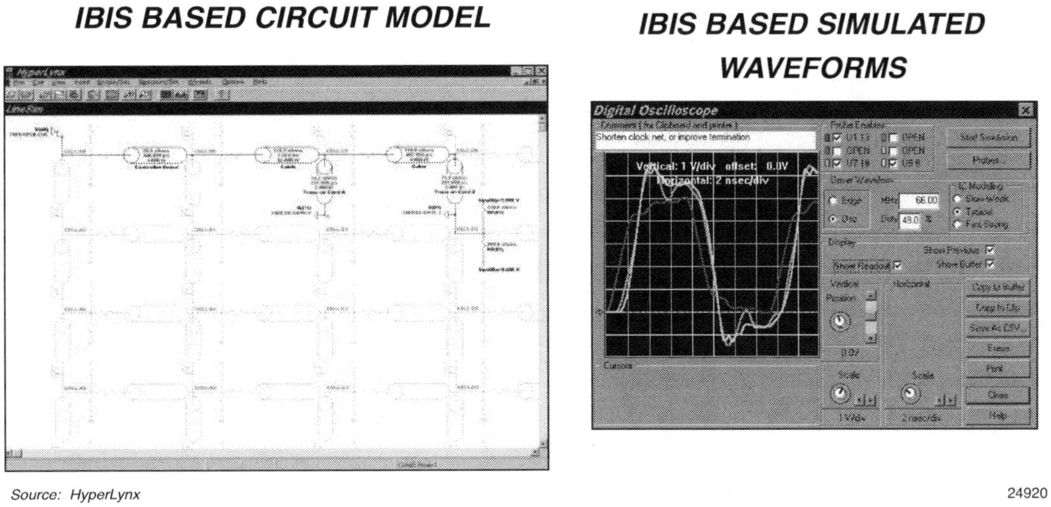

Figure 11-15. IBIS based model and simulation results.

In the past five years, over ten vendors have released IBIS based simulators, predominantly for board level simulation. Among the leaders are:

- Viewlogic
- Veribest
- Pads (Hyperlynx)
- Applied Simulation
- Cadence
- InCASES
- Mentor Graphics (Interconnectix)

The most recent trend in tool development is to perform circuit simulations during the layout process. This is part of the synthesis design process. For example in the Xynetix EDA Navigator tool, a model for each added trace is estimated and an approximation of the electrical effects or delay, reflection noise and cross talk is performed. Immediate feedback is provided to the designer so they can evaluate whether to proceed. An example of the output information is shown in Figure 11-16.

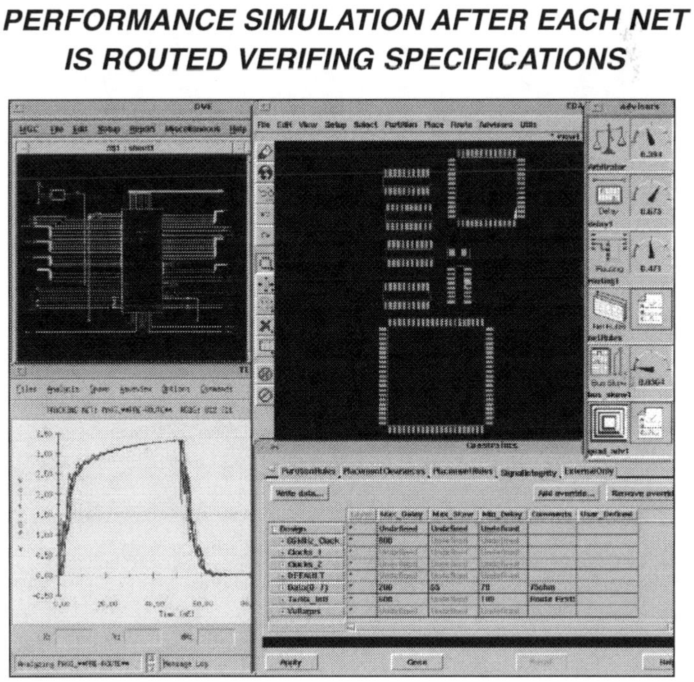

Figure 11-16. Xynetix EDA Navigator product with immediate feedback of the performance of each net as it is added.

The pioneer of synthesis tools is Interconnectix, a division of Mentor Graphics. Their tool is a true synthesis tool that will not add or route traces that do not meet a preset performance criterion. A spreadsheet is used to enter the performance constraints for each net and the waveforms are simulated at each step of the layout process. An example of this is shown in Figure 11-17.

CORRECT BY DESIGN LAYOUT PROCESS

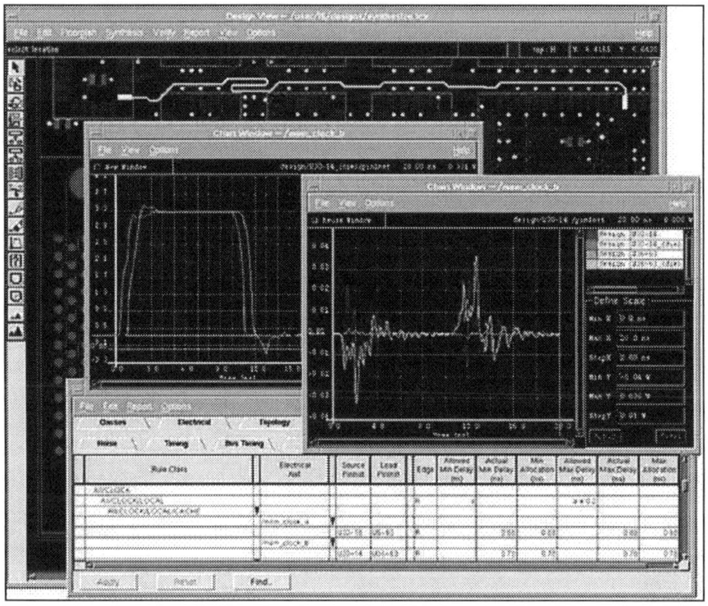

Source: Inerconnectix 24931

Figure 11-17. Synthesis of a "correct by design" layout with Interconnectix.

Though the synthesis process is still relatively new, those organizations that have tried it have found reduced total product design times. At this early phase, synthesis is being applied mostly to board level design. It is a natural evolution to apply these techniques to package design as well. As the design process moves up the path for higher productivity methods, the current leading edge design cycle times of less than 1 week can be reduced even more.

Made in United States
Troutdale, OR
11/03/2026

56845125R00082